T0321414

THOMAS NASHE

Books in the RENAISSANCE LIVES series explore and illustrate the life histories and achievements of significant artists, rulers, intellectuals and scientists in the early modern world. They delve into literature, philosophy, the history of art, science and natural history and cover narratives of exploration, statecraft and technology.

Series Editor: François Quiviger

Already published

Artemisia Gentileschi and Feminism in Early Modern Europe *Mary D. Garrard*

Blaise Pascal: Miracles and Reason *Mary Ann Caws*

Botticelli: Artist and Designer *Ana Debenedetti*

Caravaggio and the Creation of Modernity *Troy Thomas*

Descartes: The Renewal of Philosophy *Stephen Nadler*

Donatello and the Dawn of Renaissance Art *A. Victor Coonin*

Erasmus of Rotterdam: The Spirit of a Scholar *William Barker*

Filippino Lippi: An Abundance of Invention *Jonathan K. Nelson*

Giorgione's Ambiguity *Tom Nichols*

Hans Holbein: The Artist in a Changing World *Jeanne Nuechterlein*

Hieronymus Bosch: Visions and Nightmares *Nils Büttner*

Isaac Newton and Natural Philosophy *Niccolò Guicciardini*

John Donne: In the Shadow of Religion *Andrew Hadfield*

John Evelyn: A Life of Domesticity *John Dixon Hunt*

Leonardo da Vinci: Self, Art and Nature *François Quiviger*

Leon Battista Alberti: The Chameleon's Eye *Caspar Pearson*

Machiavelli: From Radical to Reactionary *Robert Black*

Michelangelo and the Viewer in His Time *Bernadine Barnes*

Paracelsus: An Alchemical Life *Bruce T. Moran*

Petrarch: Everywhere a Wanderer *Christopher S. Celenza*

Piero della Francesca and the Invention of the Artist *Machtelt Brüggen Israëls*

Pieter Bruegel and the Idea of Human Nature *Elizabeth Alice Honig*

Raphael and the Antique *Claudia La Malfa*

Rembrandt's Holland *Larry Silver*

Rubens's Spirit: From Ingenuity to Genius *Alexander Marr*

Salvator Rosa: Paint and Performance *Helen Langdon*

Thomas Nashe and Late Elizabethan Writing *Andrew Hadfield*

Titian's Touch: Art, Magic and Philosophy *María H. Loh*

Tycho Brahe and the Measure of the Heavens *John Robert Christianson*

Ulisse Aldrovandi: Naturalist and Collector *Peter Mason*

THOMAS NASHE

and
Late Elizabethan Writing

ANDREW HADFIELD

REAKTION BOOKS

For Richard Shields

Published by Reaktion Books Ltd
Unit 32, Waterside
44–48 Wharf Road
London N1 7UX, UK
www.reaktionbooks.co.uk

First published 2023

Copyright © Andrew Hadfield 2023

Printed and bound in India by Replika Press Pvt. Ltd

A catalogue record for this book is available from the British Library

ISBN 978 1 78914 687 5

COVER: Satirical woodcut of Thomas Nashe from Gabriel Harvey's
pamphlet *The Trimming of Thomas Nashe* (1597). Used by permission
of the Folger Shakespeare Library, Washington, DC (STC 12906,
image 54126), CC BY-SA 4.0.

CONTENTS

NOTE ON THE TEXT 7

Introduction: Nashe's Life, Interests and Circle 9
1 Religion 43
2 Early Style 71
3 The Theatre 101
4 Gabriel Harvey 132
5 Fiction 158
6 Late Writing, Mature Style 182
Epilogue 206

CHRONOLOGY 211
LIST OF ABBREVIATIONS 214
REFERENCES 216
BIBLIOGRAPHICAL ESSAY 241
ACKNOWLEDGEMENTS 247
PHOTO ACKNOWLEDGEMENTS 248
INDEX 249

NOTE ON THE TEXT

The spelling of quotations from sixteenth- and seventeenth-century texts has been lightly modernized: i/j, s/f, u/v have been regularized to fit modern conventions, other spellings have been made in accordance with modern usage, and punctuation has been added and regularized. Titles have generally been left in old spelling.

All translations from Latin and Greek texts are from the digital Loeb Classical Library published by Harvard University Press (www.loebclassics. com). All Bible references are to the Geneva Bible (1599). All Shakespeare references are to Stephen Greenblatt, Walter Cohen, Jean E. Howard and Katharine Eisaman Maus, eds, *The Norton Shakespeare* (New York, 2008).

Nashe's Life, Interests and Circle

Why should we read Thomas Nashe? He might now seem to be a relatively obscure figure, a writer of intricate English prose that is notoriously difficult to understand, some bits and pieces of rarely performed drama, and a bawdy poem. He is referred to in films about the Elizabethan age, often without making an appearance, and Internet sites eager to explore the question of Shakespeare's authorship routinely reference him.[1] Towards the end of *All Is True* (2018), Ben Elton's film about the last months of Shakespeare's life, Shakespeare is visited by Ben Jonson, who reminds him of his mortality and the love of his family, contrasting his fate to that of Nashe: 'No one knows how Tom Nashe died but if his filthy dildo poems are anything to go by it wasn't in the bosom of his family.'[2] Above all, Nashe is thought of as an angry satirist, a writer eager to confront and offend his readers, and not a man to cross, certainly in print.[3] The truth is that without an understanding of Nashe, a writer who was revered and feared in equal measure, the 1590s – the decade in which Shakespeare started to become famous – makes little sense. As this study will reveal, Nashe's work transformed English writing and he pushed the possibilities of the language to its limits. His achievement was widely

All Saints Church, West Harling, Norfolk.

understood at the time, but the very qualities of his writing that ensured his pre-eminence in the last decade of Elizabeth's reign led to his relative obscurity later because he was so topical and so difficult.

C. S. Lewis once argued that 'If asked what Nashe "says", we should have to reply, Nothing.'[4] Lewis, as usual, was making a serious point: that we read Nashe for his complicated, convoluted and polemical style, not for the substance of his work. Lewis is right that Nashe deliberately manipulates, wrongfoots and unsettles his readers, making it hard to work out exactly what he believes or what he is arguing at any particular point. Even his best-known work, *The Unfortunate Traveller* (1594), is hard to pin down; it is almost impossible to know whether it has a serious message and, if so, what that is. The novel seems to be a collection of bluffs and double-bluffs. We follow the journey of Jack Wilton, a page in various early sixteenth-century English armies, as he travels through France, Germany and Italy, reconstructing a nightmarish grand tour that parodies those undertaken by aristocratic young men to finish their education and make them ready for the serious responsibilities of adult life.[5] While they encountered spectacular courts, beautiful artworks and impressively grand buildings, Jack is confronted by war, crime, brutality, poverty, disease and sexual violence. Every brief instance of relief is followed by moments of terrible danger; every fleeting glimpse of beauty gives way to ugliness and terror. When he returns to England, we do not know whether he has been irredeemably corrupted by his adventures or is the same cynical rogue he was when he started his travels. Nashe appears to be demonstrating that it is impossible to tell whether one can actually learn anything from travel or if it is better to stay at home in a warm study acquiring knowledge. On the one hand, travellers may not really discover anything substantial and might be better off reading more widely than visiting places near and far; on the other, those who stay at home are vulnerable to deception because what they read – indeed, like *The Unfortunate Traveller* – may be confusing and misleading. Nashe never travelled further than the Isle of Wight, so he may have lamented his lack of experience of the wider world; or he may have thought that a world dominated by dangerous upheaval such as the French Wars of Religion, the Münster Uprising in Germany, the protracted war with Spain and the chaotic violence endemic in an Italy scarred by murderous factional conflict – events that form the European context of his work – was one best kept and understood at arm's length.[6]

If there is a central theme in Nashe's work, it is probably the need to be on one's guard in a time of immense cruelty, thoughtless violence and deadening stupidity. Even his vicious quarrel with his nemesis, Gabriel Harvey (1552/3–1631), which did so much to define Nashe's reputation and the nature of English literature in the crucial decade of the 1590s, was based on a moral principle, the need to preserve proper forms of reading to equip individuals for life. Harvey, a university teacher in Cambridge, saw himself as a forward-thinking intellectual and pedagogue, eager to import and disseminate new methods of instruction through a logical approach to rhetoric. For reasons that have never been entirely clear, Nashe took particular exception to Harvey's methods and personality, and their dispute sucked in a series of other figures, most significantly Harvey's two brothers, Richard (1560–1630) and John (1564–1592), Nashe's friend Robert Greene (1558–1592), and Richard Lichfield (d. 1630), the barber-surgeon of Trinity College, Cambridge.[7] After a number of vicious exchanges (discussed mainly in Chapters Three and Four), the authorities decided that the dispute had gone far enough and intervened to silence both men as part of a more general censorship of satire (the Bishops' Ban, 1 June 1599).[8] For Nashe, Harvey was a false teacher, too arrogant, foolish and tone-deaf to educate the young, and so capable of causing immense damage if not confronted.

Furthermore, as his angry writings in defence of the established church demonstrate (the Anti-Martinist tracts and *Christ's Tears over Jerusalem*), Nashe was a deeply religious man. However, as with so many other contemporary writers – Marlowe, Shakespeare, Donne and Jonson, to name only a few – we do not know the nature of Nashe's Christian belief, even though he provides a number of hints and clues. He was surely a Protestant of some form, prepared – or eager – to move on after the Reformation and to defend the (relatively) newly established Church of England; after all, his father was a clergyman. His writings excoriate sectarianism and defend church hierarchy, specifically the bishops, even though he is scathing of what he saw as undeserving status, authority and hierarchy often enough elsewhere. In common with many, particularly the 'church papists' (Catholics who kept quiet about their true beliefs in order to preserve church unity and their own lives), Nashe surely thought the institution was more significant than a particular confessional belief, and that any church worth serving had to be broad.[9] Perhaps the answer to Nashe's enigma, and the solution to the paradoxes he poses, is that he did not believe in 'nothing', but, like a strange Old Testament prophet, sought to confront and expose the vice and evil that threatened to overwhelm his world. His writing, which is at once populist and elitist, seeks to create a readership of like-minded thinkers equipped to confront both powerful authorities and the vulgar populace. Perhaps, given the magnitude of this almost impossible task, we should not be surprised that he dazzled his contemporaries but soon became obscure after his early death.

NASHE WAS BORN in November 1567 in Lowestoft, Suffolk, the third son of a clergyman, William Nashe (d. 1587), and his second wife, Margaret.[10] The family moved to the small village of West Harling, Norfolk, in 1573/4 and Nashe spent his childhood there, perhaps taught by his father, who was probably the schoolmaster in the village. Nashe makes little mention of his early years in his writing, which does contain a number of biographical references to other stages of his life, but it is clear that his East Anglian origins were important to him, most obviously in his last published work, *Nashe's Lenten Stuff* (1599), his strange and compelling meditation on the red herring. Nashe was certainly proud of his university education, which he mentions frequently throughout his work. He matriculated at St John's College, Cambridge, as a sizar (a student who carries out tasks in return for meals) in October 1582 and stayed in the city until 1588, when he moved to London. He may have been forced to leave and earn a living after his father died in 1587, the year he probably started his first work, *The Anatomy of Absurdity* (published 1589). A keen

The Great Gate, St John's College, Cambridge, 1890–1900.

advocate of the theatre (it is clear that his contempt for Gabriel Harvey partly stems from Harvey's lack of interest in and understanding of drama), Nashe was also probably involved in university drama. Lichfield (satirized by Nashe in the prefatory material to his most sustained attack on Harvey, *Have with You to Saffron Walden* of 1596) claims in *The Trimming of Thomas Nashe* (1597) that he co-authored the lost play *Terminus et non terminus* with Robert Mills, who was expelled from the university as a result.[11]

Nashe appears to have escaped this fate, and he kept up his relationship with Mills, staying with him in his house in Stamford, Lincolnshire. He made other friends at Cambridge, notably Robert Greene, one of the first professional writers, and the iconoclastic Christopher Marlowe (1564–1593), with whom he collaborated in some form, and whose literary laurels Nashe was keen to inherit.[12] Nashe would also have known of Harvey, and their embittered quarrel probably began while both were in Cambridge.[13]

In London Nashe started to publish his works, and a number appeared in quick succession. At the same time as the publication of *Anatomy* and the preface to *Menaphon*, he was employed by the bishops led by John Whitgift (*c.* 1530–1604), the Archbishop of Canterbury (1583–1604), who appears to have been keen to patronize Nashe. The bishops wanted to counter a series of scurrilous anti-episcopal tracts, produced anonymously on a movable hand press, that attacked the roles and character of a series of prominent Anglican churchmen. Nashe, along with the more established author and playwright John Lyly (1553–1606) and, perhaps, the extremely elusive author and spy Anthony Munday

(1560–1633), was commissioned to answer the 'Martinist' authors in kind.[14] While probably successful in the short term – although the tracts stopped only when the press was discovered in Lancashire – this was a high-risk strategy and surely encouraged Nashe to develop his satirical wit and style.[15] He undoubtedly wrote *An Almond for a Parrot* (1589), using the alias Cuthbert Curry-Knave, and probably wrote parts of *A Countercuffe Given to Martin Junior* (1589), *The Return of Pasquill* (1589) and *Pasquills Apologie* (1590). The unsettling polemical, satirical style Nashe put to good effect in the 1590s was certainly developed through his anti-Puritan writings, and the change from his early works to maturity can be gauged by comparing the studied parallel clauses of *The Anatomy of Absurdity* with the ferociously savage witty attacks on Harvey in *Have with You to Saffron Walden*. By this time Nashe had perfected the art of the long sentence, one in which clauses change tack suddenly and the reader is never entirely sure where the language is taking them or quite what it means.[16]

Richard Harvey, Gabriel's younger brother, who had leanings towards the 'hotter' form of Protestantism and some sympathy for the Martinists, took exception to the Anti-Martinist writings. It is possible that a pamphlet, *A Wonderful Astrological ... Prognostication* (1591) by Adam Foulweather, may be the work of Nashe, designed to satirize Richard's unfortunate prophecies. Richard had written an enthusiastic pamphlet, *An Astrological Discourse upon the Great and Notable Conjunction of the Two Superior Planets, Saturn and Jupiter*, in 1583, in which he had predicted great changes in the world on the day of the planets' visible union in the skies. None had happened, and Nashe dubbed him 'Astrological Richard' at the start of *Have with You* to *Saffron Walden*, so Nashe might have been the author of the earlier parody.

Nashe did write the preface to the pirated copy of Sir Philip Sidney's sonnet sequence *Astrophil and Stella* in the same year, 1591, and it is certainly possible that this work led to another, rather less obvious feud with the Sidney family, who perhaps took exception to the publication and had the edition called in by William Cecil, Lord Burghley (1520–1598), Elizabeth's chief minister. A second edition, published later in 1591, omitted Nashe's preface. Nashe frequently attacks the Sidney family in his work, referring to Sir Philip's rather embarrassing public quarrel with Edward de Vere, 17th Earl of Oxford (1550–1604), on a tennis court, and laughing at the rather botched image of the Sidney crest on the title page to *The Countess of Pembroke's Arcadia* (1593), which resembled a pig rather than a porcupine.[17]

Nashe acquired another patron, Ferdinando Stanley, Lord Strange, 5th Earl of Derby (1559–1594). Lord Strange supported a number of writers, including Thomas Kyd and Christopher Marlowe, and patronized Lord Strange's Men, the actors who performed the Henry VI plays at the Rose Theatre. The plays have long been attributed to Shakespeare, but were clearly produced by a team of writers, almost certainly including Nashe, who wrote the first act of *Henry VI, Part One*.[18] Nashe's reference to 'brave *Talbot*' in *Piers Penniless, His Supplication to the Devil* (1592) would therefore seem to be a cunning act of self-promotion rather than the disinterested praise of an impressed spectator.[19] Later, in *Nashe's Lenten Stuff*, he praises *The Case Is Altered* (published 1609, but probably first performed in 1597) as a 'witty Play', which might suggest that he played a hand in that work too.[20] The play is assigned to Ben Jonson, but bears little resemblance to his other plays, and Nashe was to collaborate with Jonson on the lost play *The Isle of Dogs*, also in 1597. Nashe is now recognized as a pioneering playwright as well as a prose writer who collaborated with Shakespeare and Jonson early in their careers, as well as with Marlowe.[21] He was also a poet of some notoriety, if not distinction; the pornographic narrative poem 'The Choice of Valentines' (also known as 'Nashe's Dildo'), written for Lord Strange, circulated widely in manuscript (Gabriel Harvey dismisses it in his long attack on Nashe titled *Pierces Supererogation* of 1593 as an unprinted packet of 'bawdy and filthy rhymes').[22]

A number of Nashe's close friends (most of his friends seem to have been male, and he rarely mentions women other than those who helped to support him) died in the early 1590s. Thomas Watson (1555–1592), best known as a Latin poet, died in September 1592 and Greene died in the same month, perhaps after a banquet of 'Rhenish wine and pickled herring', as Gabriel Harvey alleged. Nashe denied the cause, admitting that the meal had taken place but stating in *Strange News* (1592), his response to Harvey's *Four Letters and Certain Sonnets* (1592), that it had been some time earlier.[23] Most significant was the death of Marlowe in mysterious circumstances, probably murdered, in Deptford in 1593. Nashe and Marlowe appear together on the title page of the play *Dido, Queen of Carthage* (1594), another work that is unusual, as it does not read like the work of either writer.[24] It is sometimes suggested that Nashe acted as the editor of this posthumously published play, a work that is extremely hard to date (it may have been first

THE
COVNTESSE
OF PEMBROKES
ARCADIA,
WRITTEN BY SIR PHILIPPE SIDNEI.

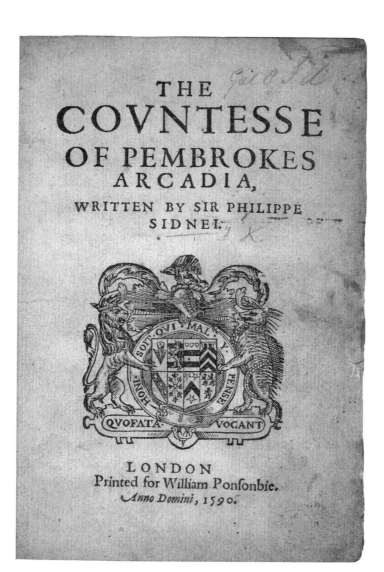

LONDON
Printed for William Ponsonbie.
Anno Domini, 1590.

Title page to Sir Philip Sidney, *The Countesse of Pembroke's Arcadia* (1590).

performed when both authors were students at Cambridge, but is more likely to have been written for the boy's company known as the Children of the Chapel, which may well be the reason for its distinctive style, neither author working otherwise with a children's company).[25] The appearance of both names on the title page might also indicate that Nashe was eager to be associated with Marlowe, a writer with whom he shared a number of qualities and affinities, not least their enthusiasm for the brilliant, scabrous anti-establishment Italian author Pietro Aretino (1492–1556).[26]

By this point Nashe was a well-known author. In the autumn of 1592 he published *Piers Penniless*, a popular work that went through five editions in three years. It offered a sweeping satirical portrait of the vices of contemporary Londoners, establishing a literary persona to rival those of other authors such as Gabriel Harvey's protégé, Edmund Spenser (1554?–1599), who had adopted the figure of Colin Clout from the early Tudor poet John Skelton (*c.* 1460–1529).[27] The name was a further sign that Nashe now saw himself as a significant English literary figure and he was immediately referred to by his pseudonym, notably in Gabriel Harvey's *Pierces Supererogation*, published the following year.

When *Piers Penniless* was published, Nashe was staying at Croydon Palace, the summer residence of the Archbishop of Canterbury. This demonstrates that he was still supported by Archbishop Whitgift, a sign that his role in counteracting the anti-episcopal threat of the Marprelate Pamphlets had met with official favour. Croydon was then a fairly small village separate from London, and the archbishop and his household retired to the country from their normal residence in Lambeth

Palace to avoid the danger of plague, a major epidemic having broken out in 1592–3.

Nashe's only surviving single-authored play, *Summer's Last Will and Testament*, was performed in October 1592. Will Somers (d. 1560), Henry VIII's famous court jester, acts as the chorus and defers to 'My lord' in the audience, indicating that the archbishop was present at the performance. The play also refers to the queen, but, although she completed her summer

Titian, *Pietro Aretino, c.* 1537, oil on canvas.

progress at about this time, she cannot have been present given her known route. The play was not published until 1600, without Nashe's usual elaborate prefatory material, and was probably pirated by the unscrupulous bookseller Walter Burre.[28] Perhaps the text was based on a copy obtained from Nashe's papers and produced without his permission, so it may be an unrevised work that refers to earlier plans that never materialized. Nashe calls the work a 'show', and it contains a series of tableaux as the dying Summer, flanked by Autumn and Winter, watches the events that signal the end of his reign. The play contains frequent allusions to the plague, which flourished in the summer, so that life is balanced by death. Plague is a central theme in Nashe's work, from God's cursing the evil behaviour of Londoners in *Piers Penniless* and *Christ's Tears over Jerusalem* (1593) to the hideous outbreak in Rome described in *The Unfortunate Traveller*.[29] *Summer's Last Will* contains Nashe's most famous and influential lyric, sung while Summer dies, which has been given the title 'A Litany in Time of Plague'.

Nashe must at this time have been at work on *Strange News*, which was probably published before the end of 1592. In this, his first serious salvo in his quarrel with Gabriel Harvey, Harvey is attacked in a bewildering variety of ways: his frequent mention of his father's profession as a ropemaker; his pride in his achievements; his absurd style of dress; his tin ear and leaden prose; his copious writings that will be used only for domestic purposes, covering pots of food and toilet paper. Nashe is keen – as he is later – to demonstrate that he really knows about Harvey's life and writing (which Nashe cites and imitates), and, therefore, his character. He is also eager to show that, unlike Harvey, he is not a pedant and can combine an appreciation of scholarship and an ability to read and write classical languages with a dextrous understanding of popular culture.

Harvey, now living in London with his publisher John Wolfe (1548?–1601; the chief English publisher of Italian books, and well known to Nashe), responded with a long and even more elaborate dissection of Nashe's character and works, *Pierces Supererogation*.[30] Supererogation, a legal and theological term, indicates the performance of works beyond those requested or required by God. An important concept in the medieval church and in later Catholic theology, as a means of ensuring salvation, the doctrine was attacked by Protestant theologians led by Martin Luther. It was criticized explicitly in the 39 Articles of the Church of England, reproduced in the Book of Common Prayer, which established the basic tenets of the Anglican church. Superogation, according to the articles, is a doctrine that

> cannot be taught without arrogancy and impiety: for by them men do declare, that they not only render unto God as much as they are bound to, but that they do more for his sake, than of bounden duty is required: whereas Christ saith plainly, When ye have done all that are commanded to you, say, We are unprofitable servants.[31]

Harvey's point in using the term is that Nashe has exceeded his limits and asked for and expected too much, and will now be repaid in kind, Harvey's attack being the reward for his 'supererogation'. As so often in Harvey's writing, there is an

anti-establishment thrust: Nashe, in common with many in
the Anglican hierarchy, Harvey implies, has lost sight of what
really matters in his eagerness to assert ideas and doctrines that
he does not really understand, and has therefore cut himself
off from proper values and core belief, ones that Harvey will
now re-state in order to correct his excesses.

Nashe appears to have left the quarrel alone for a while,
perhaps because other projects absorbed his imagination.
More likely, he was already planning his equally lengthy
response, *Have with You to Saffron Walden*, soon after the publication of Harvey's attack, even though it was not published for
another three years (perhaps Nashe did not want the quarrel
to define his writing career; perhaps he was warned that it was
already drawing critical attention from the authorities). In
1593 Nashe was working on his most popular and, for many
readers, most enduring work, *The Unfortunate Traveller*. The
first edition is dated 27 June 1593, but, for unknown reasons,
publication was delayed until 1594. The work was dedicated
to Henry Wriothesley, 3rd Earl of Southampton (1573–1624),
also the dedicatee of other works, notably Shakespeare's narrative poems *Venus and Adonis* (1593) and *The Rape of Lucrece*
(1594).[32] Unlike Nashe's relationship with Whitgift and Lord
Strange, there is no evidence of any other connection between
the two men, and Nashe's literary offering may have been one
of the many works dedicated in the hope of patronage that
came to nothing.[33]

Before the delayed publication of *The Unfortunate Traveller*,
Nashe began to write one of his most unusual works, *Christ's
Tears over Jerusalem*. It was dedicated to Elizabeth Carey (1552–
1618), sister-in-law of his patron, Lord Strange, and wife of

Sir George Carey (1547–1603). Carey had had a significant
military career and, like his brother, was a patron of the Lord
Chamberlain's Men – for whom Shakespeare worked – when
the company was founded in 1594. *Christ's Tears*, Nashe's longest
work, appears far more solemn and straightforward than many
of his other works, and contains few of the literary nuances,
devices and pyrotechnics that characterize his usual style of
writing. Nashe, in common with many impecunious writers,
had undoubtedly been in prison for debt (as he informs us in
Strange News),[34] but *Christ's Tears* led to his imprisonment on the
more serious charge of insulting London and Londoners.[35]
Nashe was characteristically fiery in his representation of the
sinful inhabitants of the capital:

> *London*, thou art the seeded Garden of sin, the Sea
> that sucks in all the scummy channels of the Realm.
> The honestest for thee (for the most) are either Lawyers
> or Usurers. Deceit is that which advanceth the greater
> sort of thy chiefest; Let them look that their retches
> shall rust and canker, being wet & dewed with Orphan's
> tears. The Lord thinketh it were as good for him to kill
> with the Plague, as to let them kill with oppression. He
> beholdeth from on high all subtle conveyances and
> recognizances. He beholdeth how they pervert foun-
> dations, and will not bestow the Bequeathers free alms,
> but for bribes, or for friendship. I pray God they take
> not the like course in preferring poor men's children
> into their Hospitals, and converting the impotents'
> money to their private usury.[36]

In the second edition a rather more anodyne passage, warning
of decay and corruption in a more generalized manner and
urging the city to do good things to inspire the rest of the
nation, was inserted instead:

> *London* thou art the wellhead of the land, and therefore
> it behoveth thee to send forth wholesome springs.
> Suffer not thy channels to overflow like full conduits.
> Let not gain outrun godliness and honesty. Make no
> trade of deceit, nor occupation of usury. Why may not
> the Lord as well kill with the plague, as suffer cruel
> extortioners to kill with oppression? He beholdeth
> from on high all subtle conveyances and crafty recog-
> nizances. No defrauder of the poor, or courteous
> perverter of foundations, but is put in the devil's black
> book. Cursed be they that give alms with the one hand,
> and take bribes with the other, that sell bequests for
> good turns, and are not ashamed to prostitute charity
> like a strumpet for ready money. I speak not this for
> I know any such, but if there be any such, to forewarn
> and reform them.[37]

Given the first text, and Nashe's ability to ventriloquize
and undermine his opponents, it is hard to read this last
sentence as anything other than subversive, drawing attention
to his earlier attack on Londoners rather than expressing his
repentance for any offence caused. The assertion that God had
killed the corrupt citizens with a plague epidemic is replaced
by a rhetorical question suggesting that he might choose to
take this drastic cause of action, but witnesses of the terrible

events of 1592–3 could, of course, draw their own conclusions. Many names had already gone into the Devil's black book.

Nashe was probably imprisoned in Newgate around 20 November 1593, before Sir George Carey appears to have been able to have him released. Nashe, as he informs his readers in *Have with You*, spent the Christmas period, and some time after, with Carey at his family home, Carisbrooke Castle on the Isle of Wight, his one known departure from the mainland. *Terrors of the Night*, Nashe's encyclopedic survey of apparitions, real and imagined, that haunt people in darkness, was published in 1594 with an effusive dedication to Elizabeth Carey (1576–1635), George and Elizabeth's only daughter.

Nashe's activities and whereabouts during the next two years are not well documented. He may have been working in the theatre in various ways, since it is likely that he was involved in a number of plays and productions between *Summer's Last Will* in 1592 and *The Isle of Dogs* in 1597 (and we have the evidence of his part in the publication of *Dido* after Marlowe's death). He appears to have visited friends in the country, such as his co-author from student days, Robert Mills, who lived in Stamford, Lincolnshire (Nashe refers to the journey there in *Have with You*).[38] It is also possible that Nashe lived a predominantly itinerant lifestyle in the mid-1590s (as he did towards the end of his life, after he fled the capital in haste), eager to escape hostile attention in London, which would further explain his lack of literary output. Nashe invariably relied on access to libraries to produce his work, and often it is possible to chart the important books and helpful guides that he used in his work. He mined Richard Hakluyt's *The Principal Navigations of the English Nation* (1589) for Russian

names to use when insulting Harvey, and he relies on Protestant martyrologies such as John Foxe's *Acts and Monuments of the Christian Church* (1563), on Holinshed's *Chronicles* (1577, 1587), on a range of Latin authors such as Juvenal, Ovid, Terence and Virgil, and, perhaps most often, on Heinrich Cornelius Agrippa's *Of the Vanity and Uncertainty of Arts and Sciences*, translated by James Sanford in 1569, a source of all sorts of bits and pieces of information and packed with useful anecdotes, one of a number of works that Nashe was happy to use frequently. Indeed, Nashe may well have owned a copy of the *Vanity*, a small octavo volume, which would have been easy to carry around, just as he undoubtedly owned a number of small books in Latin and English, such as John Leland's *Principum, ac illustrium aliquot et eriditorum in Anglia virorum encomia* (1589), which bears Nashe's signature.[39] He probably also owned a copy of Harvey's *Pierces Supererogation*, just as Harvey probably

Carisbrooke Castle, Isle of Wight, 1890–1906.

owned some of Nashe's works, each of the two deadly enemies being, in many ways, his rival's closest and best reader.[40]

Whatever the cause or reason, 'a period of intense and exhausting literary activity' ended in 1593 and it was three years before Nashe, now an established author, published another work.[41] *Have with You to Saffron Walden*, the last complete work he dedicated to insulting Harvey (there are a number of asides in *Lenten Stuff*), is seen either as a literary dead end in its relentless verbal assaults and obsessively focused loathing for its subject, or as the mark of a new sophistication and dexterity in Nashe's style, a work that justifies Lewis's judgement cited above. Nashe ventriloquizes the styles of other writers; he also shows a bewildering ability to make use of his grammar-school and Cambridge education, in particular the rhetorical practice of arguing *in utramque partem* (on either side of an argument) and, joining these literary attributes together, to write extraordinarily complicated sentences that constantly unsettle a reader by starting in one place and suddenly changing direction to look as if they are making the opposite point. These were hardly new departures: Nashe's style had always owed much to debate and oral performance.[42] But it can be argued that in *Have with You* he perfected a mature style that, had he lived longer, would have allowed him to adapt and produce ever more fanciful and imaginative literary works.[43]

Have with You gives us some clues about Nashe's life in the three years before the work's publication, although it is most likely that it was written relatively rapidly while he had access to libraries, rather than over a protracted period. We learn that he stayed for a time with his printer, John Danter (*fl.* 1589–99), in Hosier Lane, and undoubtedly worked for Danter in his print shop, probably as a proof corrector, as Harvey worked for Wolfe.[44] Throughout his writing career Nashe seems to have taken a careful interest in how his works were produced, a concern that was probably the result of his familiarity with the production of books.[45] We learn of the London-based writers in his circle – John Lyly; Henry Chettle (d. 1603–7), a printer and prolific author who had posthumously published Robert Greene's *A Groatsworth of Wit* (1592), the work that contains the phrase 'upstart crow beautified with our feathers', thought to be one of the first references to Shakespeare; the Welsh soldier-poet Sir Roger Williams (1539/40–1595); Thomas Campion (1567–1620), the composer, poet and masque writer – and Nashe demonstrates his close relationship with Marlowe by being the first writer to refer to him in print by the affectionate diminutive 'Kit'.[46]

On his return from Lincolnshire after visiting Mills in 1595, Nashe stayed at the well-known Dolphin Inn, Cambridge (now demolished, 'whose premises stretched from All Saints Churchyard to Bridge Street').[47] There, he claims, he had a room next to Harvey, who was also staying at the inn, and witnessed 'the conflict betwixt my Hostess of the Dolphin . . . and him, at my staying there, about his lying in her house, a fortnight, and keeping one of the best Chambers, yet never offering to spend a penny'.[48] Again, Nashe is demonstrating how much he knows about Harvey's life and character, so that when he exposes Harvey's offensive meanness, and defends Robert Greene from Harvey's slurs, the reader will believe him.

Have with You has an especially complicated preface, even by Nashe's standards. The work is dedicated to Richard

Lichfield, the barber-surgeon of Trinity. The dedication is anything but friendly, polite or in praise of the dedicatee, as Nashe imagines Lichfield giving Harvey a haircut as a means of cutting him down to size, and Lichfield, like Harvey, is the butt of a number of Nashe's jokes and quibbling on his name in the opening sentence of the epistle:

> Acute & amiable Dick, not *Dic mihi, Musa virum,* Musing Dick, that studied a whole year to know which was the male and female of red herrings: nor *Dic obsecro,* Dick of all Dicks, that in a Church where the Organs were defaced, came and offered himself with his pipe and tabor: nor old Dick of the Castle, that upon the news of the loss of *Calais,* went and put a whole bird-spit in the pike of his buckler: nor Dick Swash or Desperate Dick, that's such a terrible Cutter at a chine of beef, and devours more meat at Ordinaries in discoursing of his frays and deep acting of his slashing and hewing, than would serve half a dozen Brewers' Dray-men: nor *Dick of the Cow,* that mad Demilance Northern Borderer, who played his prizes with the Lord *Jockey* so bravely: but paraphrastical gallant Patron Dick, as good a fellow as ever was Heigh fill the pot hostess: courteous Dick, comical Dick, lively Dick, lovely Dick, learned Dike, old *Dick* of *Lichfield, Jubeo te plurimum salvere,* which is by interpretation, I joy to hear thou hast so profited in gibridge [gibberish].[49]

The comic inventiveness of the passage probably influenced one of Falstaff's major speeches in *Henry IV, Part One*.[50] However, it did not impress Lichfield, who responded in kind with his own satirical riposte, *The Trimming of Thomas Nashe* (1597). In one way this exchange can be read as a piece of minor Cambridge politics, with Nashe of the rich and powerful St John's College imagining a non-academic employee of an equally powerful college, Trinity, reducing its noisy small neighbour, Trinity Hall, to size. It is also a sign that satirical exchanges were becoming ever more animated and spiralling out of control, and it would not be long before the authorities who had launched Nashe's career intervened to end it, along with that of Harvey.

The only surviving letter in Nashe's hand can be dated to August or September 1596.[51] It is addressed to William Cotton, an employee of the Careys of Carisbrooke Castle, who had delivered the money to release Nashe from gaol in 1593. There is comment on the theatres, probably indicating his close involvement in drama. Nashe begins by complaining how tedious the inactive days of summer are, 'as unfortunate as a term at Hertford or St Albans to poor country clients or Jack Cade's rebellion to the lawyers, wherein they hanged up the Lord chief justice'.[52] Jack Cade (d. 1450) was the leader of an especially dangerous rebellion against the authority of Henry VI, inspired by the harsh conditions and chaos resulting from the disastrous war with France.[53] Nashe's reference to Cade is surely to the play *The First Part of the Contention* (later *Henry VI, Part Two*), which had been performed relatively recently.[54] Even though it is Lord Saye, the Lord High Treasurer, who is hanged on Cade's orders in the play, and not the Chief Justice, there is enough hostility to lawyers to indicate that Nashe's reference was undoubtedly to a sequence of plays in

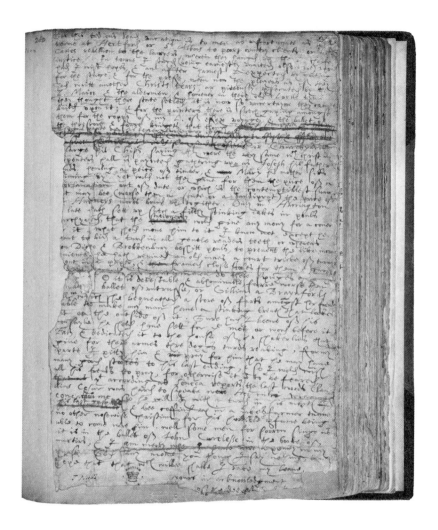

Thomas Nashe letter to William Cotton,
August/September(?) 1596.

which he was involved, rather than to a historical source, such as Holinshed's *Chronicles*.

Nashe complains that he is not being employed properly and would like to be writing rather more, and to have work in the theatre:

> I expected by writing for the stage & for the press, when now the players as if they had writ another Christ's tears, are piteously persecuted by the Lord Mayor & the aldermen, & however in their old Lord's time they thought their state settled, it is now so uncertain they cannot build upon it.

Nashe is referring to the uncertainty generated in the Lord Chamberlain's Men by the death of the company's patron, Henry Carey, Lord Hunsdon (1526–1596), in July. Nashe's benefactor, Sir George Carey, had taken over, but he was not yet invested as Lord Chamberlain (the figure who oversaw the running of the theatres), a fact that had presumably caused the impasse. The comment also demonstrates that the episode of *Christ's Tears* was an ever-present fear in Nashe's mind and that the theatres were, as so often, at odds with the authorities.

Much of the rest of the letter contains a series of scatological observations on the recent publication of Sir John Harington's *A New Discourse about a Stale Subject: The Metamorphosis of Ajax* (1596), notorious as the first treatise to describe the flushing toilet, but also one that contained a large number of discreetly placed allusions to the poisoning of the land by its chief political figures, specifically Robert Dudley, 1st Earl of Leicester (1532–1588), and the persecution of Catholics.[55]

Nashe would have understood the allusions and known that
Harington had been banished from court – and nearly suffered
a worse fate – as a result of a publication that was possibly
influenced by Nashe's own style of prose.[56] The influence was
surely mutual: the woodcut of Harvey, 'ready to let fly upon
Ajax', in *Have with You* may have been inspired by Harington's
treatise, and Nashe refers again to the work in *Lenten Stuff*.[57]

Nashe was writing for the theatre once more soon afterwards, when he collaborated with the young Ben Jonson
(1572–1637) on the comedy *The Isle of Dogs*, performed at the
Rose Theatre on the south bank of the River Thames, near
the Globe, in July 1597. It was probably Jonson's first play, an
obviously important work for him, and he appears to have
recalled his collaboration with Nashe in later works.[58] The
content of the play is unclear, since no trace of it remains; it
may well have been a satirical work attacking various sycophantic courtiers, either because the Isle of Dogs was where
the queen was thought to keep her hounds or because, being
a prominent bend in the slow-moving Thames of the time,
the island was where the city's refuse – including human and
animal waste – collected. As has recently been argued, the
play may not have been as offensive as critics have assumed,
but was merely cited as a convenient target by an informer
eager to advance his own career with the authorities.[59] Whatever the truth behind the lost work, it was clear that the
theatres had become a target for the authorities. Three actors,
one of them Jonson, were imprisoned; the play was denounced
as 'lewd . . . seditious and slanderous'; and an order was issued
by the Privy Council demanding that the theatres be closed
(which they were for a brief period) and pulled down (which

did not happen).[60] The notorious priest-hunter, torturer and interrogator Richard Topcliffe (1531–1604) was sent to arrest Nashe, but it seems he had already fled London, as he describes in *Lenten Stuff*, for the familiar territory of East Anglia.

Nashe was in Great Yarmouth in the autumn of 1597, and there he was probably sheltered by one of the town's civic dignitaries. Certainly, he had access to the town records, stored in the 'Yarmouth Hutch', a large chest kept in the town hall that contained records of the town's history, and which played a vital and unusual role in making Yarmouth's citizens aware of their past and of their particular rights, liberties and privileges.[61] He was to make good use of these in *Lenten Stuff*, his extraordinary story of his escape from London that merges with the history of Great Yarmouth and the red herring, the abundant, easily caught fish in the North Sea and the Baltic that made many rich in the coastal regions of Scandinavia, Holland, England and Scotland. While the Scandinavians and the Dutch liked to preserve herring in vinegar, the English tended to smoke it so that it turned red, principally because of a shortage of salt. Great Yarmouth was the centre of the English herring industry and had become an extremely wealthy and powerful independent borough, proud of its history and traditions.[62] Although Nashe was from Lowestoft, Yarmouth's principal coastal rival, his praise of the independence, liberty and wealth of the town that sheltered him in his hour of need can be taken at face value.[63]

Nashe probably stayed in the Yarmouth area for most of 1598, perhaps at a number of houses, including those of his brother, Tom, and half-sister, Mary, who were both married and lived nearby.[64] He complained about his lack of books and papers, which had undoubtedly been left behind in his London lodgings when he fled in great haste.[65]

Lenten Stuff was published in early 1599, having been entered in the Stationers' Register on 11 January by Cuthbert Burby (1565–1607), who had also published *The Unfortunate Traveller* and, along with Danter, was one of the booksellers with whom Nashe worked most closely.[66] The preface indicates that Nashe was now back in London. His dedications to Humphrey King (*fl.* 1595–1613) – a minor poet who seems to have little obvious relationship to Nashe and may even have been one of his enemies, since he was associated with Harvey – and to 'To his Readers, he Cares not what they be', would appear to indicate a fierce defiance of hostile interpretation as well as an acknowledgement that no significant patron would want to be associated with his work after the *Isle of Dogs* affair.[67] Nashe promises to answer the '*Trim Tram*', Lichfield's inconsequential work, but nothing ever appeared.[68]

Perhaps Nashe was aware that the authorities were closing in and that he was not likely to be able to publish much more, if anything at all. Archbishop Whitgift, his former supporter, acting under orders from the Privy Council in his capacity as chief censor, issued a decree on 1 June 1599 banning a series of satirical literary works by prominent authors, including Joseph Hall, Marlowe, John Marston and Thomas Middleton, for their bad taste and, presumably, capacity to undermine public morality. Nashe and Harvey were to be silenced for ever: 'all Nashe's books and Dr Harvey's books be taken wheresoever they may be found, and that none of their books be ever printed hereafter'.[69] Nashe was a former gamekeeper who had turned poacher.

The Bishops' Ban, unlike the closure of the theatres, was indeed permanent and effective. Harvey lived on for another thirty years but published nothing more, retiring to Saffron Walden and probably practising medicine, his few attempts to re-enter public life proving unsuccessful.[70] Nashe probably wrote nothing else. *Summer's Last Will* was published at the end of 1600 (it was entered in the Stationers' Register on 28 October), and it is possible that he was already dead by this point, given the unusual appearance of that work. He may have played a part in the publication of the anonymous translation of Tommaso Garzoni's *The Hospital of Incurable Fooles* (1600), since the preface to that work is signed 'Il Pazzissimo' (the maddest one), which could well be a Nashe epithet. Nashe appears to have been fairly fluent in Italian (he seems to have had access to the Italian translation of the Quran), so translation of such a work, a mixture of medicine and satire along Rabelaisian lines, would surely have appealed to him.[71] Equally, however, the author of the preface – who may or may not have been the translator – could have been one of the many writers in the 1590s eager to be associated with one of the most influential authors of the time.

Nashe was dead by 1601, as epitaphs started to appear. He was lamented in measured lines in the witty *The Second Part of The Return from Parnassus*, performed at St John's College, Cambridge, Nashe's alma mater: 'His style was witty though it had some gall,/ Some things he might have mended, so may all.'[72] Thomas Dekker and Thomas Middleton paid tribute to their fellow writer.[73] The most touching tribute, discovered only recently, was a manuscript poem by Jonson, further emphasizing the close nature of the two men's relationship.[74]

The poem tells us a great deal about how Nashe was viewed by his friends, a counterbalance to his public persona and the comments of his enemies. Jonson, like the author of the Parnassus play, celebrates Nashe's acute wit:

> Here lies
> Conquered by destiny & turned to earth
> The man whose want hath caused a general dearth
> Of wit; throughout this land: none left behind
> to equal him in his ingenious kind.

Nashe's death, according to Jonson, has deprived English literature of a crucial element. Jonson valued wit, and his volume of epigrams in his first folio (1616) is indebted to one of his favourite authors, the witty Roman poet Martial, who makes a brief appearance towards the end of Nashe's last work, *Lenten Stuff*.[75] Jonson also valued friendship, one of the virtues most prized in Renaissance Europe.[76] At a time when hierarchies structured everyday life, friends could act as equals speaking freely and openly to each other without fear of hostile intervention. Jonson is clear that he was not praising Nashe as a 'parasite', and acknowledges that Nashe certainly knew how to insult his enemies:

> But to his friends her faculties were fair
> pleasant and mild as the most temp'rate air
> O pardon me dear friend if fear control
> the zealous purpose of my wounded soul
> fear to be censured glorious in thy praise.

Jonson – a writer, like Nashe, frequently at odds with the authorities who supported his career at other times – brings to the foreground the issue of censorship, reminding readers of the forces that silenced Nashe just before his death (which might explain why Jonson never published the poem). The poem makes it clear that Nashe was a good friend, and was able to trust younger companions such as Jonson, who knows more about the dead writer than he can reveal here. For Jonson, Nashe cannot be properly known by those who see only his public profile and read his published works. Jonson tells his readers that Nashe had a good death, secure in his faith and ready for the afterlife: 'thou diedst a Christian faithful penitent/ Inspir'd with happy thoughts & confident,' an appropriate end for a writer whose career began defending the established church.

There is no known likeness of Nashe apart from the woodcut in *Trimming*, a hostile work. He was generally represented as slender and youthful in appearance, even boyish, a description he endorsed as late as *Lenten Stuff*, when he was in his early thirties, where he refers to himself as a 'stripling'.[77] Much is made of Nashe's inadequate facial hair, which led Richard Lichfield to joke that the sparseness may be owing to treatment for syphilis (although the jibe is as likely to be revenge for Nashe's slurs against the Harvey brothers for their alleged sexual misdemeanours).[78] It is possible that Nashe had red hair, since he appears to represent himself as a fox in his writings, notably in *Have with You*, in which he threatens to pour scalding ink on Harvey's scalp, an allusion to the myth that foxes killed hedgehogs by urinating on them.[79] Harvey describes him as 'gag-toothed' (with prominent, protruding teeth), so

that, in Charles Nicholl's words, Nashe was probably 'youthful, beardless, scruffy, long-haired'.[80]

We know little of his private life beyond his capacity for making close friends and deadly enemies, and for a tendency to bite the hand that fed him. He appears never to have owned property, and lived in a variety of lodgings or in other people's houses, especially when on the run from the authorities. He never married and there is no mention of a partner or serious

Satirical woodcut of Thomas Nashe from Gabriel Harvey's pamphlet
The Trimming of Thomas Nashe (1597).

affective relationship beyond a number of friendships. He hints at a casual attitude towards prostitutes, which is repeated by his enemies, but whether this is a mixture of bravado and common insult is hard to determine.

ONE

Religion

etween 1588 and 1590 a series of scurrilous and libellous pamphlets appeared attacking the ecclesiastical hierarchy of the relatively newly established Church of England. The message of the pamphlets, produced on a portable press, was simple and familiar enough: that the church had lost sight of the proper aims and message of Christianity. Protestants had left the late medieval church, inaugurating the Reformation, because they thought that the corruption of the worldly established church had obscured and distorted the true message of Christ, and they wished to return to fundamental principles. Many Catholics and traditional theologians warned that this was a dangerous manouevre and that it would be hard – as it indeed proved – to stop the revolution once it had started. A state Protestant church was always vulnerable to the accusation that its structures and divisions simply replicated those of the over-elaborate medieval church it had left, and that yet more change was needed.[1]

This charge – that the Church of England was complacent, self-serving and corrupt, that it was designed to protect and promote its own while preaching a hypocritical message of salvation for all – was the substance of the Marprelate tracts. They were not doctrinally or theologically complicated, and their message was therefore easily understood. Their challenge to the established church came principally through their aggressive, polemical style, in particular the use of colloquial, demotic language. While the established church sought to maintain elaborate hierarchies of curates, vicars, rectors, bishops and archbishops, the authors of the Marprelate tracts removed these distinctions by addressing all clerics and their congregations in identical terms. In doing so they were following the Lutheran dictum that the church functioned through 'the priesthood of all believers', based on Matthew 18:20: 'For where two or three are gathered together in my Name, there am I in the midst of them.' For the Marprelate authors and their supporters, the Church of England was sliding back to the Catholicism they had worked so hard to overthrow.

The first writer to confront the unknown authors, Thomas Cooper (*c.* 1517–1594), Bishop of Winchester, understood the nature and extent of the challenge. In Joseph Black's words, 'Cooper's reading of Martinist style as a threat not only to the dignity of the libeled bishops, but ultimately also to the country's fundamental religious, political, legal, and social structures, would become the core message of the Anti-Martinist campaign.'[2] For the bishops, if the language of the church was overthrown then so was the church itself. Accordingly, Cooper and his fellow bishops employed a series of sympathetic writers, including John Lyly and Thomas Nashe, to answer the Marprelate writers in kind and, so they hoped, restore order. Together these writers became the 'Anti-Martinists', their style and diction tailored – perhaps rather too closely – to confront the Martinists (which is why it is not always clear who wrote which tract, or whether they were a collective effort).[3]

A good sense of the style of the Marprelate pamphlets is provided by one of the later tracts, *The Just Censure and Reproof of Martin Junior* (July 1589). Here and elsewhere in the series a family of irascible but true believers is imagined. The *Reproof* was purportedly written by Martin Marprelate's eldest son, Martin senior, and addressed to his younger brother, Martin junior. Martin senior reprimands Martin junior for his hasty publication of their father's *Theses Martinanae*, which had appeared earlier that same month. Here, Martin Junior had outlined 110 principles – with commentary – which demonstrated why episcopacy was un-Christian. It began with the axiom 'That all the officers of a true and lawful church government, in regard of their offices, are members of the visible body of Christ, which is the church' (p. 149), signalling the attack on existing church government.

Martin senior paraphrases the words of Archbishop Whitgift in order to provide advice to his hotheaded younger brother. Whitgift is cited as claiming that 'These Martinists are all of them traitors and enemies unto her Majesty' (p. 174), worse than the Jesuits, which enables Martin to respond in kind and at length:

> And trust me, Jack, I commend thee for thy plainness, and do so still, boy, for truth never shames the Master, I warrant thee, and take it o' my word. For indeed thine uncle Canter[bury] is no less than a most vile and cursed tyrant in the church. And a plain Antichrist he is even by the doctrine of the Church of England, and so by

the doctrine of our church are the rest of our cursed
bishops, in the proof of which point by-and-by I will
a little insist. And because many take snuff that my
father should account them, yea, and prove them petty
antichrists, I will manifestly prove them to be so, even
by the doctrine of the church of England, maintained
by statute and her Majesty's royal privilege. For my
father now hath taught us such a way to reason against
these Caiphases, in the Theses set down by thee, as

Magdalena de Passe and Willem de Passe, after G. Paul,
John Whitgift, Archbishop of Canterbury, c. 1620, engraving.

will anger all the veins in John Canterbury's heart. And
that is, to show that they are enemies to the doctrine
of our church. (p. 177)

The thrust of the attack is clear enough. Whitgift's own words
can be used to condemn him, and Martin junior should have
understood that point. The exchange between Martin senior
and Martin junior works as a ruse to elaborate, extend and
explain Marprelate hostility to the established church,
demonstrating the democratic arguments that their form of
religion permits and encourages.

It is the details that make this passage powerful. The
Marprelates are staging a debate so that they can expose what
they see as Whitgift's prejudices before answering them in
kind. There is the emphasis on 'plainness', which by implication indicates that other styles of argument are excessively
ornate and designed to confuse, mislead and assert an unjus-
tified superiority over opponents. Accordingly, Whitgift is
stripped of his ecclesiastical titles and referred to in familiar
terms as 'uncle Canter' and 'John Canterbury', in line with the
Marprelate claims made in the first published work in the
assault on the church, that 'all true pastors, and all pastors that
are under Jesus Christ, are of equal authority' (*The Epistle*,
October 1588, pp. 11–12). Martin senior is therefore asserting
his right to address Whitgift as an equal, challenging the pri-
mate to object and so declare his unfitness to govern the church.

Just as Protestants routinely dismissed the pope as the
Antichrist, so does Martin senior dismiss the archbishop. The
passage is replete with studded colloquial phrases challenging
ecclesiastical language: the clergy 'take snuff' (that is, care, take

offence) that they are labelled 'petty antichrists', and so they will have to answer the charges outlined in the pamphlets; the archbishop will feel anger in his veins and heart. It adopts and imitates formal and everyday reasoning in ways that every reader will be able to understand, making it clear that the Marprelates wish to inaugurate a revolution in church government by which the congregations will take control of their churches and not have the church imposed on them by an alien, self-serving elite (again, deliberately mirroring Protestant arguments that they must reclaim their church from the tyranny of Rome). The bishops and their supporters have become 'Caiphases', after the Jewish high priest who oversaw the trial of Jesus and had him punished for blasphemy (Matthew 26:56–67).

Nashe appears to have been supported by Whitgift at this point in his writing career, possibly through connections via his clergyman father (William Nashe obtained his preferment in West Harling through the Gawdy family, who had links to Whitgift).[4] It is not certain which of the Anti-Martinist pamphlets Nashe wrote, and whether he cooperated with other writers, but it is likely that he played a prominent role in the response coordinated by the bishops.[5] A *Countercuffe Given to Martin Junior* (1589), written by the pseudonymous Pasquill of England, is probably wholly or in part by Nashe. In this pamphlet, the role of the bishops is forcefully defended and the Martinists answered with interest, as Nashe parodies their style and arguments:

Down with learning and Universities; I can bring you a Free-mason out of *Kent*, that gave over his occupation

twenty years ago. He will make a good Deacon for your
purpose: I have taken some trial of his gifts; he preach-
eth very prettily over a Joynd-stool. These Bishops are
somewhat too well grounded for green-heads; so long
as they keep their place and power, it is impossible for
thee to cast the Religion of this Land into a new Mould
every new Moon. The whole state of the Land per-
ceives it well enough, that to deliver up the Prelacy to
Martin is a canker more dangerous to the Church and
Realm, than it was for the *Athenians* to deliver their
Orators to *Phillip* of *Macedon* their utter enemy: or than
it is for the Sheep to betray their Shepherds to the
Wolf.[6]

The passage concludes that the Marprelates will see 'Religion
haled with violence into her grave' (I, p. 62). It is a brilliant
answer to the Martinist challenge and contains a number of
themes that Nashe was to develop throughout his life.

The passage begins with a respect for learning, achievement and status, reminding readers that democratizing the
clergy may also mean employing many enthusiasts and
time-servers who do not have the ability, training or aptitude
for the profession. With such a transformation comes the
related fear that the church will be forced to change endlessly
according to whatever fashion has caught the imagination of
the zealots who have seized control of the institution, and
that this is prevented by the wisdom and experience of the
very bishops whom the Martinists are so keen to deride. Far
from being the hypocritical Antichrists of their opponents'
imagination, the bishops are the just and sensible elders who

ensure that all can worship safely and properly, free from the aggressive bigotry of their opponents. Nashe (assuming he is the author) turns the Martinist arguments against them; to counter the Marprelate assertion that they speak the language of the people, Pasquill alleges that the 'whole state of the Land' realizes that the status quo is preferable to manic change, and that an ordered hierarchy is required to run the church properly. He neatly juxtaposes a story from Greek literature, to show his learning and fitness to defend the bishops (his source is the history of Diodorus Siculus), with a familiar Protestant image usually applied to Catholics, that of wolves infiltrating the flock of the good shepherd. In doing so, he justifies the conclusion of Archbishop Whitgift, parodied and ridiculed in *The Just Censure and Reproof of Martin Junior,* that the Martinists are 'worse than the Jesuits' (p. 174).

The comparison is developed in other writings that Nashe produced either alone or with others, notably the preface to *An Almond for a Parrot* (1590) by Cuthbert Curry-Knave. Adopting the identity of an Englishman returning from Europe who has heard little about the current situation in England, the author claims to have experienced a loud peal of bells and singing and shouting in an unnamed Catholic country, 'as though Rhodes had been recovered, or the Turk quite driven out of Christendom'.[7] Instead, it transpires that the celebrations are for Martin Marprelate,

Who by his books, libels, and writings, had brought that to pass which neither the Pope by his Seminaries, Philip by his power, nor all the holy League by their underhand practices and policies could at any time

effect: for whereas they lived at unity before, and might
by no means be drawn unto discord, he hath invented
such quiddities to set them together by the ears that
now the temporality is ready to pluck out the throats
of the Clergy, & subjects to withdraw their allegiances
from their Sovereign.[8]

Again, the satire is both incisive and based on the longer
history of Reformation polemic, labelling the Martinists as
the schismatics and traitors who undermine the unity that
others have worked so hard to create. All the efforts of the
pope, the Spanish and the Holy League of Catholic States
(1571) pales into insignificance when compared to the success
of the ignorant Marprelates, who are undermining the church
from within and leaving England vulnerable to attack. The
implication is that triumphs such as that over the Armada
two years earlier will have been in vain unless the Marprelate
threat is properly identified and countered.[9]

The Marprelate threat did indeed cease, but not because
of the writings defending the bishops. The press was seized
in Newton Lane (now Oldham Road) near Manchester on
14 August 1589. Some type had spilled out of the cart in which
it was being carried ten days earlier, in the village of Warrington,
Lancashire, and bystanders – although not initially realizing
what they had seen, and believing the small metal objects to
be lead shot – evidently reported the incident so that the
authorities caught up with the itinerant printers.[10] Neither
of the two principal authors of the tracts were ever directly
accused or convicted, even though they were identified by the
Elizabethan authorities.[11] Job Throckmorton (1545–1601),

assumed by most scholars to be the principal author, was exposed in 1594 but denied his involvement; his collaborator John Penry (1563–1593) was captured and executed for sedition, but for another, unpublished work. It is a sign of the significance of the episode for Nashe that in his last work, *Nashe's Lenten Stuff* (1599), he refers to a 'parish in Lancashire [where] we have a flying voice dispersed'. By that he means the capture of the Marprelate press and the silencing of its dangerously uncontrollable message (although there may be rather more sympathy from Nashe at this point, since he had also been the target of unwelcome attention from the Elizabethan censors for his part in *The Isle of Dogs*).[12]

The Marprelate controversy was not the first major polemical exchange over religion in England; the conflict between Thomas More and William Tyndale in the 1520s and 1530s had been, if anything, even more vituperative.[13] In terms of the theological nature of religious debate, it changed very little, and similar positions were assumed and argued with equal vigour in the seventeenth century, including throughout the English Civil War.[14] What did change was the nature and style of English writing and satire in the 1590s, so much so that eventually the authorities intervened to impose the Bishops' Ban in 1599.[15] We have only a limited idea of how Nashe wrote before he was employed to counteract the Martinists – the one work we can date to his student career in Cambridge, *Terminus et non terminus*, is no longer extant, and *The Anatomy of Absurdity* (1589) is obviously developed from his studies – but indications are that he was developing an acerbic, satirical style, which was probably the reason he was employed in the first place. Certainly, the controversy enabled him to develop a mode of writing that he was able to put to good effect and which established his reputation for the rest of his career.

Nashe wrote one other didactic Christian work, *Christ's Tears over Jerusalem* (1593), but references to religion are legion throughout his works and it is clear that his religious faith shaped his life. Beyond a few basic principles we learn little of the nature of his belief, but that is not unusual; we know almost nothing about the confessional allegiances of many of his contemporary writers – hardly surprising at a time of dangerous sectarian conflict, when an unequivocal declaration of faith was either brave or foolhardy.[16] The main animating principle in Nashe's writings is not doctrinal, but a hostility to sectarian schism. Anything that threatened the unity of the church was treated with hostility and contempt, and he attacks both Catholics and the 'hotter' sort of Protestants in numerous places. In *The Unfortunate Traveller* the narrator, Jack Wilton, is horrified by the rebellion he witnesses in the German city of Münster. The charismatic John of Leiden (1509–1536), a Dutch Anabaptist, led a violent revolt against the Catholic authorities, his followers believing his claim that he was a prophet inspired by God who had been sent to save them in the Last Days.[17] Nashe/Wilton's condemnation of the delusions of the prophet's egalitarianism and destruction of established authority marks the rebellion as a more extreme version of the assault on the Church of England by the Marprelates. Anticipating the reader's imagined objection, the narrator counters:

> You may object that those which I speak against are more diligent in reading the Scriptures, more careful

to resort unto Sermons, more sober in their looks, more modest in their attire, than any else. But I pray you, let me answer you, Doth not Christ say that before the Latter day the Sun shall be turned into darkness, and the Moon into blood? Whereof what may the meaning be, but that the glorious Sun of the Gospel shall be eclipsed with the dim cloud of dissimulation; that that which is the brightest planet of salvation shall be a means of error and darkness; and the Moon shall be turned into blood, those that shine fairest, make the simplest show, seem most to favour religion, shall rent out the bowels of the church, be turned into blood, and all this shall come to pass before the notable day of the Lord, whereof this Age is the Eve? . . .

Did not the Devil lead Christ to the pinnacle or highest place of the Temple to tempt him? If he led Christ, he will lead a whole army of hypocrites to the top or highest part of the temple, the highest step of Religion and Holiness, to seduce them and subvert them . . . Remember then, imprint in your memory; your pride and singularity will make you forget them; the effects of them many years hence will come to pass. Whosoever will seek to save his soul shall lose it; whosoever seeks by headlong means to enter into heaven, and disannul God's ordinance, shall, with the giants that thought to scale heaven in contempt of Jupiter, be overwhelmed with Mount Ossa and Pelion, and dwell with the devil in eternal desolation.[18]

IOHAN·VĀ·LEIDEN·EY·KONINCK·DER·WEDERDOPER·
THO·MONSTER·WA ____ ERHAFTICH·GŌTER·

HÆC·FACIES·HIC·CVLTVS·ERAT·CV·SEPTRA·TENE·
REX·ανα βαπ̄τjisc̄p·SED·BREVE·TĒPVS·EGO·
HENRICVS·ALDEGREVER·SVSATIĒ·FACIEBAT·
·ANNO·M·D·-·XXXVI·
GOTTES·MACHT·IST·MYN·CRACHT·

Of course, *The Unfortunate Traveller* is a fictional text, and such language and representations of religious positions can be learned – as Nashe, a writer especially adept at ventriloquism, demonstrates time and again. However, the horror of pointless and unnecessary violence caused by the destruction

Heinrich Aldegrever, *Jan van Leiden*, 1536, engraving.

of the city's religious and social infrastructure and ideological glue, and the vain hope of salvation, suggest that this passage is not simply a fictional chimera designed to challenge the reader's sense of reality. Nashe represents the Münster Anabaptists, who believe in the freedom of choice of adult believers confirmed and publicly demonstrated by adult rather than child baptism, as similar to the Marprelates and their fellow travellers. Indeed, the episode demonstrates where such Protestant sectarian logic leads, according to Nashe. The Münster Anabaptists imagine that faith and worship should be simple and that following clear rules is best and a certain means of securing salvation. Accordingly, they remove all signs of distinction between believers, a dangerous manoeuvre that the narrator argues is a sign of their ignorance, hypocrisy and stupidity. Not only does it imperil their souls, but this misconceived equality prevents others from learning how to obtain a state of grace. Objections that the Anabaptists are saintly in their self-denying behaviour are therefore equally deluded and must be countered. In fact, the Anabaptists are right that what is happening in the world is a sign that the last days before the Apocalypse are upon us, but they do not realize that they are in thrall to the Devil and are tempting the faithful with false solutions of immediate salvation that must be resisted. True Christians will find their faith strengthened by resistance to the false religion of those who have overthrown the church in Münster.

Nashe may or may not have believed that the End of the World was nigh: it is quite possible that he did, given the prevalence of Millenarian thought in England – and throughout Europe – in the aftermath of the Reformation.[19] It is much

more certain that, in common with many other writers, he
was very worried about challenges to the authority of the
church and believed that chaos was likely to follow the undermining of ecclesiastical unity.[20] He also had a series of intellectual and aesthetic objections to the style and nature of
Protestants eager to accelerate the Reformation and return
to the simpler style of worship in the early church. In his preface to Robert Greene's prose romance *Menaphon*, which was
entered into the Stationers' Register on 23 August 1589, Nashe
demonstrates that the religious issues he was considering in
the Anti-Marprelate tracts were at the forefront of his mind:

> Epitaphers and position Poets we have more than a
> good many, that swarm like Crows to a dead carcass,
> but fly, like Swallows in the Winter, from any contin-
> uate subject of wit.

> The efficient whereof I imagine to issue from the
> upstart discipline of our reformatory Churchmen, who
> account wit vanity, and poetry impiety . . . I deem him
> far unworthy the name of a scholar, and so, conse-
> quently, to sacrifice his endeavours to Art, that is not
> a Poet, either in whole or in part.[21]

Again, it is not clear how seriously Nashe's argument should
be taken, but the link he makes between religious polemic
and poetry is both suggestive and important. Bad poetry –
the insincere work of inferior writers who exploit the grief
of family and friends because they are presumably in no fit
state to realize how poor is the verse offered to them for

comfort – stems from the assaults on poetry and drama by such writers as Stephen Gosson (1554–1624). In his *School of Abuse* (1579), Gosson condemned poetry and plays because he thought they were a waste of time and lured people away from the true teachings of the church. His argument inspired a number of attempts at refutation, most famously that of the work's unwitting dedicatee, Sir Philip Sidney, with his *Defence of Poetry*.[22] In the preface, Nashe argues by implication that good poetry and proper religion are bound inextricably together. Bad writing goes with the poor theology and the simplistic, leaden arguments of the 'reformatory Churchmen' who want to break down distinctions in the name of an undesirable and mistaken equality that occludes proper religious thought.

The quality that Nashe claims as truly religious in his preface is 'wit', a major feature of Renaissance writing, which described the ability, both innate and learned, to make startling connections.[23] Without 'wit', proper understanding, nothing makes any sense because neither writers nor readers are able to forge the connections necessary to secure salvation, and neither will they be able to write well. Just as Counter-Reformation Catholics argued that churches should be made as beautiful as possible to celebrate the glory of God and to distinguish them from the bare formality of austere Protestantism, Nashe is hostile to claims that ingenuity and true religion are at odds, and that faith requires the rejection of pleasure, sophistication and complexity.[24] As he does in his depiction of the ignorant preachers in Münster in *The Unfortunate Traveller*, in the preface Nashe reserves his particular ire for bad preachers who assume that they have the right to instruct others in a faith they do not understand themselves: 'I know not how it cometh to pass by the doting practise of our Divinity Dunces, that strive to make their pupils pulpit-men before they are reconciled to *Priscian* [one of the most basic grammar books, studied very early on in school].'[25] The cycle of witless instruction and bad writing continues as the teachers train in their own image new generations of clergymen who, in turn, train their flocks to misread and misunderstand, and so it will go on unless someone – such as Nashe – intervenes to break the spell.

Nashe's most extended discussion of religion is to be found in his longest work, *Christ's Tears over Jerusalem*, entered into the Stationers' Register on 8 September 1593 and published later that year (that is to say, before 25 March, when the new year formally began; the calendar was not adjusted to start the year on 1 January until 1752), when a terrible epidemic of plague was still raging in London. It is surely appropriate that 'the most serious of Nashe's works should also be his most stylistically ambiguous. The humour in *Christ's Tears* does indeed pull the reader in contrary directions, creating the entertainment it ostensibly castigates.'[26] The comic nature of the stock situations and the familiar, often religious rhetoric are in pointed contrast to the grim nature of the subject matter and the serious message of the tract, that some way has to be found to cope with the horror of the plague. Perhaps, in other words, there can be no understanding without the use of paradox and wit, and a simple and straightforward belief in God's grace is unlikely to be enough in such times. God's mysterious ways require a deep and profound response from men and women, which only educated and nimble thinkers

such as Nashe can provide. Nashe advises his readers more than halfway through the text, 'That religion which is soon ripe, is soon rotten.'[27] A more substantial, sustaining and witty faith is required, especially in times of plague.

Nashe makes the need for wit one of the central planks of true faith in *Christ's Tears*, a crucial requirement for avoiding the excessive and misleading piety of schismatic clergy inclined to the puritanical belief of those such as the Marprelates:

> Get you some wit in your great heads, my hot-spurred Divines, discredit not the Gospel: if you have none, dam up the Oven of your utterance, make not such a big sound with your empty vessels. At least, love men of wit, and not hate them so as you do, for they have

Plague in London, illustration from the title page of Thomas Dekker's pamphlet *A Rod for Run-awayes* (1625).

what you want. By loving them and accompanying with them, you shall both do them good and your selves good; they of you shall learn sobriety and good life, you of them shall learn to utter your learning and speak movingly. (p. 124)

Religion requires a balance of faith and wit properly combined, and the 'hot-spurred Divines' are urged to read the Gospels. This is a calculated insult, since the 'hotter sort' of Protestants invariably argued that they were the Christians returning the faith to its original biblical principles. These clergy wanted to remove the extraneous layers of church practice that had accumulated over the centuries, while their opponents – presumably including Nashe – argued that they were simply 'things indifferent' in terms of worship, and did not interfere with the truth of the Christian message.[28] The combination in the adjective 'hot-spurred' not only implies self-righteous certainty and enthusiasm, but is later linked by Nashe to the virulent spread of disease.[29] In Rome, Jack Wilton observes 'such a hotspurd plague as hath not been heard of', suggesting that, if *Christ's Tears* is read alongside *The Unfortunate Traveller*, extreme Protestant belief is an epidemic that threatens to overwhelm the institution of the church in the same way that plague destroys helpless city-dwellers.[30]

Nashe's narrator is also clear that the neglect of aptitude, ability and the proper training to explain the Bible to a lay audience has disastrous consequences. The universities and the church have done the country a serious disservice by preferring

A number of young hypocrites, who else had never known any such sin as dissimulation to the Commonwealth. It is only ridiculous dull Preachers (who leap out of a Library of Catechismses, into the loftiest Pulpits) that have revived this scornful Sect of Atheists . . .

They boldly will usurp *Moses'* chair, without any study or preparation. They would have their mouths reverenced as the mouths of the *Sibyls*, who spoke nothing but was registered; yet nothing comes from their mouths but gross full-stomached tautology. They sweat, they blunder, they bounce & plunge in the Pulpit, but all is voice and no substance: they deaf men's ears, but not edify. Scripture peradventure they come of thick and three-fold with, but it is so ugly daubed, plaistered, and patched on, so peevishly specked & applied, as if a Botcher (with a number of Satin and Velvet shreds) should clout and mend Leather-doublets & Cloth-breeches. (pp. 123–4)

It is a vivid and memorable description – as it is meant to be. The undereducated and incompetent clergy are unable to preach, a serious fault in a Protestant country when the sermon was the main way for most people to access religious instruction and have the Bible explained to them.[31] Performance allied to proper instruction was vital, and preachers needed to be educated in the art of rhetoric and delivery as well as doctrine.[32] Nashe is providing his own version of how to write properly, tailoring his message to the written medium, in representing bad preachers as 'botchers', unskilled tailors who repaired old, worn-out clothes, or simply those who performed such tasks badly.[33] These botchers desperately try to repair garments with the unsuitable materials they have to hand so that everyday working clothes such as ordinary cloth breeches (trousers) and doublets made of a hard-wearing material such as leather and suitable for the working day are patched with strips of such expensive, luxury materials as satin and velvet. In the same way preachers who have not the skill or wit to combine the learned and the demotic – as Nashe demonstrates that he has – simply patch things together and produce something ugly, distorted and, at best, useless, rather than a carefully wrought verbal artefact that will lead people to a better understanding of the faith.[34]

In asserting the necessity of a symbiotic link between style and substance, good writing and sound doctrine, Nashe connects religion and literature.[35] In doing so, he avoids questions of confessional allegiance and doctrine, so that literature is cast as good writing, witty and able to move dextrously and easily between high and low culture; true religion should be the correct obedience to the established church and the desire to understand the Bible in an intelligent, non-dogmatic manner. While excessive devotional piety is one particular sin, uncontrolled wit is another because it 'is the superabundance of wit that makes Atheists' (p. 124), those who imagine that they are so self-sufficient that they do not require instruction from the church.

It is easy to see why Nashe might have appealed to the bishops as a suitable author to defend them from hostile Puritans: he values a *via media*, a course that avoids excess and which expresses the familiar desire for proportion and balance.[36] Unfortunately, his attacks on his enemies and those whose ideas he saw as dangerous to the commonwealth were expressed with what his opponents clearly regarded as a superabundance of wit, writing that they found excessively challenging, defamatory and slanderous. A particularly purple passage excoriating the sins of Londoners had to be replaced for the second edition of 1594.[37]

In design *Christ's Tears* is a relatively straightforward work. It was dedicated to Sir George Carey's wife, Elizabeth, one of the Spencers of Althorp, who was well known for supporting authors, including Edmund Spenser. Nashe writes of his 'Tear-stubbed pen', which he has turned to a 'Theological subject', and claims that he would not have written on divinity 'if aught else might have consorted with the regenerate gravity of your judgement' (pp. 10–11).[38] Nashe praises Lady Carey elsewhere as a properly Christian and learned woman, demonstrating the obvious sincerity of this dedication.[39] She was also the dedicatee of more playful, secular works such as Spenser's strange animal fable *Muiopotomos* (1590) and, later, John Dowland's *First Book of Songs or Airs* (1597), which contained many obviously sexually orientated lyrics, indicating that her preferences were not limited to the pious and that she had a robust and catholic enough taste to appreciate the wit of *Christ's Tears* and other works.

Nashe's longest work can be divided into two distinct sections. Arguing that London has been overwhelmed by sin, he claims that the city is in danger of encouraging the horrors the Jews experienced after their rebellion against Rome in 66 CE.[40] The first part, loosely based on Josephus'

The Jewish War (75–9 CE), recounts the suffering of the Jews under siege, largely in the form of a long sermon delivered by Christ, who warns the Jews to repent and to return to God. The second, delivered by the narrator, follows the rough outline of the seven deadly sins, to warn Londoners that they will suffer the same fate if they do not abjure their vices.[41]

The prophet Jeremiah – one of the major figures of the Old Testament, who prophesied that Jerusalem would be captured by the Babylonians, for which he was persecuted by the Jews – links the two sections of *Christ's Tears*. In his sermon Christ laments that he lacks a prophet of Jeremiah's stature with whom he might discuss the dire state of the nation: 'Good *Jeremy*, now I desire with thee, that I had a Cottage of wayfaring men in the Wilderness, where I might leave my people and live, for they be all Adulterers and a band of Rebels' (p. 35). This may well be a piece of grim humour, Christ desiring to retreat from Jerusalem to escape the vice of a city that shocks even the Son of God.[42] At least the Londoners understand the significance of Jeremiah's prophecies and the particular relevance of those prophecies to their current suffering:

> At this instant is a general plague dispersed throughout our Land. No voice is heard in our streets, but that of *Jeremy, Call for the mourning women, that they may come and take up a lamentation for us, for death is come into our windows, and entered into our Palaces.* God hath stricken us, but we have not sorrowed, of his heaviest correction we make a jest. We are not moved with that which he hath sent to amaze us. (p. 157)[43]

Michelangelo, *Jeremiah*, 1508–12, Sistine Chapel, fresco.

Nashe demonstrates that he can imitate conventional sermon styles when he thinks it appropriate: here, the Jeremiah-inspired lament at the sins of the people and the exhortation that they return to good behaviour to deflect the wrath of God. The passage emphasizes the word 'jest', ostensibly reprimanding Londoners for not reflecting seriously enough on their fate and so risking God's further anger. But is this actually a 'jest' at some level, an acknowledgement perhaps that the plague may well be a punishment from God but one that is hard to fathom and even harder to assuage? Nashe can use his wit to list all the sins and vices of the Londoners, but this may not help them to stem the plague, which keeps returning whatever is done to prevent it. The outbreak of 1592–3 was the worst in recent memory, but there had been an equally serious outbreak in 1563 and several serious epidemics between 1585 and 1587. The way to cope with the disease is probably to realize that repeating familiar lamentations may not be enough, and that true wit does not require weeping and wailing but an understanding that plague is unfathomable, an aspect of God's 'infinite jest'.[44]

Certainly, it is hard to believe that Nashe thinks a Jeremiah-like response the best way to deal with the crisis when he compares the situation to a well-known play on the London stage. Drama was the frequent target of moralistic popular theologians such as Gosson, a sign of a debauched society spiralling out of control, and a position Nashe had already confronted. Near the start of *Christ's Tears* Nashe invokes Tamburlaine's system of flying three different flags during the siege of Damascus:

To desperate diseases must desperate Medicines be applied. When neither the White-flag or the Red which *Tamburlaine* advanced at the siege of any City, would be accepted of, the Black-flag was set up, which signified that there was no mercy to be looked for; and that the misery marching towards them was so great, that their enemy himself (which was to execute it) mourned for it. Christ, having offered the Jews the White-flag of forgiveness and remission, and the Red-flag of shedding his Blood for them, when those two might not take effect nor work any yielding remorse in them, the Black-flag of confusion and desolation was to succeed for the object of their obduration. (p. 20)

In Marlowe's play, despite the pleas of the virgins of Damascus, the black flag has been raised and Tamburlaine kills the virgins, hangs their bodies on the city walls and resumes the siege.[45] Nashe's narrator notes that the black flag was 'waved or displayed' in Matthew 23 with the domination of the scribes and Pharisees in Jewish religion and society so that there can be no mercy shown and any appeal will fall on deaf ears. The lesson is surely complicated and challenging: taken at face value, it means there can be no respite for these sinners and, therefore, would suggest that the same may be the case for Londoners. Furthermore, theatregoers who had attended the second part of *Tamburlaine* would have known that he is defeated by death only after he has burned multiple copies of the Quran. Again, Nashe would appear to be suggesting that God does indeed move in mysterious ways and that,

whatever harsh moralists might claim, the theatre is a more
valuable source of information and insight into the world's
affairs than many assume.

Christ's Tears concludes with an exhortation to its readers to
repent of their sins, and tries to provide them with a strategy
for individual – if not collective – salvation. The experience
of the world being bad enough, the fears of hell's pains may
not work to turn people to God, because they will fail to
understand just how much worse eternity in hell will be than
life on Earth. Only the prospect of being deprived of heavenly
bliss can work properly, since mankind – tormented as was
Tantalus, the Greek mythological figure who could never
eat or drink because water and fruit would recede from him
as soon as he moved towards them – needs to try to move
towards a goal, however impossible it might seem. Nashe's
solution sounds very close to the atheism he condemns so
resolutely earlier in the work:

> Our best method to prevent this excluding [from
> heaven], or separating from God's presence, is here
> on earth (whatsoever we go about) to think we see
> him present. Let us fancy the firmament as his face, the
> all-seeing Sun to be his right eye, and the Moon his left
> (although his eyes are far more fiery pointed and subtle,)
> that the Stars are but the congemmed [condensed into
> gems? A Nashe coinage] twinklings of those his clear
> eyes, that the winds are the breath of his nostrils, and
> the lightning & tempests the troubled action of his ire.
> (pp. 170–71)

If men and women want to save themselves, they will have to use their wit and imagination and not simply bewail their fate like a bad preacher. That way they may not see God, but might be able to use what talents God has given them to understand a modicum of his majesty. If they are serious enough about their religion and salvation, they will know that the process cannot be without some humour, as the narrator's labours to depict the face of God demonstrate. The right eye of Horus, the Egyptian god and son of Osiris and Isis, represented the sun, and his left eye the moon. Nashe knew of Egyptian sources, as *The Anatomy of Absurdity* demonstrates.[46] For puritanical Christians Nashe's representation here could seem absurd, even blasphemous; for Christians who knew their classics or had a grounding in and sympathy for ancient forms of knowledge, the attempt probably seemed a bold effort to combine Christian and pantheistic sources with some wit to conjure up what was surely beyond the limits of human imagination.[47]

TWO

Early Style

ashe was certainly busy in the late 1580s and early 1590s; he was writing drama, poetry and prose, and probably had a hand in other works hitherto unidentified. His first published work, *The Anatomy of Absurdity*, which pre-dates the pseudonymous Anti-Marprelate tracts, was entered into the Stationers' Register on 19 September 1588, but was probably written in the summer of 1587.[1] It was undoubtedly something he had been working on while in Cambridge, and it appears to have grown out of a scholarly exercise or to have been written in imitation of popular encyclopedias with handy lists. The work was published by Thomas Hacket (active 1556–90), an established publisher who had been a member of the Stationers' Company since 1569.[2] Hacket had recently published books by Arthur Golding (*c.* 1536–1606) – a prolific translator of Latin works best known for his version of Ovid's *Metamorphoses* (1567) and Calvin's *Institutes of the Christian Religion*; and Thomas Kyd (1558–1594), whose work Nashe knew and who may well have been responsible for the 'Ur-*Hamlet*' to which Nashe refers in his preface to Greene's *Menaphon*, as well as the stage blockbuster *The Spanish Tragedy* (before 1588), quoted in *Strange News*; and also Nicholas Udall's comedy *Ralph Roister Doister* (1566–7).[3] A writer with

Nashe's range of literary interests and evident ambition could
hardly have placed his work better. Hacket clearly recognized
that Nashe, who may have caught his attention through his
involvement in various dramatic works (*Terminus et non terminus*
and, possibly, *Dido, Queen of Carthage* and other unknown works),
had a literary talent that was likely to make him money.

The relatively long dedicatory epistle to Charles Blount
(1563–1606) has a sly, knowing and rather arch tone. Blount,
later Lord Mountjoy (from 1594) and Earl of Devonshire
(from 1604), was a successful soldier in the wars in the Low
Countries, known as an intellectual rather than a courtier,
and a generous patron to whom a number of books by prominent authors were dedicated (perhaps most significantly by
Robert Greene). Mountjoy was already well known as the
long-standing partner of Penelope Devereux (1563–1607),
who had been betrothed to Sir Philip Sidney and was given a
literary life as Stella in his sonnet sequence *Astrophil and Stella*,
for the pirated edition of which Nashe later wrote a preface.[4]
There is no evidence of a link between the author and dedicatee, before or after the work appeared, and Nashe may well
have dedicated the *Anatomy* to Blount in hope rather than
expectation, and failed to secure patronage. If so, the opening
would seem to be an extraordinary performance, a mixture
of mock humility and stylistic brio, one that draws attention
to the writer and his significance even as it acknowledges his
dependence on his patron:

> If (right worshipful) the old poet *Perseus*, thought it
> most prejudicial to attention, for *Verres* to declaim against
> theft, *Gracchus* against sedition, *Catiline* against treason:

MOVNTIOY · HONORAT·D̄ · CAROLI·BLVNT· CO:DEVION BAR ·

The
Right honourable CHARLES BLVNT
Earle of Deuon, Baron Mountioy
and Knight of the Garter.

Henry Balaam, *Charles Blount*, c. 1612–16, engraving.

what such *supplosus pedum* may sufficiently entertain my presumption, who, being an accessary to Absurdity, have took upon me to draw her Anatomy. But that little alliance which I have unto Art, will authorize my folly in defacing her enemy: and the circumstance of my infancy, that brought forth this *Embrion*, somewhat tolerate their censures, that would derive infamy from my unexperiencest infirmities. What I have written, proceeded not from the pen of vain-glory but from the process of that pensiveness, which two Summers since overtook me: whose obscured cause, best known to every name of curse, hath compelled my wit to wander abroad unregarded in this *satyricall* disguise, & counselled my content to dislodge his delight from traitors' eyes.[5]

The opening sentence draws attention to Nashe's knowledge of Latin literature, as he provides a series of cases to illustrate hypocrisy, and so deny that he has any particular claims to learning. He cites three celebrated instances from the history of the Roman Republic: the notoriously corrupt government of Gaius Verres (*c.* 115–43 BCE), exposed by Cicero in one of his most celebrated forensic orations; the attempted *coup d'état* by Lucius Sergius Catilina (*c.* 108–62 BCE); and the sedition of the tribune Gaius Gracchus (*c.* 153?–121 BCE), who was assassinated after his attempts to stir the populace against the senate got out of hand.[6] Nashe links the examples through the use of a technical Latin phrase, which is not strictly necessary, *supplosus pedum*, stamping of the feet to indicate disapproval.[7] In doing so he highlights his learning through a conspicuously clever series of references while ostensibly proclaiming his unsuitability for the task ahead, and so, it would seem, providing the first example of a form of absurdity. What looks like modesty is, of course, nothing of the sort, a familiar witty paradox that many Renaissance writers employed.[8] That might not seem unusual in itself, but to address a prominent figure in such terms in the very first paragraph demonstrates extraordinary self-confidence.

The rest of the paragraph is equally self-promoting and conspicuously foregrounds the book's literary pretensions. Nashe refers to the *Anatomy* as an 'embrion', a live birth that is the produce of his youth, contrasting his inexperience with his sophisticated literary achievement (perhaps not entirely successfully).[9] In proclaiming that his work was not the result of pride and ambition, but grew out of an introspective melancholy (pensiveness), he places emphasis on his status as a writer and the importance of his compulsion to write, perhaps indicating that he and Blount are similar in their characters and desires, setting both against the courtier who wants to climb the greasy pole to the top. Blount is drawn into Nashe's world through this publication of their apparently personal communication, the patron manipulated by the writer so that it is obscure and undecipherable details of Nashe's life – his pensiveness two years ago – that take centre stage. Nashe states that he is compelled to write about absurdity, and to adopt the guise of a satirist: ironic, detached, disgusted by the follies of the world but forced to speak out to chastise the ignorant and the sinful and so provide relief for his readers. In doing so he will sacrifice his chance of worldly success, but will have the satisfaction of knowing that he has put his talents to proper use even if it comes at the expense of proper reward.

We do not know whether Blount was impressed by the young writer's chutzpah, but his subsequent lack of support may tell its own tale. The *Anatomy* consists of a series of vignettes outlining various types and examples of absurdity, a form that was to characterize Nashe's work until he developed a more polyphonic style of narration in his later works *Have with You to Saffron Walden* and *Lenten Stuff*. Many of the work's pages are taken up with anti-feminist diatribes (Nashe's work in general is notable for its lack of interest in, and contemptuous attitude towards, women). A short way in, Nashe lists the faults of women outlined by serious writers from ancient Greece onwards. He observes that Plato doubted whether women had the capacity to think rationally; that Aristotle railed against early marriages because they might bring too many women into the world; and that Homer invariably represented women such as Juno as unnecessarily confrontational:

> But what should I spend my ink, waste my paper, stub my pen in painting forth their ugly imperfections, and perverse peevishness, when as how many hairs they have on their heads, so many snares they will find for a need to snarl men in; how many voices all of them have, so many vices each one of them hath; how many tongues, so many tales; how many eyes, so many allurements. What shall I say? They have more shifts than *Jove* had sundry shapes, who in the shape of a Satyr inveigled *Antiope*; took *Amphitrios'* form, when on *Alcmena* he begat *Hercules*, to *Danae* he came in a shower of gold, to *Leda* in the likeness of a Swan, to *Io* like a Heifer; to *Aegina* like a flame; to *Mnemosyne* like a Shepheard; to *Proserpina* like

a Serpent; to *Pasiphae* like a Bull; to the Nymph *Nonacris* in the likeness of *Apollo*. For cruelty, they seem more terrible than Tigers: was not *Orpheus* the excellentest Musician in any memory, torn in pieces by Women, because for sorrow of his wife *Eurydice*, he did not only himself refuse the love of many women, and lived a sole life, but also dissuaded from their company? Did not merciless *Minerva* turn the hairs of *Medusa*, whom she hated, into hissing Adders? Therefore see how far they swerve from their purpose, who, with Green colours, seek to garnish such Gorgonlike shapes. Is not witchcraft especially upholden by women? Whither men or women be more prone unto carnal concupiscence, I refer them to *Thebane Tyresias*, who gave judgement against them long ago: what their impudencie is, let Antiquity be Arbiter. Did not *Calphernia's* impudencie (who was so importunate and unreasonable in pleading her own cause) give occasion of a Law to be made, that never woman after should openly plead her own cause in Courts of judgement? (pp. 16–17)

The passage is more complicated than it appears at first reading, and demands more careful scrutiny than the straightforward attacks on women that are easy to find and on which Nashe relies.[10] It begins with what looks like a familiar criticism of the inconstancy of women and the unscrupulous wiles they employ to trap and abuse men. However, by way of illustration, the narrator cites Jove and the shape-shifting that the notoriously lecherous king of the gods underwent in order to seduce/rape numerous goddesses and mortal women.

The examples are largely taken from Ovid's *Metamorphoses* and *Heroídes*, works that would have been familiar to all male readers who had attended a grammar school.[11] The joke would appear to be on the narrator, a figure so opposed to women that he is prepared to cite entirely inappropriate – and very familiar – evidence to argue against them, examples of brutal male treatment of women. By implication, a reader who reads this without wit or irony has fallen into a trap. In order to satisfy his lust, Jove is prepared to transform himself into a satyr, another man, a shower of gold, a swan, a bull and another god. As readers of Ovid would have known, although the usual explanation for such changes was that gods had to turn themselves into less frightening forms when they interacted with humans, such examples also expose the weakness of the

god rather than that of the women unfortunately connected to him.[12]

    The examples of women's cruelty are perhaps more double-edged. As the narrator explains, Orpheus was dismembered by the Thracian maenads, angered by his failure to pay them adequate attention, but his story is also one of his devotion to his wife, Eurydice, who perishes as he leads her out of the underworld but, in his excitement at having her back, turns to look at her too early. The shift to Minerva's hatred of Medusa and witches being predominantly women indicates a wild, uncontrolled series of uncoordinated and angry attacks by a choleric speaker who is not building an argument, as rhetorical manuals dictated, but twisting and turning from one subject to another as he lashes out at his target.[13]

Jacopo del Sellaio, *Orpheus, Eurydice and Aristaeus*, 1475–80, oil on panel.

The last two examples also do not serve the ostensible subject of the narrator's attack. Tiresias supported Jove in his argument with Juno. Jove claimed that women experience more pleasure from sex than men, a subject on which Tiresias was an authority, as he was transformed into a woman for seven years after he attacked two copulating snakes with a stick and was punished by Juno; crossed for the second time in the argument about sexual pleasure, she strikes the now male Tiresias blind. The final example, Calpurnia, is even more complicated. Calpurnia was the loyal wife of Julius Caesar, who, despite her husband's infidelity, did all she could to prevent his murder. However, the law that was passed to prevent women from pleading a case in court was the result of the actions of Gaia Afrania, a notably successful advocate. She angered male lawyers such as Ulpian, who was eager to prevent women from participating in the legal process, arguing that it was immodest for them to do so.[14] Nashe's narrator appears to have confused these two figures, and he may also be thinking of Carfania, another successful lawyer in the Roman courts, who was notorious for baring her behind at key moments in trials.[15] It is unlikely that this is the author's mistake, but it would seem to be part of a parody of misogynistic arguments made by intemperate and semi-educated men, who confuse female figures as they garble the historical record to support their case.

Nashe would appear to be less interested in defending women than in exposing absurd and ridiculous arguments in *The Anatomy of Absurdity*, and the text itself often demonstrates false logic rather than exposing its use elsewhere. In doing so, it sets tests and traps that the reader must negotiate. As the narrator is concluding, he argues that 'Young men are not so much delighted with solid substances, as with painted shadows' (p. 46), forcing the thoughtful reader to reflect on what they have read and how exactly the short book makes this case.

Similarly inventive, challenging and often disturbing lists characterize and define most of Nashe's early work. In the letter from the author to the printer prefacing *Piers Penniless, His Supplication to the Devil* (1592), Nashe cautions, 'let the interpreter beware; for none ever heard me make Allegories of an idle text' (p. 155). The key word here is 'idle', which should indeed make interpreters beware, and they must ask when, if ever, a Nashe text is an idle text. George Puttenham, in *The Art of English Poesie* (1589), defined allegory as 'false semblant or dissimulation', a passage that seems to have one meaning but which really has another, and which defines the nature and tenor of Nashe's early work, where the reader is never secure that what they might think a passage means is really right.[16] *Piers Penniless* is a good example of such dissimulation. It starts as the plea of a frustrated, neglected and poor writer, before becoming a means of listing (in some ways similar to *Christ's Tears*) the manifestations of the seven deadly sins in contemporary England as Piers submits his supplication to the Devil to help him increase his hoard of souls and so enable Piers to make a better living on Earth. When he asks the Knight of the Post, who claims he can act as an intermediary, about the nature of devils, he receives a long reply with a number of digressions, before Piers concludes with an address to the reader on the nature of publishing (including a hilarious comment on Edmund Spenser's search for preferment through

the sonnets prefacing his long poem *The Faerie Queene* of 1590),
bringing the work back to where it started.[17]

Piers Penniless was a major success and established Nashe
as the persona Piers, so that when Gabriel Harvey attacked
him in a complete work in the following year (1593), it was
entitled *Pierces Supererogation* (Pierce's performance of more
work than is required, indicating – as Nashe would have done
– that his opponent had written far too much).[18] Nashe ingen-
iously links brief sketches of vices, in the manner of traditional
homilies and sermons, with assaults on his enemies. Wrath
is characterized as someone who

> respecteth no degrees nor persons, but is equally armed
> against all that offend him. A hare-brained little Dwarf
> it is, with a swarth visage, that hath his heart at his
> tongue's end, if he be contraride, and will be sure to
> do no right nor take no wrong. If he be a Judge or a
> Justice (as sometimes the Lion comes to give sentence
> against the Lamb), then he swears by nothing but by
> Saint Tyborne, & makes Newgate a Noun Substantive,
> whereto all his other words are but Adjectives. Lightly,
> he is an old man (for those years are most wayward
> and teatish [irritable, peevish]), yet be he never so old
> or so froward, since Avarice likewise is a fellow vice of
> those frail years, we must set one extreme to strive with
> another, and allay the anger of oppression by the sweet
> incense of a new purse of angels: or the doting planet
> may have such predominance in these wicked Elders
> of *Israel*, that, if you send your wife, or some other
> female, to plead for you, she may get your pardon upon

promise of better acquaintance. But whist, these are
the works of darkness, and may not be talked of in the
day time; Fury is a heat or fire, & must be quenched
with maid's water. (pp. 187–8)

It is a characteristically vivid description with a wealth of
significant detail. Wrath is a small man, impotently railing
against the world. There is the irate judge, a bully who likes
nothing better than to convict the accused, regardless of –
perhaps even despite – guilt or innocence. Tyburn, where
most convicted criminals in London were executed, has
become a carelessly and frequently uttered oath from his
mouth, a common curse rather than the solemn promise it
should be from someone assuming his office. Grammar rules
his speech, with Newgate Prison, known for its cramped and
unpleasant conditions, serving as a common noun, and other
words becoming merely adjectives describing it, as the accused
are sentenced, their fate determined in advance. Nashe shows
that a prison sentence for such an irate judge means no more
than uttering a simple grammatical sentence, his mind already
fixed on the noun he repeats so often. Bad justice and bad
language are connected, just as the abuse of religion was
inextricably linked to poor rhetoric in the Anti-Martinist
writings.[19] Furious such judges may be, but they are old and
greedy and can be bought off with gold, or with the promise
of sexual favours, like the wicked elders who would pardon
criminals if they were sent pliable wives as a favour.[20] However,
with a flourish and a twist at the end of the paragraph that
he was to exploit more carefully in his later writings, Nashe
acknowledges that anger generally happens in the light, not

under cover of darkness, because the wrathful are not keen
to hide their sin but, convinced of the justice of their cause,
want to trumpet it abroad.

Nashe exhibits a particular fascination with spirits, ghosts
and devils that was to reappear in many of his subsequent
works. In his oration on devils delivered after Piers has concluded his survey of sins, the Knight of the Post (specifically
a professional perjurer in cony-catching literature, which
described the petty crime of the Elizabethan underworld)
provides details of a subterranean spirit encountered by King
Eritus (Eric) of Sweden.[21] Asmundus and Asvitus are two
friends who promise that the one who outlives the other
shall be buried alive with the corpse of the other. Asvitus dies
and Asmundus, with his horse and his dog and copious sup-
plies, vows 'to finish his days in darkness, and never depart
from him that he loved so dearly' (p. 233). Eric and his army
pass by and, suspecting that the barrow contains treasure, dig
down,

> Whereupon was discovered the loathsome body of
> *Asmundus*, all too besmeared with dead men's filth, &
> his visage most ugly and fearful: which, imbrued with
> congealed blood and eaten & torn like a raw ulcer, made
> him so ghastly to behold, that all the beholders were
> affrighted. He, seeing himself restored to light, and so
> many amazed men stand about him, resolved their
> uncertain perplexity in these terms. Why stand you
> astonished at my unusual deformities? when no living
> man converseth with the dead but is thus disfigured.
> But other causes have effected this change in me: for

I know not what audacious spirit, sent by *Gorgon* from
the deep, hath not only most ravenously devoured my
horse & my dog, but also hath laid his hungry paws
upon me, and tearing down my cheeks as you see, hath
likewise rent away one of mine ears. Hence is it that my
mangled shape seems so monstrous, and my human
image obscured with gore in this wise. Yet scaped not
this fell Harpy from me unrevenged: for as he assailed
me, I raught his head from his shoulders, and sheathed
my sword in his body. (pp. 233–4)

Most of this description is taken straight from the Latin *History
of the Danes* (early thirteenth century) by Saxo Grammaticus
(*c.* 1150–*c.* 1220), although some details are omitted. Saxo's
work was well known in sixteenth-century England and was,
directly or indirectly, the most important source for *Hamlet*.[22]

In both Saxo and Nashe's accounts, it is the inexplicable
nature of the event and encounter that is most significant.
There is no stated reason for the spirit of friendship turning
to fierce and terrifying conflict, nor why Asmundus's loyalty
to his friend is so harshly and irrationally punished, other
than an understanding that the living and the dead who come
up from the underworld must be at odds. Readers are not led
to believe that Asvitus has behaved either badly or well when
alive, and so cannot tell whether his dead spirit is his true
essence or an inversion of his earthly character. Saxo's account
has a refrain that Asmundus repeats, 'Why are you dismayed
to view me so bereft of colour? How can any man who lives
with dead men not grow somewhat faded there?', which
explains the sad and unfathomable mystery of death and the

underworld.[23] In Nashe Asmundus has become an evil spirit,
a Harpy sent by a Gorgon, as he makes the story more classical
in nature, rather than a more specifically pagan Germanic or
Norse myth, perhaps gathering the collection of pre-Christian
beliefs into a whole.

However, this would seem to be crediting *Piers Penniless*
– or, at least, its sections – with rather too much coherence,
whereas it is probably best read as a diverse, imaginative but
not fully worked out piece of literature. The Asvitus/Asmundus
episode has more of the transgressive thrill of the horror
story, defying explanation and so exciting or even titillating
the reader, who is unsettled and not quite sure how they
should understand what they have just read. More coherent
– although not necessarily more interesting – is *The Terrors of
the Night; or, A Discourse of Apparitions* (published in 1594, but
completed in 1593). In this work, Nashe combines his fascination with the supernatural with his interest in stylistic and
structural transformation. As in *The Anatomy of Absurdity*, his
dedicatory letter to Elizabeth, the daughter of Sir George
Carey, publicly demonstrates his intimacy with his upper-
class patrons. He states that he wrote the 'foolish' work some
time ago but that it was wrested out of his hands by a friend,
and the copy was passed from one print shop to another,
forcing the author to publish in order to reap the rewards of
his own labour and not to 'let some unskillful pen-man or
Noverint-maker [scrivener] starch his ruff and new spade
his beard with the benefit he made of them' (p. 341).[24] As
with the story of the composition of *The Anatomy of Absurdity*,
we have no means of knowing whether it is actually true. The
claim does suggest that Nashe was on familiar, friendly terms

with his dedicatee, that they were intimate enough to share a joke, and that, therefore, the professions of modesty are indeed a topos.

Terrors of the Night opens with a flesh-crawling image that devils are legion, inhabiting every conceivable crevice and space in the human body:

> What do we talk of one devil? there is not a room in any man's house, but is pestered and close packed with a camp royal of devils. *Chrysostome* saith the air and earth are three parts inhabited with spirits. Hereunto the Philosopher alluded, when he said, Nature made no voidness in the whole universal: for no place (be it no bigger than a pockhole in a man's face) but is close thronged with them. Infinite millions of them will hang swarming about a worm-eaten nose.
>
> Don *Lucifer* himself, their grand *Capitano*, asketh no better throne than a blear eye to set up his state in. Upon a hair they will sit like a nit, and over-dredge a bald pate like a white scurf. The wrinkles in old witches' visages, they eat out to entrench themselves in.
>
> If in one man a whole legion of devils have been billeted, how many hundred thousand legions retain to a Term at *London*? (p. 349)

The passage is a mixture of the serious – with the citation of St John Chrysostom (347–407 CE), one of the most significant Church Fathers, to warn readers that devils are everywhere, even in the most unexpected places – and the ghoulish, making the point of the ubiquity of demons in a memorable, spectacular fashion designed to induce unease and disgust. Aristotle's famous dictum 'Nature abhors a vacuum' is employed to argue that even the tiniest openings on the surface of the body will contain vast communities of devils, as Nashe combines a popular understanding of physics with a queasily imaginative account of the body penetrated by and populated with hostile alien organisms.[25]

The passage owes much to Nashe's understanding of rhetoric and the need to make particular points in memorable fashion in order to persuade the reader or listener – specifically, here, the sermon.[26] The style and technique as the author explores a particular point through a series of images, approaching it from a variety of positions and worrying away at its significance, are reminiscent of passages in meditations and sermons by Nashe's contemporary John Donne (1572–1631).[27] Even so, it is hard to read the passage entirely straightforwardly as a serious argument about the conflict between good and evil. Nashe frequently employs images of unattractive noses, pockmarked, disfigured with blotches and swellings, the result of an indulgent lifestyle of excessive drink and sex. In particular, he jokes about the nose of a well-known ballad writer, the recently deceased William Elderton (d. 1592), who appears to have been a frequenter of taverns and often encountered by Nashe. In the dedicatory epistle to *Strange News*, written at about the same time as *Terrors*, Nashe refers to 'Elderton's *parliament of noses*' (1, p. 256).[28] The image is not quite clear, but would seem to refer to a lost ballad by Elderton, and also to his drink-scarred, nodule-encrusted nose. In *Piers Penniless* Nashe launches a scathing attack on Richard Harvey for his ludicrous prognostication following the conjunction of Jupiter and Saturn in 1583, noting that '*Elderton* consumed his ale-crammed nose to nothing in bear-baiting him [Harvey] with whole bundles of ballets [ballads]' (p. 197). Read together, the images of Elderton suggest that Nashe has a particular fascination for self-induced bodily decay and imagines Elderton's nose as a well-populated site teeming with tiny creatures.

Reading these passages alongside the passage in *Terrors*, it becomes harder to understand the description of the devils in the nose as simply a religious insight into the nature of the world suspended between heaven and hell. Of course, it works as an example of Nashe's insistence that we must employ wit if we are to have any understanding of religious truth. But the vigour and style of the description also suggest that there is much to be enjoyed in the representation of the grotesque juxtaposition of the incongruous and the startling, forcing readers to think imaginatively about unusual and disturbing connections between things and subjects they had never before seen as connected.[29]

A few pages later the short work changes dramatically. While the opening sections appear to be warning readers that they should not ignore the malign supernatural forces that surround them, as even the most obscure and apparently insignificant place is brimming with malignity, the narrator now warns readers that much of the terror they experience in the night is the product of their own overheated imagination and ignorant fear:

Our cogitations run on heaps like men to part a fray, where every one strikes his next fellow. From one place to another without consultation they leap, like rebels bent on a head. Soldiers just up and down they imitate at the sack of a City, which spare neither age nor beauty; the young, the old, trees, steeples & mountains, they confound in one gallimaufry [confused jumble].

Of those things which are most known to us, some of us that have moist brains make to our selves images of memory: on those images of memory whereon we build in the day, comes some superfluous humour of ours, like a Jackanapes, in the night, and erects a puppet stage, or some such ridiculous idle childish invention.

A Dream is nothing else but the Echo of our conceipts [conceits] in the day. (p. 356)

As in the earlier passage, Nashe employs striking images to make the point, one that counterbalances the earlier memorable description. Here, the narrator tells us that what we think is a real terror is in fact nothing of the sort. Our overactive brains do not shut down in the night, so that what we learned and memorized during the day returns at night to haunt us as though it were real. The description of the devils living in the nose is now revealed to be nothing more than a chimera, a striking image that has been implanted in the mind and which will undoubtedly reappear in terrifying form when the sun goes down. The narrator further notes that the most intelligent people – those with moist, functioning brains – are the most susceptible to night terrors, which is, presumably, the justification for the work.[30] We may not be able to prevent ourselves from dreaming, but we should be able to combat the fears our dreams inspire if we understand that they do not signal an external reality or provide evidence of a hostile spirit world shadowing our own.

Nashe's description of night terrors as a chaotic jumble, like rebel soldiers overwhelming a city and sacking it after a siege, is another arresting image carefully placed to persuade the reader that belief in the reality of such terrifying dreams is dangerous. Enforcing discipline in armies was a major problem; moreover, cities were sacked after sieges, and commanders allowed soldiers to run riot, looting, pillaging and raping the inhabitants as a means of compensating them for the dangers they faced and to avoid paying them more than they had to.[31] The most notorious example in living memory was the destruction Antwerp experienced after it was sacked

Anon., *The Spanish Fury*, 1576–85, oil on canvas.

by Spanish troops in November 1576, an event that was described by an eyewitness, George Gascoigne (*c*. 1539–1577), in a widely circulated pamphlet, *The Spoil of Antwerp* (1576), and which became known as the Spanish Fury.[32] In describing the brain experiencing night terrors as a city overrun by marauding soldiers, Nashe aims to inspire terror in his readers and so shock them into disbelief.[33] What is most disturbing here is the chaotic and random nature of the confusion depicted: just as the soldiers attack indiscriminately, assaulting whomever and whatever they happen to encounter, so do night thoughts. The list of targets – the beautiful, young and old, trees, steeples, mountains – merges the probable and the absurd, exactly as night terrors appear in the mind, a jumble (gallimaufry) of the real and the impossible. And, just as citizens under attack are vulnerable to the assault of dangerously armed, angry and resentful soldiers, so is the brain when subject to the confusing horror of night terrors. Yet the last sentence – standing alone as a paragraph for emphasis – strikes a deliberately bathetic note: there is no substance to something that simply reflects, distorts and inverts the thoughts of the day.

Terrors concludes with another list of rhetorically patterned exhortations urging different groups of people to mend their ways and reclaim the night as a time of rest and peace, an assemblage of images that represents the belief in the power of the imagination to make startling and surprising connections:

You, whosoever or wheresoever you be, that live by spoiling and over-reaching young Gentlemen, and make

but a sport to deride their simplicities to their undoing, to you the Night at one time or other will prove
terrible, except you forthwith think on restitution: or,
if you have not your night in this world, you will have
it in hell. (p. 384)[34]

The list might well seem as random as the gallimaufry of night
terrors, and the tone is certainly more upbeat than solemn,
with the somewhat jaunty acknowledgement that if such
criminals do not experience night terrors in this world, they
will when they descend to hell, sidestepping or even undoing
the narrative trajectory of the work. *Terrors* concludes that
Christianity is the key to combating superstition: 'Had we no
more Religion than we might derive from heathen fables, me
thinks those doleful Querristers [choristers] of the night, the
Scritch-owle, the Nightingale and croaking Frogs, might over-
awe us from any insolent transgression at that time' (p. 386).
A pious enough sentiment, but hardly one inspired by the wit
that Nashe claims true religion requires. *Terrors* surely unsettles
its readers and makes them think hard about whether what
they experience is the result of an overactive imagination or
inspired by devils, precisely because it refuses to provide a satis-
fying answer to the question. We all want to follow the truth,
but how can we know what it is or how to find it?

Nashe was extraordinarily productive between 1591 and
1593. Alongside prose, he produced two works that were not
published in those years (and there may have been others lost
or undetected): the play *Summer's Last Will* (published when he
was dead or dying) and the pornographic poem 'The Choice
of Valentines', also known as 'Nashe's Dildo'.[35] The poem has

tended to receive rather adverse comment, and is a work that has frequently embarrassed Nashe's champions.[36] Written for Lord Strange, the poem is significant, whatever the objections to its content, as (probably) the first work to use the word 'dildo' to mean prosthetic penis, and because it circulated widely in manuscript and was read by and influenced a number of major and minor writers, and so forms an important chapter in the history of pornography.[37]

The poem, as Linda Grant has demonstrated, is 'unequivocally a response to Ovid', in particular the *Amores*.[38] It combines a certain knowing wit with voyeuristic sexual detail and a level of humour often found in similar works, such as Shakespeare's *Venus and Adonis* (written a year or so later) and Marlowe's *Hero and Leander* (also written at about this time), a work that had an impact on Nashe's writing. Taken together, these poems – often defined as epyllia, small epics – show the central importance of Ovid's influence in establishing the nature of erotic or pornographic literature.[39] Such poetry was, of course, designed to arouse almost exclusively male readers, but it also worked through humour, irony and wit, along with a certain moralism, derived from Ovid's ever-darker tales of the price of adulterous passion in his *Elegies*.

Nashe's poem is a case in point. His story involves a young man, Tomalin (it is implied that he is yet another of the author's personae), who visits a brothel where he encounters Francis, to whom he was once engaged. Exceptionally eager to renew what had been an exciting sexual relationship, he is initially impotent, then, after a brief, more successful passage of lovemaking, he ejaculates, leaving his frustrated partner to satisfy herself with a dildo she has to hand. The poem employs

Unknown artist, *Ferdinando Stanley, 5th Earl of Derby*, 1594, oil on canvas.

a number of familiar pornographic tropes: the scene is set with nature urging men and women to behave 'naturally'; Francis's body is then envisaged in terms of the natural world, specifically the countryside; her undressing is described at great length; and, most importantly, it represents the male lover as inadequate, partly to generate humour, but also to demonstrate to a male reader that women are insatiable and desire sex more often than the most libidinous man could imagine.[40]

Nashe describes the lovers as affectionate and sharing mutual desire, principally in order to undermine the Petrarchan and Neoplatonic conceptions of love so frequently adopted by poets. Their common desire/lust is a force that transcends the physical:

> On him her eyes continually were fixt,
> With hir eye-beams his melting looks were mixt,
> Which like the Sun, that twixt two glasses plays
> From one to th'other cast's rebounding rays.
> He like a star, that to reguild his beams
> Sucks-in the influence of Phoebus' streams,
> Imbathe's the lines of his descending light
> In the bright fountains of hir clearest sight.
> She fair as fairest Planet in the Sky
> Hir purity to no man doth deny. (155–64)

The last line wittily undercuts the poetic/scientific description that precedes it. Francis does not deny her purity to any of her clients, which further suggests that for some she pretends for their gratification to be untouched, and reminds us of her profession and the duplicity that it inevitably entails. The lovers' eyes reflect each other, like astronomers observing the sun using mirrors to prevent their eyesight from being damaged. Tomalin becomes a star using the sun to strengthen his beams as he looks down on her, a romantic and fetching image but one that is a prelude to their physical encounter.

As Tomalin's physical prowess fails, Francis laments his inability to satisfy her:

> Stay, stay sweet joy, and leave me not forlorn,
> Why shouldst thou fade, that art but newly born?
> Stay but an hour; an hour is not so much,
> But half an hour; if that thy haste be such:
> Nay but a quarter; I will ask no more,
> That thy departure (which torments me sore)
> May be alighted with a little pause,
> And take away this passion's sudden cause. (213–20)

Her words may owe something to the desperation of Doctor Faustus's final speech in Marlowe's play, as he tries to stop the clock and prevent his impending damnation:

> Ah *Faustus*,
> Now hast thou but one bare hour to live,
> And then thou must be damned perpetually:
> Stand still you ever moving spheres of heaven,
> That time may cease, and midnight never come:
> Fair Nature's eye, rise, rise again, and make
> Perpetual day, or let this hour be but a year,
> A month, a week, a natural day,

That *Faustus* may repent and save his soul,
O *lente lente currite noctis equi*:
The stars move still, time runs, the clock will strike,
The devil will come, and *Faustus* must be damned.[41]

Nashe knew the play (which was not published until 1604, after his death) exceptionally well, and copied out quotations in a book he possessed; he could even have been its co-author.[42] The apparent reference to time hastening on at a terrifying rate as Faustus has to realize the bargain he has made at the conclusion of Marlowe's play further demonstrates the wit of a poem that draws more obviously on Ovid's *Amores*, in particular 3.7, in which the poet's erection fails before the beauty of Corinna:

> Was she then not beautiful, not attractively groomed, not longed for a thousand times in my dreams? And yet when I held her in my arms, I was unhappily limp and could not perform, but lay a shameful burden on an idle bed; but though I was eager for it, and she no less, I could not use the pleasurable part of my languid loins. Her ivory arms, gleaming more brightly than Thracian snow, she cast about my neck and with eager tongue implanted wanton kisses, and lasciviously slid her limbs beneath mine. She whispered endearments, calling me master, and all the natural rapturous utterances as well. But my body, as if drugged with chill hemlock, was paralysed and failed to achieve my intent. I lay like a dead tree-trunk, a mere spectacle, a useless weight, and it was unclear whether I was body or ghost.[43]

While Ovid's narrator and the Ovidian Tomalin exist suspended between life and death (and Faustus hastens to his terrible end), Francis is very much alive and demands sexual satisfaction, a matter she now takes into her own hands with her dildo:

Upon a chariot of five wheels he rides,
The which an arm strong driver steadfast guides,
And often alters pace, as ways grow deep;
(For, who in paths unknown, one gate can keep?)
Sometimes he smoothly slideth down the hill;
Another while the stones his feet do kill:
In clammy ways he treaddeth by and by,
And plasheth and sprayeth all that be him nye.
So fares this jolly rider in his race,
Plunging and sourcing forward in like case.
(277–86)

The description is both graphic, in representing Francis inserting the dildo into her vagina and mimicking the movements of intercourse, and comic in depicting sex as an uncomfortable journey through muddy countryside. The poem ends with Francis lying breathless after her orgasm and Tomalin confessing that he has been 'taken down' (312) as he leaves the brothel.

In the envoy, Nashe hopes his patron will smile at what he has written (13, III, p. 416), and the circulation and influence of 'The Choice of Valentines' would indicate that it was received with pleasure by a wider group of readers. It may not be Nashe's wittiest work, but it is proficiently written, demonstrates a clear understanding of what its audience would want, and is often inventive in the connections it makes between literature and science, the poem and a wider literary tradition, the body and humour, and sex and death.

THREE

The Theatre

ashe has not been given due credit for his role in the development of the theatre in the 1590s. One reason for this is that he is generally known as a writer of prose, and has been since the early seventeenth century. The poet Michael Drayton (1563–1631), an often astute and opinionated literary critic, refers to Nashe as a 'proser' nearly twenty years after Nashe's death, a sign of how deep-seated his reputation as a writer of biting satire had become.[1] For Drayton Nashe's satirical wit is a literary quality that should be valued alongside the work of England's most celebrated poets:

> And surely *Nashe*, though he a Proser were
> A branch of Laurel yet deserves to bear,
> Sharply *Satiric* was he, and that way
> He went, since that his being, to this day
> Few have attempted, and I surely think
> Those words shall hardly be set down with ink;
> Shall scorch and blast, so as his could, where he,
> Would inflict vengeance.[2]

Another reason is that many of Nashe's theatrical works have been lost (a common problem), so that we have a

distorted sense of his achievement.[3] As a student, he wrote
Terminus et non terminus with Robert Mills, and he was clearly
involved in the dramatic culture that flourished at Cambridge,
often written in Latin.[4] University drama was a flourishing
art, developed out of schoolroom and college practices in
which students learned from debating major issues with their
fellow students and their tutors. Much was highly satirical,
caricaturing unpopular figures at the university – such as
Gabriel Harvey. Some authors, including Nashe and Thomas
Watson, went on to work in the commercial theatre in London,
and the relationship between the two theatrical cultures
remains largely underexplored.[5] Others – such as Thomas
Legge (1535–1607), author of a Latin play about Richard III
that may well be the first history play – remained in Cambridge
to pursue an academic career.[6]

Nashe refers to this often riotous culture in *Have with You
to Saffron Walden*, claiming that Harvey and his brothers were
the particular objects of widespread student ire. He cites
Pedantius (1581), Edward Forsett's satirical Latin play, the central character of which was obviously a version of Gabriel
Harvey. Harvey is represented as a pompous, hair-splitting
academic whose excessive faith in the value of his erudition
leads to his distorted understanding of life, and who is the
mainspring of the comedy:

> I'll fetch him aloft in *Pedantius*, that exquisite Comedy
> in *Trinity College*; where, under the chief part, from which
> it took his name, as namely the concise and firking
> finicaldo fine School-master, he was full drawn & delin-
> eated from the soul of the foot to the crown of his head.

The just manner of his phrase in his Orations and Disputations they stuffed his mouth with, & no Buffian-ism [buffoonery] throughout his whole books, but they bolstered out his part with.[7]

Harvey was ridiculed mercilessly on stage, as was his protégé, Edmund Spenser, who was represented as his helpless dupe. Nashe's recollection of the performance concentrates on Harvey's false, dull-witted learning and his inability to trans-late what he has read into meaningful advice and engagement with the world, the signs of a bad reader and a poor teacher.[8] Nashe implies that he was also involved in works that lam-pooned Gabriel Harvey and his brothers, Richard and John:

And if I should reveal all, I think they borrowed his gown to play the Part in, the more to flout him. Let him deny this (and not damn himself) for his life if he can. Let him deny that there was a Show made at *Clare-hall* of him and his two Brothers, called;
  Tarrarantantara turba tumultuosa. Trigonum, Tri-Harveyorum, Tri-harmonia.
    Let him deny that there was another Show made of the little Minnow his Brother *Dodrans Dicke* at *Peterhouse*, called; *Duns furens*. Dick Harvey in a frenzy.
    Whereupon *Dick* came and broke the College glass windows; and Doctor *Perne* (being then either for himself or Deputy Vice-chancellor), caused him to be fetched in, and set in the Stocks till the Show was ended, and a great part of the night after. (pp. 80–81)

In providing the detail of the actor playing Gabriel Harvey using his gown for the first show and describing Richard Harvey's furious and violent reaction after the second, Nashe hints strongly that he was present at both events; in challenging Harvey to deny the existence of such satirical performances attacking the three Harvey brothers, he would seem to be suggesting that he was involved in one or both productions, and is calling Harvey's bluff by goading him to deny part or all of the information recollected here. Even so, Nashe indicates that he knows much more that he could tell if provoked ('I should reveal all').

The title of the first show has three parts: *Tarrarantantara* imitates the sound of a trumpet; *turba tumultuosa* means 'disorderly crowd'; and *Trigonum, Tri-Harveyorum, Tri-harmonia* means 'a triangle of three Harveys in triple harmony'. The play, if it did exist, was performed circa 1581–6, and was probably based on Harvey's own writings, in particular his rather sycophantic collection of Latin verse dedicated to various public figures, *Gratulationes Valdinenses* (1578); it may also make use of Forsett's *Pedantius*.[9] Richard Harvey's furious reaction to a play that would appear to have been designed to incite him to violence is not noted elsewhere (neither is the play). There is no record in the college accounts of any windows being broken, so the play and subsequent events may be either invented or based on hearsay pre-dating Nashe's time in Cambridge.[10] However, there are earlier examples of windows being broken during or after the performance of college drama. The junior bursar's book at Trinity College, Cambridge, where *Pedantius* was performed, records for 1578–9, 'It[em] for thirty foot of new glass after the plays in the hall windows xv [15] s[hillings]/

It[em] for new leading of thirty foot in the great hall windows v[5] s[hillings]'.[11] Breaking windows was either a result of frustration at not being permitted entry to a popular event, or a way of expressing extreme disapproval.

The evidence Nashe provides indicates that he was not only involved in student drama at Cambridge, but keen to advertise that involvement, to show that he was closely connected to the cut and thrust of stage action. Indeed, one of his principal criticisms of Gabriel Harvey in their extended quarrel – which, as the passages cited here suggest, may have started at Cambridge – was that Harvey had little knowledge of drama, never went to see plays, and wrote in a plodding, lifeless style that lacked the wit of drama.[12]

Nashe probably worked on other plays, and it is possible that he was involved in commercial drama soon after he moved to London in the late 1580s, a period from which very few theatrical records survive. There is, however, a copy of John Leland's *Principum, ac illustrium aliquot et eruditorum in Anglia virorum encomia* (Some of the Leading Men and Illustrious Scholars in England; 1589), now in the Folger Shakespeare Library, which

Nashe's signature on the back of the title page of the Folger copy of John Leland, *Principum, ac illustrium aliquot . . .* (1589).

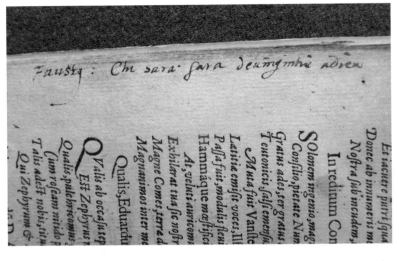

Marginalia in Thomas Nashe's hand quoting lines from *Doctor Faustus*:
'che sera sera, divinity adieu' and 'Faustus: study in Indian Silke',
in the Folger copy of John Leland, *Principum, ac illustrium aliquot . . .* (1589).

has Nashe's signature as well as quotations from *Doctor Faustus* copied out in the same hand.[13] This evidence is often used to date Marlowe's play to 1588.[14] Nashe has written 'Faustus: che sara sara devinynitie adieu', which refers to the key lines near the end of Faustus's opening soliloquy, 'What doctrine call you this? *Che sara, sara:*/ What will be, shall be! Divinity, adieu!'[15] The second marginal annotation, which is rather smudged, reads, 'Faustus: studie in indian silk'. Nashe is referring to Faustus's second soliloquy, which follows swiftly on from the first after the brief visit of the good and bad angel.[16] Faustus, turning to necromancy, announces how 'glutted' he is with the prospect of luxury, wealth and power, of being able to control the world as he has always wished he could, having spirits fetch him what he pleases, including gold from India, and, some lines later, being able to 'fill the public schools with silk/ Wherewith the students shall be bravely clad.' The marginal comment is not an exact quotation, but it definitely refers to the lines in Marlowe's play.[17]

Nashe cites Leland's book in his preface to Robert Greene's *Menaphon* (1589), the same year as *Principum, ac illustrium* was published. This is an indication that it caught his attention when it first appeared, suggesting that the marginalia date from 1589 or soon afterwards (which is why it is used to date *Doctor Faustus* to 1588). The comments have also been used to suggest that Nashe was Marlowe's co-author for *Faustus*, but the evidence is inconclusive.[18] If Nashe's annotations are simply echoes of Marlowe's play, at least one of the following suppositions must be true: Nashe must have had access to the manuscript of the play, because the first quarto of *Faustus* was not published until 1604, after Nashe's death; he must have known Marlowe personally and discussed the play with him (which is quite likely); he must have had an exceptional memory and have been able to remember specific performances of plays in impressive detail; or he took careful notes when he attended the theatre, especially when he was watching a Marlowe play.

However we read the evidence, it is clear that Nashe was closely involved in the theatre as a participant as well as a spectator. His only sole-authored play, *Summer's Last Will and Testament*, was performed at the Archbishop of Canterbury's palace at Croydon at the end of summer 1592.[19] The exact circumstances are somewhat obscure. The play contains extravagant praise of the queen, which has led many commentators to assume that it was performed for her as she completed her summer progress, but the dates and path of her return to London make this impossible.[20] The lines in which Summer asks Autumn to provide the queen with the harvest fruits he has produced after his death suggest that the printed version of the play anticipated the queen's presence:

> Unto *Eliza*, that most sacred Dame,
> Whom none but Saints and Angels ought to name,
> All my fair days remaining I bequeath,
> To wait upon her till she be returned.
> Autumn, I charge thee, when that I am dead,
> Be pressed and serviceable at her beck,
> Present her with thy goodliest ripened fruits,
> Unclothe no Arbors where she ever sate,
> Touch not a tree thou thinkst she may pass by.[21]

Why this strange discrepancy? It is hard to account for exactly, but is undoubtedly linked to the odd publication history of the play. Nashe's other works contain elaborate and carefully planned prefaces, paratexts that are important parts of the work itself and indicate how much the author cared about how his work was printed and produced (as we might expect from someone who had worked in print shops and who was close to his publishers).[22] *Summer's Last Will* contains no such preface, probably because it was printed as he was dying or after his death.[23] It would seem that Whitgift, having used Nashe to counteract the Marprelate threat, now employed him as a member of his household to write an entertainment, perhaps for a proposed visit by the queen that never took place, and perhaps as a means of passing the time fruitfully during plague outbreaks. Puns and quibbles throughout the work indicate that the part of Will Summers was played by 'Toy', who was probably a professional actor. However, the rest of the cast, including Harry Baker (who played Vertumnus) and Dick Huntley the prompter, were probably members of the archbishop's household, and possibly mainly boys.[24] The show took place in the Great Hall of the Palace at Croydon, which still stands, one of the few authentic acting spaces from the period to survive.[25]

Like Nashe's early prose works, *Summer's Last Will* consists of a series of tableaux or a procession of scenes, rather than a polyphonic narrative combining and integrating diverse elements into a coherent whole. The famous jester Will Summers (Somers) was surely chosen for his name, since the character bears no obvious relation to the historical figure and is a vehicle for Nashe to draw the audience into the play and then

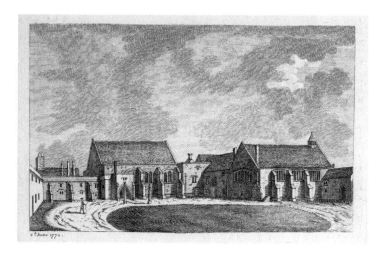

comment on the nature of the action, perhaps as a member of the audience.[26] When Back-Winter, a Nashe coinage for the bitingly cold winter of January and February (exceptionally severe in the Little Ice Age of the 1590s), exits, Will addresses the audience in part to emphasize the neologism, in part to provide a break before Summer's dramatic final dying speech, and in part to draw attention to dramatic conventions that connect actors and players as part of the show:

> This *Back-winter* plays a railing part to no purpose; my small learning finds no reason for it, except as a Back-winter or an after-winter is more raging tempestuous and violent than the beginning of Winter, so he brings him in stamping and raging as if he were mad, when his father is a jolly mild quiet old man, and stands still and does nothing. The court accepts of your meaning; you might have writ in the margent of your play-book, Let

Croydon Palace, 1772, engraving from Francis Grose, *The Antiquities of England and Wales*, vol. III (1775).

there be a few rushes laid in the place where *Back-winter*
shall tumble, for fear of raying [dirtying] his clothes,
or set down, Enter *Back-winter*, with his boy bringing
a brush after him, to take off the dust if need require.
(ll. 1805–18, p. 290)

The text presumably signals a pratfall, the actor playing Back-
Winter having fallen over and Will now drawing attention
to the need to lay rushes on the floor to prevent him from
damaging his costume (the lines indicate that it is the clothes
that matter, not the actor himself). The interlude of physical
comedy provides dramatic emphasis for Summer's bitter last
words, at the end of which he expires on stage:

Summer, Autumn and Winter from a performance of *Summer's Last Will and
Testament*, Old Palace of John Whitgift School, Croydon, 30 September 2017.

This is the last stroke my tongue's clock must strike,
My last will, which I will that you perform:
My crown I have disposed already of.
Item, I give my withered flowers and herbs
Unto dead corses [corpses], for to deck them with;
My shady walks to great men's servitors,
Who in their masters' shadows walk secure;
My pleasant open air and fragrant smells
To Croydon and the grounds abutting round;
My heat and warmth to toiling labourers,
My long days to bondmen and prisoners,
My short nights to young married souls,
My drought and thirst to drunkards' quenchless throats.
(ll. 1822–34, pp. 190–91)

Yet another comparison to Faustus's final speech might
be made.[27] Despite the local joke about Croydon, which probably works because the town was known as a centre for
industries that produced noxious smells (tanning, brewing
and charcoal), the list serves as a dying man's curse, envious
of the good fortune of those who have more time than he.[28]
Summer's last will, the title of the play, turns out to be a sad
legacy of useless and unattractive gifts, being based on the
resentment of time passing. The withered flowers for dead
bodies surely reminded the audience that they were living in
times of plague, and that it was hard to follow the ordinary
rites for the dead.[29] The gift of shady walks serves only to
remind the audience that many – undoubtedly including
Nashe himself – had to live in the shadow of the good and the
great to whom they were beholden, and giving hot days to

labourers, short nights to newlyweds and thirst to drunkards casts the dying king as a petty and spiteful creature.

The play's plot, such as it is, is straightforward enough. Will Somers appears on stage and delivers a long prologue, in which he states that Summer is dying and now wishes to make his will before Autumn and Winter. Will is clear that Summer is dying not just because time has moved on, but 'because the Plague reigns in most places in this latter end of summer, Summer must come in sick' (p. 235), a reminder of what is taking place in the world outside the hall, and, perhaps, why they might be there in the first place. The sickly Summer enters and announces that he will show what he is leaving to his heirs. This is the cue for a series of scenes resembling a progress throughout the year to match that of the queen throughout the country (*'Eliza*, England's beauteous Queen,/ On whom all seasons prosperously attend,/ Forbad the execution of my fate,/ Until her joyful progress was expir'd' (ll. 133–6, p. 237).

Flanked by Autumn, Winter and Vertumnus (the god of seasons and change), with whom he often converses, Summer witnesses songs, dances and pageants. These begin with the figure of spring, Ver, who celebrates the abundance he produces – much to the chagrin of Summer, who curses Vertumnus with the promise of Lent, a counterbalance to his profligacy. The aged figure of Solstitium, the summer solstice, carries balances to symbolize 21 June as the pivotal point of the year, midsummer, an anxious time when things could go either way, leading to feast or famine (there were good harvests in 1591–3, but then four terrible years, 'perhaps the worst sequence of the entire century').[30] Summer is angered – a common theme of the encounters – that Solstitium brings him no more than an understanding of proportion, which is of no use to a dying man. Sol, the blinding figure of the sun, also irritates Summer, reminding him of the season's lack of balance as his hot rays scorch the land and bring disaster as well as pleasure ('The *Thames* is witness of thy tyranny,/ Whose waves thou hast exhaust for winter showers,' ll. 543–4, p. 250).[31] Orion appears next, the mighty hunter with his huge array of dogs. The constellation appears as one of the most prominent in the night sky, but the link here is to the dog days, the hottest and most uncomfortable of the summer, which usually took place after the heliacal rising of Sirius, the Dog Star. Dogs were thought to run mad at this time, and the plague to flourish (as it had in 1592). The episode generates a series of dog references and jokes, from fawning courtiers (which possibly prefigures the subject matter of Nashe and Jonson's lost play *The Isle of Dogs*) to the chaos on stage appearing like a dog's dinner, as Will also intervenes.

Harvest is the next to be summoned, appearing singing with his reapers, and he confirms that this year has yielded a good crop, earning Summer's praise. It is the first time he has seemed pleased, which undoubtedly reflects the anxious nature of a life dependent on the seasons and the feeling of relief after a successful harvest.[32] A bibulous and rather debauched Bacchus follows, whose over-familiarity irritates Summer. The pageants are now ended and Summer decides to make his will, which he realizes he has already made as Autumn is declared his successor. Winter claims he should be next, making a series of long speeches against the scholars who refuse to acknowledge what he sees as his right; his diatribe becomes more of a generalized attack on the faults of the learned, akin to a work such as *The Anatomy of Absurdity*. Autumn and Winter argue about their right to follow Summer, Winter arguing that after Carnival, there should be Lent ('The fields have surfeited with Summer fruits;/ They must be purg'd, made poor, oppressed with snow' (ll. 1553–4, p. 282). Summer asks for some music to signal his approaching death and the song, frequently extracted from the play as 'A Litany in Time of Plague', is performed accompanied by a lute:

Adieu, farewell, earth's bliss,
This world uncertain is,
Fond are life's lustful joys,
Death proves them all but toys,
None from his darts can fly;
I am sick, I must die;
    Lord, have mercy on us.

Rich men, trust not in wealth,
Gold cannot buy you health;
Physic himself must fade.
All things to end are made,
The plague full swift goes by;
I am sick, I must die:
    Lord, have mercy on us.

Beauty is but a flower
Which wrinkles will devour,
Brightness falls from the air,
Queens have died young and fair,

Dust hath closed Helen's eye.
I am sick, I must die:
Lord, have mercy on us.
(ll. 1574–94, pp. 282–3)

The song is a stark reminder that the play is not simply about the death of Summer, but about the deaths caused by this particular summer. The refrain 'Lord, have mercy on us' reproduces the words painted on the fronts of houses known to be infected with plague, as they were nailed shut and those within left to their fate.[33] The poem forces the audience to think about the reality of death and what happens to a body when life has disappeared, in particular the tantalizingly ambiguous 'Brightness falls from the air', which involves a pun on air/hair. If we read it as 'air', we have a frightening image of darkness descending and enveloping everything, a pointed contrast to the brilliant light and colours of summer. If we read it as 'hair', we have an equally disturbing image of a dead body, as all signs of life disappear and an individual's hair becomes dull, losing its sheen.[34] Nashe is reminding the audience of how a dead body looks, and that they will see many more in the coming months, if they do not themselves succumb to the disease. When Summer later devotes his withered flowers and herbs to corpses, the gift is already associated with the plague and death through the same stanza in the song ('Beauty is but a flower,/ Which wrinkles will devour'). The song serves as a poetic version of the ubiquitous image of the dance of death, showing a skeleton leading its victims away, as it merges a moral and religious message: do not trust in gold; beauty is ephemeral; life is uncertain, and death a random event;

powerful people, as well as poor ones, die young; and medicine often cannot save you.[35] There is an added poignancy in the publication of *Summer's Last Will* when Nashe was either dying or dead, especially if he died from the plague.

Summer is visibly moved by the song, but the play moves to a more comic moment with the entrance of the miserable and miserly figure of Christmas, who is as niggardly as Ver was generous. Christmas, anticipating Dickens's Scrooge by some centuries, is particularly hostile to feasts, exaggerating their extravagance as he is carried away by his own eloquence:

> Feasts are but puffing up of the flesh, the purveyors for diseases; travel, cost, time ill spent. O, it were a trim thing to send, as the *Romanes* did, round about the world for provision for one banquet. I must rig ships to *Samos* for Peacocks, to *Paphos* for Pigeons, to *Austria* for Oysters, to *Phasis* for Pheasants, to *Arabia* for Phoenixes, to *Meander* for Swans, to the *Orcades* for Geese, to *Phrygia* for Wood-cocks, to *Malta* for Cranes, to the Isle of Man for Puffins, to *Ambracia* for Goats, to *Tartole* for Lampreys, to *Egypt* for Dates, to *Spain* for Chestnuts, and all for one feast! (ll. 1685–94, p. 286)

Will's response, 'O sir, you need not; you may buy them at London better cheap' (ll. 1695–6), is suitably deflating. As well as re-establishing the play as a comedy, Nashe's point is probably that, while it is true that earthly pleasures are ephemeral, this does not mean they cannot be enjoyed at all, a further attack on the Puritan attitudes of those such as the Marprelates, who argued that nothing that was not in the Bible could be tolerated in a religious ceremony, and so were opposed to the extravagant celebrations for Christmas, Easter and other festivals.[36] Even the hitherto surly Winter apologizes for the behaviour of his ill-mannered son, Christmas. Back-Winter then explains that he loves darkness, cold and suffering, and Winter, hitherto eager to claim his due after the impending demise of Summer, realizes that his time will come as well, all too soon.

The play moves to its conclusion. Summer makes his final speech and is carried out by the satyrs and wood nymphs, singing another song. Will Summers cues the audience to get ready to clap the actors; an epilogue is delivered on their behalf, which, in pleading for tolerance for any faults in the performance, yet again reminds the audience of the plague raging abroad:

> The Romans dedicated a temple to the fever quartane [time of plague], thinking it some great God, because it shook them so: and another to ill fortune in *Exquilliis*, a Mountain in Rome, that it should not plague them at Cards and Dice. Your Graces frowns are to them shaking fevers, your least disfavours the greatest ill fortune that may betide them. They can build no Temples, but themselves and their best endeavours, with all prostrate reverence, they here dedicate and offer up wholly to your service. (ll. 1921–30, p. 294)

Any laughter this passage generates is surely uneasy, making the comic conclusion distinctly uncomfortable. The equation in the opening sentence between being isolated because of fever and ill fortune looks back to the song that so moved

Summer, and the words on the doors of plague houses warning passers-by to stay away. The point is rammed home with the metaphorical use of 'plague' to represent misfortune in games of chance. The furrowed brows of the audience are then likened to plague, disfavour spreading through the theatre like disease through the city, in itself also a reminder that any involuntary movement might be a sign of the onset of illness. The actors are not builders and so rely on the goodwill of the audience for their survival, a further reminder that the epilogue is about more than the actors' need for praise; that everyone will be leaving the hall and going out into a dangerous and uncertain world; and that they will all need some luck if they are to get through the current crisis.

Summer's Last Will, while it lacks dramatic sophistication, is a verbally dextrous and engaging play. It is characterized by end-stopped lines, a familiar feature of Nashe's dramatic poetry, as it was of Christopher Marlowe's.[37] Orion's representation of the various characters of his dogs is a case in point:

> *Chrysippus* holds dogs are Logicians,
> In that, by study and by canvasing,
> They can distinguish twixt three several things:
> As when he cometh where three broad ways meet,
> And of those three hath stayed at two of them,
> By which he guesseth that the game went not,
> Without more pause he runneth on the third;
> Which, as *Chrysippus* saith, insinuates
> As if he reason'd thus within himself:
> Either he went this, that, or yonder way,
> But neither that, nor yonder, therefore this.

> But whether they Logicians be or no,
> Cynics they are, for they will snarl and bite;
> Right courtiers to flatter and to fawn;
> Valiant to set upon the enemies,
> Most faithful and most constant to their friends.
> (ll. 698–713, p. 255)

Dogs have the basis of reasoning and so can act with self-interest, working out how best to get what they want. Accordingly, they are cynics, selfish and critical of others, but able to advance themselves like courtiers through an extravagant display of love and devotion. But they have good qualities, too, being brave and loyal to their real friends.

The end-stopped nature of Nashe's verse, which is clear throughout *Summer's Last Will*, is one of the main reasons why he is thought of as the most likely author of the first act of *Henry VI, Part One*. That section of the play also contains stage directions that resemble those of *Summer's Last Will*, a number of particular phrases and words used by Nashe rather than Shakespeare, and references to some of Nashe's favourite sources (among them Cornelius Agrippa's *Of the Vanity and Uncertainty of Arts and Sciences*, c. 1530).[38] In particular, the act is characterized by inversions, the reversal of subject and object. In *Summer's Last Will* we have 'Not raging *Hecuba*, whose hollow eyes/ Gave suck to fifty sorrows at one time' (ll. 1782–3, p. 289), and then in *Henry VI, Part One*, 'Wounds will I lend the French, instead of eyes' (1.i.87) and 'Thy heart-blood I will have for the day's work' (1.iv.80).[39]

Many critics now believe that *Henry VI, Part One* is a prequel, in the manner of many modern film series. A team of writers including Shakespeare had written *The First Part of the Contention of the Two Famous Houses of York and Lancaster* and *The True Tragedy of Richard Duke of York and the Good King Henry the Sixth*, which were staged at some point between 1590 and the first half of 1592. It seems that they were so popular in representing the course of the Wars of the Roses, up to their conclusion with the death of Richard III and the accession of Henry VII as the first Tudor monarch, that a third play was commissioned at some point in 1592 to consolidate their success. This would probably have been written rapidly, to build on public interest in the wars, and this may well have been why Nashe – especially if he was a known writer for the theatre – was commissioned to join the team of writers and write the first act.

Henry VI, Part One tells the story of the conflict that developed as soon as the warrior king Henry V died, when aristocratic rivalry in England fatally undermined English military campaigns in France, despite the heroic efforts of John Talbot, 1st Earl of Shrewsbury ('brave Talbot'). The *Contention* and the *True Tragedy* appeared as quartos (1594, 1595), and all three plays were then published in the first folio of Shakespeare's works (1623). By this point, seven years after his death, Shakespeare had eclipsed the fame of many of his contemporaries, which is probably why plays that he co-wrote with largely forgotten writers were attributed to him.

Henry VI, Part One was therefore probably written just before or just after *Summer's Last Will*, the most recent calculation placing it in March 1592, soon before Nashe began work on *Summer's Last Will*.[40] However the evidence is interpreted, Nashe was surely working on the plays at more or less the same time. While he worked alone on *Summer's Last Will* (unless passages are by Robert Greene), he was writing as part of a team on *Henry VI, Part One*, as he was on the Anti-Martinist tracts, probably with Marlowe and at least one other from the list of Greene, George Peele (1556–1596) and Thomas Kyd.[41] Shakespeare's role is more complicated. He was undoubtedly one of the sequence's co-authors, but he may also have revised the whole text later, at some point before 1599, probably in the mid-1590s.[42]

Act One opens with the English nobles squabbling beside the coffin of Henry V. The Duke of Gloucester will become Lord Protector because the new king, Henry VI, is still a minor, but he is opposed by the Bishop of Winchester, the king's great-uncle. The conflict between those who should be leading the country undermines the military campaign in France, and as a result Lord Talbot is left short of support and captured by the French. There are numerous verbal flourishes in the act that seem distinctively Nashean. When the French fire their heavy guns during the siege of Orleans, Salisbury and Gargrave, who are standing on the battlements, fall down and cry out,

> SALISBURY O Lord have mercy on us, wretched sinners!
> GARGRAVE O Lord have mercy on me, woeful man!
> (I.vi.48–9)

If a link to the refrain in the song in *Summer's Last Will* seems unconvincing, Talbot's subsequent speech, with its carefully patterned end-stopped lines, does sound like the work of Nashe:

What chance is this that suddenly hath crossed us?
Speak, Salisbury – at least, if thou canst speak.
How far'st thou, mirror of all martial men?
One of thy eyes and thy cheek's side struck off?
Accursed tower! accursed fatal hand
That hath contrived this woeful tragedy!
In thirteen battles Salisbury o'ercame;
Henry the Fifth he first trained to the wars;
Whilst any trump did sound, or drum struck up
His sword did ne'er leave striking in the field.
Yet liv'st thou, Salisbury? though thy speech
        doth fail,
One eye thou hast to look to heaven for grace.
The sun with one eye vieweth all the world.
Heaven, be thou gracious to none alive
If Salisbury wants mercy at thy hands. –
Sir Thomas Gargrave, hast thou any life?
Speak unto Talbot. Nay, look up to him. –
Bear hence his body; I will help to bury it.
                [Exit one with Gargrave's body]
Salisbury, cheer thy spirit with this comfort:
Thou shalt not die whiles –
He beckons with his hand, and smiles on me,
As who should say, 'When I am dead and gone,
Remember to avenge me on the French.'
Plantagenet, I will; and like thee, Nero,
Play on the lute, beholding the towns burn.
Wretched shall France be only in my name.
(1.vi.50–75)

Talbot heroically defies the French almost single-handedly as they overwhelm the English forces in France and take back the conquests of Henry V seized a generation earlier.[43] The style of the play, especially this first act, owes much to Marlowe's *Tamburlaine*, and it is surely his own work on the play that Nashe praises in *Piers Penniless*, the quotation used to date *Henry VI, Part One*:

> How would it have joyed brave *Talbot* (the terror of the French) to think that after he had lyen two hundred years in his Tomb, he should triumph again on the Stage, and have his bones new embalmed with the tears of ten thousand spectators at least (at several times), who, in the Tragedian that represents his person, imagine they behold him fresh bleeding.
> (*Works*, I, p. 212)[44]

Talbot's speech consists of the end-stopped lines that characterize the long speeches in *Summer's Last Will*, and the surprising and unsettling comparison the speaker makes of himself to Nero is also characteristic of Nashe's style of reference, using an easy familiarity with classical literature to startling effect. Here, Talbot will, like Nero playing an instrument while devastation raged around him, oversee the destruction of the fertile French countryside.[45] Attempting to revive Salisbury (although he is mortally wounded, and we learn of his death in the next scene), Talbot reminds him of his past heroic feats that predate those of Henry V, the great warrior; urges him, in lines that contain considerable grim humour, to look out with his one good eye like the sun; and then interprets Salisbury's feeble movements as a sign that Talbot must carry the fight to the French in Salisbury's name. The audience witnesses Talbot watching Salisbury die on stage while creatively interpreting the signs his fallen comrade makes to suit his purposes. The link to the behaviour of the characters in *Summer's Last Will*, who see the world from their particular perspective, is clear. Even if it is not in itself proof of Nashe's authorship of this act – other evidence provides that – it demonstrates how he established a particular dramatic style and suggests that there may be more work of his that has not yet been identified.

Nashe's role in *Dido, Queen of Carthage* is much harder to determine. The play contains many words and phrases that may be evidence of Nashe's authorship, but other stylistic tests have proved inconclusive and the work does not resemble Nashe's characteristic end-stopped style of dramatic verse.[46] It is perhaps the case that we would not consider this to be a work to which Nashe contributed were it not for the title page, which states that the play was performed by 'the children of her Majesty's chapel' and was 'written by Christopher Marlowe and Thomas Nash. Gent.' On the other hand, we should also bear in mind that *Dido* does not sound much like Marlowe either, and neither Nashe nor Marlowe worked with the company named on the title page.

That *Dido* also names Nashe as co-author has troubled critics ever since. It has been suggested that it is significant that Nashe is named in smaller script and below Marlowe, but this has not won widespread acceptance and looks more like a convention to most critics.[47] Other commentators have concluded that Nashe must have played some part in the production of the text, and they suggest that he may have

THE
Tragedie of Dido

Queene of Carthage:

Played by the Children of her
Maiesties Chappell.

Written by Christopher Marlowe, and
Thomas Nash. Gent.

Actors

Iupiter.	*Ascanius.*
Ganimed.	*Dido.*
Venus.	*Anna.*
Cupid.	*Ach..es.*
Iuno.	*Ilioneus.*
Mercurie,or	*Iarbas.*
Hermes.	*Cloanthes.*
Æneas.	*Sergestus.*

AT LONDON,
Printed,by the Widdowe *Orwin,* for *Thomas Woodcocke,* and
are to be solde at his shop, in Paules Church-yeard,at
the signe of the blacke Beare. 1594.

Title page to Christopher Marlowe and Thomas Nashe, *The Tragedie of
Dido Queene of Carthage* (1594).

acted as a plotter, a role that we know existed, as playhouses employed a writer to sketch an outline of a play that was then written by different authors.[48]

Might Nashe have acted as a plotter for Marlowe? The case against is that Nashe's extant play, *Summer's Last Will*, does not look obviously like the work of a plotter, with its episodic drama in which one encounter follows another. Yet if Nashe played no role in writing *Dido*, contributing neither scenes nor plot, why is his name on the title page? The attribution to two authors in 1594 is not just exceptional but unique, coming at a time when few plays were attributed to one author. It is therefore very unlikely to be a simple error, suggesting, at the very least, that Nashe was eager to be closely connected to Marlowe; that if anyone was playing a sly game it was surely Nashe himself; and that if he was able to do this, he undoubtedly played some role in writing, staging or publishing the play.

The date of *Dido* is as uncertain as its authorship, and it may well have been first performed in the late 1580s, placing it alongside the lost works *Terminus et non terminus* and the anti-Harvey satires (although there is an added complication because the Children of the Royal Chapel do not appear to have performed plays between 1584, when they lost their lease, and 1599).[49] The play is principally an adaptation of Virgil's *Aeneid*, Books 1, 2 and 4, the story of Aeneas' sojourn in Carthage and his romance with its queen, Dido, before he feels compelled by the injunction of the gods to abandon her and sail off to Italy to found Rome. Dido kills herself, perhaps the most potent sign of *translatio imperii*, the shift of power and authority from the old empire of North Africa to the newly emerging forces of Rome.

If Nashe did write parts of the play, it is most likely that he contributed to the early sections, given his role in the Henry VI plays and his statement in Lenten Stuff about his contribution to The Isle of Dogs. Jupiter's dialogue with Ganymede does indeed contain more Nashean features than other sections of the play. When Ganymede urges Jupiter to avenge a slight he has suffered at the hand of Juno, Jupiter replies indignantly that he has granted his favourite almost everything he has ever asked for:

> What ist, sweet wag, I should deny thy youth?
> Whose face reflects such pleasure to mine eyes,
> As I, exhal'd with thy fire darting beams,
> Have oft driven back the horses of the night,
> When as they would have hal'd thee from my sight:
> Sit on my knee, and call for thy content,
> Control proud Fate, and cut the thred of time.
> Why, are not all the Gods at thy command,
> And heaven and earth the bounds of thy delight?
> *Vulcan* shall dance to make thee laughing sport,
> And my nine Daughters sing when thou art sad;
> From *Juno's* bird I'll pluck her spotted pride,
> To make thee fans wherewith to cool thy face;
> And *Venus'* Swans shall shed their silver down,
> To sweeten out the slumbers of thy bed:
> *Hermes* no more shall show the world his wings,
> If that thy fancy in his feathers dwell,
> But, as this one, I'll tear them all from him,
>   *[Plucks a feather from Mercury's wings.]*
> Do thou but say, their colour pleaseth me:

Hold here, my little love, these linked gems, *[Gives jewels.]*
My *Juno* ware upon her marriage day,
Put thou about thy neck, my own sweet heart,
And trick thy arms and shoulders with my theft. (*Works,*
III, p. 342, I.i.23–45)

The use of 'exhal'd' in the third line of the speech has a parallel
at the end of *Terrors* ('he whom in the day heaven cannot exhale,
the night will never help'; I, p. 386); and the image of Vulcan's
dancing inspiring scorn is a possible connection to the epilogue
of *Summer's Last Will*:

> To make the gods merry, the celestial clown, Vulcan,
> tuned his polt-foot to the measures of Apollo's lute,
> and danced a limping galliard in Jove's starry hall. To
> make you merry, that are the gods of art and guides
> unto heaven, a number of rude Vulcans, unwieldy
> speakers, hammer-headed clowns (for so it pleaseth
> them in modesty to name themselves) have set their
> deformities to view, as it were in a dance here before
> you. (III, p. 294)[50]

The link is no better than suggestive – as are other connections
to Nashe's writings in the play – and Jupiter's homoerotic
speech here could be the work of either writer (it probably
sounds rather more like Marlowe). Nashe's link to *Dido* seems
more mysterious and rather less solid than his connection to
Henry VI, Part One.

Nashe may well have continued writing for the theatre
in the middle years of the 1590s, but nothing has survived

and no unattributed play has been discovered that may be his work. He did co-author the lost play *The Isle of Dogs* with Ben Jonson in July 1597, which caused him to flee London for East Anglia.[51] He recounts the episode at the start of *Lenten Stuff*, refers to the play as 'That infortnate imperfit embrion of my idle hours' and admits that it attracted the hostile attention of the authorities, perhaps acknowledging that he had not been as cautious or wise as he might have been ('Too inconsiderate headlong rashness this may be censured in me, in being thus prodigal in advantaging my adversaries': pp. 153–4).[52]

This last statement would appear to provide evidence that the play was a satirical attack on prominent courtiers, as many have assumed, or, at least, an offensive work.[53] Nashe's marginal note to 'embrion' (embryo) – a word he had used to describe *The Anatomy of Absurdity* – confirms that he was the author of the opening sections of the play as he attempts to distance himself from the rest of the work, indicating that this may have been his general role: 'An imperfit Embrion I may well call it, for I having begun but the induction and first act of it, the other four acts without my consent, or the least guess of my drift or scope, by the players were supplied, which bred both their trouble and mine too' (pp. 153–4). Perhaps Nashe knew his work was likely to be banned, as it was on 1 June 1599, when the bishops clamped down on the proliferation of satire, naming him as one of the proscribed authors. In that case his comments at the start of *Lenten Stuff* are either a plea for mitigation or an acceptance of his fate and an acknowledgement that from now on he was likely to receive the meagre, austere fare of Lent for his writing.

Lenten Stuff, like *Piers Penniless*, singles out a play for extravagant praise, in a section of the work unconnected to any immediate context. Referring to a joke about herrings, Nashe poses a rhetorical question: 'hath it any more sense in it than it should have? is it not right of the merry cobbler's cut in that witty Play of *the Case Is Altered?*' (III, p. 220). In Jonson's *The Case Is Altered* (his first known play), Juniper 'begins the play in song, and proceeds to mangle the language in comic misuse', appearing on stage for much of the play, hence 'cobbler's cut', meaning a ham-fisted, clumsy style.[54] Jonson's play combines plots from two of Plautus' plays, *The Captives* and *The Pot of Gold*.[55] It was probably first staged in 1597, and performed by Pembroke's Men, for whom both Jonson and Nashe wrote *The Isle of Dogs* that same year. The play does not appear in Jonson's 1616 folio of his *Works*, which may be because he did not own copyright, or because, as many critics have suggested, it was a collaborative work that he no longer wished to acknowledge.[56] Nashe may be praising the work of his co-author, but it is also quite possible that he is again referring to a play in which he had a hand. Whatever the truth, his crucial role in the development of commercial English theatre in the 1590s is a story that has not yet been fully told.

FOUR

Gabriel Harvey

riting in 1589, Nashe laments the dearth of proper Neo-Latin poetry written in England, a sign of the nation's backward culture and lowly place in European letters:

> I know not almost any of late days that hath showed himself singular in any special Latin Poem; whose *Amintas*, and translated *Antigone*, may march in equipage of honour with any of our ancient Poets. I will not say but we had a *Haddon*, whose pen would have challenged the Laurel from *Homer*, together with *Car*, that came as near him as *Virgil* to *Theocritus*. But *Thomas Newton* with his *Leland*, and *Gabriel Harvey*, with two or three other, is almost all the store that is left us at this hour.[1]

At the start of his career he clearly had a respect for the man whose work he was to savage for the rest of his writing life. There is a neat irony in Nashe's praise, as one of his principal targets was Harvey's Latin hexameters, later taken by Nashe to be an indication of his opponent's inability to write or think.

It is hard to fathom what happened to change Nashe's good opinion.[2] As already noted, Nashe sneers at Gabriel and his

brother Richard's behaviour at university, and relishes Harvey's
appearance as the central character in the satirical play *Pedantius*,
so he clearly had memories of their failings and unpopularity
dating back to the early 1580s.[3] The long-running dispute
may have originated as an offshoot of the public quarrel
between Sir Philip Sidney (1554–1586) and Edward de Vere,
17th Earl of Oxford (1550–1604), in August 1579, and in John
Lyly's reporting to Oxford that Gabriel Harvey – who was
keen for support from both Oxford and Sidney – had satirized him [Oxford] in the poem *Speculum Tuscanismi*, published
in *Three Proper, Witty and Familiar Letters* (1580). By the late 1580s
Nashe was associated with Lyly, most obviously through their
very public roles as champions of the bishops against the
Marprelate authors.

Any residual ill feeling seems to have lain dormant – Nashe
was still a teenager in 1580, and he had then praised Harvey's
Latin poetry – until 1590, when Richard Harvey published
his long theological diatribe *The Lamb of God*. The book attacks
the Marprelate authors, but, in a prefatory epistle added after
the book was first published, Richard turns his guns on Nashe:

> Many a man talketh of *Robin Hood*, that never shot in
> his bow; and that is the rash presumption of this age,
> that every man of whatsoever quality and perfection
> is with every man of whatsoever mediocrity, but as
> every man pleaseth in the abundance of his own swell-
> ing sense. Iwis [certainly] this *Thomas Nash*, one whom
> I never heard of before (for I cannot imagine him to
> be *Thomas Nash* our butler of *Pembroke Hall*, albeit per-
> adventure not much better learned) showeth himself

none of the meetest men to censure *Sir Thomas More*, *Sir John Cheke*, Doctor *Watson*, Doctor *Haddon*, Master *Ascham*, Doctor *Car*, my brother Doctor *Harvey*, and such like, yet the jolly man will needs be playing the doughty *Martin* in his kind, and limit every man's commendation, accord-ing to his fancy, profound no doubt, and exceeding learned, as the world now goeth in such worthy works.[4]

The contemptuous putting of a young upstart in his place is clear enough. Richard Harvey asserts that Nashe is less well known to authorities such as him than his college butler, yet he imagines he can pass judgement not only on contemporary

Woodcut of Robert Greene, illustration from the title page of Thomas Dekker's pamphlet *Greene in Conceipte* (1598).

writers but on important, well-known figures, past and present.[5] And, like those who believe in the significance of the legends of Robin Hood, he is a lowbrow fantasist, too mediocre even to write one of those poor pieces. Nashe is an arrogant, conceited writer who is yet to earn his spurs, but who loves the sight of his own writing.

As a polemical attack, it is reasonably effective, lining up a wealth of authorities to intimidate a callow opponent and combining social and academic snobbery in wittily compressed form. Richard also attacked his brother's old adversary, John Lyly, as 'vain Paphatchet', alluding to Lyly's Anti-Martinist tract *Pap with an Hatchet* (1589), in which he satirizes Gabriel for writing so ridiculously about the earthquake of 6 April 1580 and libelling Oxford.[6] Robert Greene was the first writer to reply to these salvos from Richard. He provided a savage thumbnail portrait of the Harvey brothers in his *Quip for an Upstart Courtier* (1592) – removed soon after publication, so it obviously caused offence – attacking Richard for living immorally (and, therefore, being a hypocrite) and Gabriel for having spent time in prison and for writing bad Latin poetry.[7]

Nashe then joined in with attacks on Richard in *Piers Penniless*, responding directly to the assault on him in *The Lamb of God*. Richard is excoriated for being a terrible philosopher and a bad writer, and for being very short and boastful, a '*Pigmy Braggart*'.[8] Nashe, like Lyly, reminds his readers of Richard's rash astrological prediction of the cataclysmic consequences that would follow the conjunction of the planets Jupiter and Saturn on Sunday 28 April 1583, based on the prophecies of the Bohemian astrologer Cyprian Leowicz (Leovitius):

Gentlemen, I am sure you have heard of a ridiculous Ass that many years since sold lies by the great, and wrote an absurd *Astrological Discourse* of the terrible Conjunction of *Saturn* and *Jupiter*, wherein (as if he had lately cast the Heavens water, or been at the anatomizing of the Skies' entrails in Surgeons hall) he prophecieth of such strange wonders to ensue from stars' distemperature, and the unusual adultery of Planets, as none but he that is Baud to those celestial bodies could ever descry. What expectation there was of it both in town and country, the amazement of those times may testify: and the rather because he pawned his credit upon it in these express terms: *If these things fall not out in every point as I have wrote, let me for ever hereafter lose the credit of my Astronomy.* Well, so it happened, that he happened not to be a man of his word; his Astronomy broke his day with his creditors, and *Saturn* and *Jupiter* prov'd honester men than all the world took them for.[9]

If Richard's attack on Nashe was neat and well crafted (albeit as self-regarding as he claimed his opponent was), Nashe has returned the favour with interest. He argues that Richard should have known better than to believe such astrological nonsense in the first place and, the rejoinder implies, to throw stones when living in a glass house. Even those not inclined to give credit to pagan deities and forces will thank them for demonstrating their unexpected moral probity, exposing the absurdity of Richard's credulous and stupid version of Christianity. If Richard wanted to imply that many of the Anti-Martinists were actually very like their opponents

– a fair charge, as the subsequent development of the Nashe–
Harvey quarrel demonstrates – then Nashe can show that
Richard is himself as deluded as the Martinists.

Richard did not reply to Nashe, but Gabriel did in *Four
Letters and Certain Sonnets* (1592), surely provocatively, given
Lyly's attacks on his earlier published letters, an indication
that he intended to use the letter form in the war with his
opponents. In the fourth letter, Harvey attacks Nashe as a
flashy, incompetent and semi-educated writer whose superficial literary virtues have led a new generation of writers badly
astray:

> God help, when Ignorance and want of Experience,
> usurping the chair of scrupulous, and rigorous Judgment,
> will in a fantastical Imagination, or percase in a melan-
> choly mood, presume farther, by infinite degrees, than
> the learnedest men in a civil Common-wealth or the
> sagest counsellors in a Prince's Court. Our new-new
> writers, the Loadstones of the Press, are wonderfully
> beholding to the Ass, in a manner the only Author, which
> they allege: the world was ever full enough of fools, but
> never so full of Asses in print: the very Elephant, a great
> Ass; the Camel, a huge Ass; the Bear, a monstrous Ass;
> the Horse, an absurd Ass; the Fox himself, a little Ass, or,
> for variety, an Ape: who not an Ass, or an Ape in good
> plain English, that chanceth to come in the wise Ass-
> makers & mighty Ape-dubbers' way?[10]

Building on his brother's description, Gabriel casts Nashe as
a limited, second-rate writer who has had undeserved and

somewhat unexpected success in attracting a large group of followers, all of whom are even worse writers than he. Against this rabble of talentless writers, who can do nothing more than pander to popular taste, Gabriel sets true scholarship and discernment, represented by his own achievements, work that is based on scrupulous, informed judgement rather than flights of fancy and fashionable moodiness. On the one hand he sees the manic taste for newness, discarding something as soon as it becomes unfashionable (as, he implies, will soon be the fate of Nashe's writings); on the other, writing such as his is recognized by the learned as already having achieved the status of a classic. Harvey's satire is rather leaden, and there is little wit in the heavy and obvious repetition of 'ass' for impact and his pursuit of the animal metaphors to characterize other writers. More significantly still, he manages to be grand and pompous, failings that Nashe exploits mercilessly in their subsequent exchanges.

Nashe replied with a fairly long and somewhat incoherent work, *Strange News* (1592). Its subtitle, *Of the intercepting certain Letters, and a convoy of verses, as they were going privily to victual the Low Countries*, imitates the titles of news books, many of which contained accounts of recent events in the Low Countries. In doing so Nashe casts Harvey's work as news that quickly becomes obsolete, demonstrating how carefully he was reading and responding to Harvey's attacks on him, and representing his opponent exactly as he did not want to be seen. The pun on 'privily', meaning both private and connected to the latrine, implies further that Harvey's works do not feed any intellectual appetites or satisfy bodily needs, but are best used as toilet paper.

Nashe then published an apology to Harvey in the preface to *Christ's Tears over Jerusalem*, a serious and solemn work of which Harvey may well have approved. In the prefatory letter to the reader, Nashe declares that he desires 'to be at peace with all men, and make submissive amends where I have most displeased', continuing, 'Even of Master Doctor *Harvey*, I heartily desire the like, whose fame and reputation (though through some precedent injurious provocations, and fervent incitements of young heads) I rashly assailed: yet now better advised, and of his perfections more confirmedly persuaded, unfainedly I entreat of the whole world, from my pen his worths may receive no impeachment.'[11]

Unfortunately, while there appear to have been some attempts to patch up the quarrel, in the meantime Harvey had published *A New Letter of Notable Contents* (1592), which describes *Strange News* as 'the most desperate and abominable Pamphlet'. Harvey also boasts that he plans to 'bounce Nashe like a barn door, thump him like a drummer from Flushing, knead him like a cake of dough, churn him like a dish of butter' so that he could have his '*Penny-worths* of his *Penniless wit*'.[12] On its own, this not terribly witty barrage might have reignited the quarrel, but Harvey ensured the battle would continue by producing his long, carefully scripted and expensively published attack *Pierces Supererogation; or, A New Praise of the Old Ass* (1593). The work is in three parts: an introductory section that laments how tiresome it is for a serious man of letters to have to become embroiled in such a pointless literary quarrel; a second part, written earlier and now incorporated into his wars with Nashe, replying to *Pap with an Hatchet*; and a third detailing Nashe's faults and his malign influence on a

generation of writers, and responding to many of the taunts
in *Strange News.*

Following Nashe's attacks on his writing, Harvey takes
particular exception to Nashe's own style and vocabulary,
focusing on what he sees as Nashe's hypocritical double
standards:

> For his Eloquence passeth my intelligence, that cleapeth
> himself a *Calimunco,* for pleading his Companion's cause
> in his own Apology: and me a *Pistlepragmos,* for defending
> my friends in my Letters: and very artificially *interfuseth*
> *Finicallitie, sillogistrie, disputative right, hermaphrodite phrases,*
> *declamatorie stiles, censorial moralizers, unlineal usurpers of judge-*
> *ment, infamizers of vice, new infringement to destitute the inditement,*
> *deriding dunstically, banging abominationly, unhandsoming of divin-*
> *ityship, absurdifying of phrases, ratifying of truthable and eligible*
> *English, a calm dilatement of forward harmfulnesse, and backward*
> *irefulnesse.*[13]

Here, when he has had time to assemble a case, Harvey's attack
on Nashe is far more reasoned and effective than it is elsewhere.
He shows that what Nashe has found wanting in Harvey's
writing is actually characteristic of his own, a sign that, at
times, the two antagonists were not as far apart as they liked
to imagine. Harvey also argues that Nashe is far worse than
the inkhorn writers whose use of outlandish, unnecessary
terms he effects to despise:

> I have seldom read a more garish, and piebald style in
> any scribbling Inkhornist; or tasted a more unsavoury

slaumpaump of words, and sentences in any sluttish
Pamfletter; that denounceth not defiance against the
rules of Oratory, and the directions of the English
Secretary, which may here and there stumble upon some
tolerable sentence, neighbourly borrowed, or featly
picked out of some fresh Pamphlet: but shall never find
three sentences together, worth any allowance.[14]

The comparison may not be entirely apt. Nashe's complaint
against Harvey in *Strange News* was that he imported words
and phrases from Cicero in order to make his own banal
thoughts seem more impressive. The criticism is implicit in
his goading of his opponent with an image of schoolboys
baiting him in the street:

From this day forward shall a whole army of boys come
wandering about thee as thou goest in the street, and
cry *kulleloo, kulleloo, with whip hoo*, there goes the Ape of
Tully, tis he, steal *Tully*, steal *Tully*, away with the Ass in
the lion's skin.

Nay, but in sadness, is it not a sinful thing for a
Scholar & a Christian to turn *Tully*? A Turk would never
do it.[15]

Nashe deliberately places his inventiveness in producing
onomatopoeic words imitating the sound of the boys against
Harvey's desire to make himself grander and more academic
by trying to imitate the most flowery version of classical Latin.
The imitation of Cicero's eloquent rhetoric, with its carefully
distinguished sections of speech designed to play on the

emotions of the reader/listener and its erudite vocabulary emphasizing the linguistic command of the speaker/writer, had by the end of the sixteenth century become something of a cliché.[16] The schoolboys recognize Harvey's unimpressive attempts to impress everyone, which is why they can insult him as an ape, a creature that copies without having the reason to understand what it is doing.

Nashe returns Harvey's insult with considerable interest: Harvey is not merely a foolish ape, but the ridiculous creature in Aesop's fable who pretends that he is a lion, a ruse that works for a time but which leads to his abject humiliation when he finally has to speak in his own voice, a problem he should have foreseen but did not because he was so carried away with his unmerited success. In Aesop's fable, the fox exposes the lion, who has successfully terrified the other animals, suggesting that Nashe is the creature sly and wise enough to see through the modern Cicero, although his vainglorious and empty boasts can be spotted by schoolboys with only the most basic grasp of a classical literary tradition (an insult Nashe commonly levels at Harvey). To round the insult off, Nashe quibbles on the familiar proverbial phrase 'to turn Turk', meaning to become a traitor and help the enemy willingly or unconsciously.[17] Harvey has 'turned Tully [Cicero]', something that is impossible to do, the attempt destroying the nature of the English language.

Three years after the publication of *Pierces Supererogation*, Nashe replied with his equally substantial *Have with You to Saffron Walden* (1596), a sign that the quarrel had moved into a new phase after the manic confusion of late 1592, when hastily compiled insults flew off the press. The antagonists' serious analyses of each other's writings made the quarrel one of the dominant features of the literary landscape of the 1590s. The titles the two men chose reveal much about their respective approaches. Harvey uses a Latinate, theological word, replacing Nashe's 'Penniless', the persona of the poor scholar who has not got his just deserts, with 'supererogation', the mistaken belief that performing numerous good works will be rewarded by the state of grace.[18] For Harvey, Nashe is a fool who imagines that producing ever more works will save him, when they actually expose his superficial failure to think properly and to repent of his pointless, distracting and often dangerous writing. For Nashe, Harvey is a writer wearing the emperor's new clothes to dress up his lack of original thought, mistaking leaden solemnity for true seriousness. He deliberately uses the idiomatic 'have with you', meaning 'go away, be off', to contrast his light-footed, nimble critique with Harvey's desire to batter his opponent into submission with his mighty erudition and scholarship. He also reminds Harvey of his origins in a relatively obscure market town in middle England, even though it was one that had grown affluent through the production of the main crop used in producing yellow dye.[19] It is a sign that the Nashe–Harvey quarrel never really concluded but just ended that Nashe's last work, *Nashe's Lenten Stuff*, formally names in the title its author, rather than his persona, and contrasts the humble but important fare produced in his native East Anglia, the preserved herring, to the luxurious, aspirational dye that flourished in Harvey's home town.[20]

Have with You is probably Nashe's most underrated work. While *Strange News* scores a number of palpable hits and is frequently witty in its ability to balance different registers

to outmanoeuvre a lumbering opponent, *Have with You* is a
carefully synthesized demolition of all that Harvey stands for,
and is frequently funny and enjoyable to read. It is carefully
organized and orchestrated – in contrast to *Strange News* –
developing arguments with care and paying attention to their
construction so that the reader is more likely to be persuaded
that they are fair and right. In doing this, Nashe is demonstrating that it is he, not Harvey, who understands the classical
rhetorical tradition, and that he is the true heir of Cicero.
Cicero is indeed frequently mentioned; the significance of
his writing is duly acknowledged, and the author argues that
proper understanding means adapting and transforming a
style into one's own idiom, not the slavish, apish imitation of
Harvey. In response to Harvey's learned treatise Nashe produces a dialogue, a new departure, one designed to exploit his
interest in and knowledge of drama, enabling him to capture
a series of voices and so break up the monotony of reading a
long treatise. It also enables him to include more cruxes,
changes of scene, style and voice, developing his long-standing
claim that wit is the vital essence that marks out human
achievement, and that style and argument cannot and should
not be separated.

Nashe had long produced involved and intricate sentences
that held together different ideas and which shifted from one
position to another, often unsettling the reader with shifts
of tone, style and meaning, sentences that frequently concluded by stating the opposite of what they had appeared to
mean at the start. Here, he found a way of transforming that
witty method from the syntactic units that made up a work
to the structure and design of the work itself. Accordingly,

Have with You marks the successful advent of his mature style, and he was able to exploit his interest in different voices, dramatic shifts of scene, the exchange of ideas and argument, imitation, parody and satire, and so on.

In *Have with You* Nashe claims that the two protagonists did meet when they had adjacent rooms at the Dolphin Inn, Cambridge, when they were both visiting their alma mater.[21] Nashe claimed that Harvey desired a meeting, 'wherein all quarrels might be discussed and drawn to an atonement', but that he 'had no fancy to it', because he did not wish to waste what he had recently written, an apparently cynical claim that is qualified by the more serious moral point that 'a public wrong in Print was to be so slightly slubbered over in private, with Come, come, give me your hand, let us be friends, and thereupon I drink to you.'[22] We have no independent verification that this meeting took place – Harvey does not mention it – nor whether, if it did, it happened as Nashe claimed. Certainly, if Harvey was keen to avoid a reconciliation earlier, now Nashe was the party more eager to continue the quarrel.

Have with You is dedicated to Richard Lichfield, who later responded with *The Trimming of Thomas Nashe*. As with the meeting in the Dolphin, we have no proper explanation of why Lichfield became embroiled in the quarrel. Perhaps he was another associate of Harvey, and therefore assumed to be fair game; perhaps the joke about the barber cutting the hair of the doctor and so cutting him down to size was too good for Nashe to ignore; perhaps he stands as a substitute for Harvey's brother Richard, given the outrageous liberties taken with his name; perhaps the two united against a common enemy.[23] Nashe's baiting of Lichfield may not have been a sensible move, and could have had some influence on the eventual decision of the authorities to stem the proliferation of satire before it developed further and had more drastic effects.

The *Trimming* makes great play with Nashe's tribulations after the *Isle of Dogs* affair in ways that surely anticipate the opening of *Lenten Stuff* and, possibly, refer to the Orion passage in *Summer's Last Will*, indicating that the link between Nashe and dogs was firmly set for many people by the mid-1590s:

> Since that thy Isle of Dogs hath made thee thus miserable, I cannot but account thee a Dog, and chide and rate thee as a Dog that hath done a fault. And yet do not I know why I should blame Dogs? for *Can*, which signifieth a Dog, is also a most trusty Servant; for that Dogs are faithful Servants, to whom their Masters in the night time give in charge all their treasure. They are at command to wait upon their Masters, whether they bend their journey, to fight for them against their Enemies, and to spend their lives to defend them, and to offend their adversaries . . .
>
> . . . thou art no such dog; these were all well nurtured when they were whelps, you not so: the worm was not plucked out from under your tongue, so that you have run mad, and bit venom ever since: for these are the properties of a mad dog.
>
> First, the black choler which reigneth in them turneth to madness most commonly in the Spring-time and in Autumn: and you, though you are mad all the year, yet have showed the sign of it especially this last Autumn; they always run with their mouths open and

their tongues hanging out: we know Howe wide your
mouth is, how long your tongue; your mouth is never
shut, your tongue never tied: slaver and foam fall from
their jaws as they run, and tis but slaver that proceed-
eth from thy mouth: though their eyes be open, yet
they stumble on every object; so though thou seest who
offends thee not, yet thou all offendest.[24]

Nashe is cast here as a cynic, the word for the disaffected
and angry Greek school of philosophy founded by Diogenes
(d. 323 BCE). The term 'cynic' derives from the image of a dog
barking at everything without any sense of proportion or
judgement, happy to live homeless like a mad dog if that enabled the philosopher to rail at everything in sight.[25] Nashe
is therefore a Diogenes – or even a mad dog – snarling at
whatever he encounters, incapable of telling whether his
criticism and carping have any significance, so enveloped is he
in the black bile that causes anger. Far from being the rational
critic of his own judgement, correcting the faults of clod-
hopping and dim-witted thinkers such as Harvey, Lichfield sees
Nashe as a fatally unbalanced man, prey to the force of his
bodily humours, which override any residual use of reason.[26]

Have with You has a clear and organized structure.[27] It has
the most elaborate paratextual prefatory apparatus of any
Nashe text, beginning with the dedicatory epistle to Lichfield,
described as 'the most orthodoxal and reverent corrector of
staring hairs, the sincere & finigraphical ratifier of prolix-
ious rough barbarism, the thrice egregious and censorial
animadvertiser of vagrant mustachios, chief scavenger of
chins, and principal Head-man of the parish wherein he

dwells'.[28] The teasing description, with ever more elaborate qualifications of Lichfield's profession using conspicuously Latinate terms, parodies Harvey's Ciceronianism, and warns the reader not to take the letter at face value as a sincere dedication to a friend or patron. Lichfield is used as a metaphor for Nashe's concerted attempt to puncture Harvey's ludicrous pomposity, cutting him down to size and reminding him that the practical matters of everyday life are as important as academic ones, especially when that academic culture has become deracinated from ordinary life and, as a result, pointless and answerable only to itself. Harvey may imagine that he is the very definition of civility and civilized debate, but he is really the epitome of 'prolixous rough barbarism'.

After the letter to Lichfield, which contains a parodic grace to the Harveys, Nashe addresses his Christian readers, blaming his critics for the fact that he has been forced to reply to Harvey: 'I do not write against him because I hate him, but that I would confirm and plainly show, to a number of weak believers in my sufficiency, that I am able to answer him' (p. 19). He explains that his reply will be in the form of a dialogue, with himself as respondent explaining his actions and words before four interlocutors: Senior Importuno, the 'opponent'; Grand Consiliadore, the 'chief Censor or Moderator'; Domino Bentivole, supporting Importuno; and Don Carneades de boone Compagniola. The work is organized as a formal rhetorical exercise, a fictitious university examination of Nashe's judgement of Harvey, the purpose being to humiliate Harvey further by finding him wanting in his own chosen arena.

In the first section of the work proper – Nashe's works invariably make good use of prefatory material and integrate it into the argument – the author explains to the interlocutors that he has delayed his response to Harvey not because he cannot write one, but because he has been forced to act as a pen for hire (which may be a defence of works his opponents have attacked, such as 'The Choice of Valentines') and so has needed time to plan his assault on Harvey. He follows this with some comments on Harvey's work, in particular criticizing the vast bulk of *Pierces Supererogation*. To make his point more graphically, Nashe inserts a picture of Harvey 'as he is ready to let fly upon Ajax' (p. 38), continuing the scatological humour of *Strange News* ('Ajax' being the term for a privy, topical because of Sir John Harington's *Metamorphosis of Ajax*, published earlier that year).[29] The interlocutors ask for a sample of Harvey's style, and Nashe argues that only those with no judgement could possibly praise what Harvey writes. He then composes a short oration in Harvey's style, which is punctuated by shocked comments from the interlocutors, unable to believe the extent of dire writing that Harvey produces.

The longest section of the book follows, a biography of Harvey that is a mixture of fact and fiction. Nashe mercilessly lampoons Harvey's pride in his origins, in particular his father's trade as a rope-maker. Nashe claims that all three sons bear the mark of their genesis in their names: '*Gabriel*, his eldest son's name, beginning with a G., for Gallows, *John* with a J. for Jail, *Richard* with an R. for Rope-maker; as much to say as all his whole living depended on the Jail, the Gallows, & making of Ropes' (p. 58). He satirizes Gabriel's education, claiming that his vast reading encouraged his father to imagine that he was destined for great things (although his mother was rather more worried by the disturbing dreams she had had before he was born). Gabriel was an aggressive and litigious youth, always involved in fights that he started. At Cambridge his serious interest in literature was activated, and Nashe imagines a letter written by Harvey's tutor, which begins as though in praise of Harvey but eventually has to acknowledge that his obsession with logic made him an intellectual laughing stock and that his attempt to impress various ladies was even more reprehensible.

Nashe outlines Harvey's humiliations when he starts to publish poetry and pamphlets, including his faux pas with the Earl of Oxford. Building on his description of Harvey as exceptionally vain, Nashe outlines his opponent's incessant pursuit of honour, which includes the memorable description of Harvey attempting to impress the queen on her progress to Audley End in 1578, when he came out to deliver his oration 'ruffling it out, huffty tuffty, in his suit of velvet' (p. 73). Nashe also sneers at Harvey's pride in Elizabeth's comment 'that he looked something like an Italian' (p. 76).[30] This remark triggers a less than impressive makeover, as Harvey's self-love reaches new, unbearable heights:

> But now he was an insulting monarch above *Monarcha*, the Italian, that wore crowns on his shoes; and quite renouncst his natural English accents & gestures, & wrested himself wholly to the Italian *punctilios*, speaking our homely Island tongue strangely, as if he were but a raw practitioner in it, & but ten days before had entertained a school-master to teach him to pronounce it. Ceremonies of reverence to the greatest States (as it were not the fashion of his country) he was very

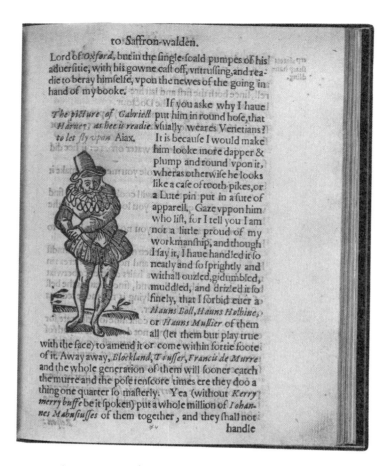

parsimonious and niggardly of . . . to whom I wish no better fortune than the forelocks of Fortune he had hold of in his youth, & no higher fame than he hath purchased himself by his pen, being the first (in our language) I have encountered that repurified poetry from art's pedantism, & that instructed it to speak courtly. (pp. 76–7)

Page including woodcut of Gabriel Harvey about to let fly on Ajax, from Nashe's pamphlet *Have with You to Saffron Walden* (1596).

Nashe again points out how deficient and inadequate Harvey's English is, diminished precisely by his attempts to be more sophisticated than his countrymen and women. The praise of the queen does not create something new, but activates what has been latent within him since his arrogant youth. Harvey imagines that he has purified the language and instructed the court how to speak proper English.

Returning to Cambridge only exposes Harvey to the play *Pedantius*, in which he is ridiculed for his clumsy and inappropriate language and overweening pride. He leaves to live and practise as a lawyer in London, where his confidence in his poetry leads him to plan to translate the corpus of English law into hexameters. Finding himself embroiled in the controversy with Nashe, Harvey lodges with his publisher, John Wolfe, where he has to make ends meet by producing plague bills for his host, making him one of the few people who do well out of outbreaks of the disease and who long for them to continue. He is now so deep in debt that he has to flee London because he owes Wolfe £36 for the publication of *Pierces Supererogation*, which has been a vanity project, not a commercial proposition. Eventually justice catches up with him and he is imprisoned, but through the good offices of the gaoler's wife and a minister, as well as his own self-regarding trickery, he is released and slinks off to Saffron Walden, even though the minister and a sergeant have stood bond for him.

The interlocutors are convinced that Harvey is a rogue and a fraud, in life as well as in language, but Importuno alleges that, even so, 'there is some good matter in his book against' Nashe (p. 102). Accordingly, Nashe provides a summary of the flaws of *Pierces Supererogation*. Looking back to his comment that only the deluded and incapable could praise Harvey's writing, Nashe argues that the first flaw is that Harvey has got three incompetent writers, Barnabe Barnes, John Thorius and Anthony Chute, to write in his honour. Barnes is mocked for some vulgar lines in one of his sonnets, in which the narrator imagines the wine his mistress drinks passing through her body ('Or that sweet wine, which down her throat doth trickle,/ To kiss her lips, and lie next at her heart,/ Run through her veins, and pass by pleasure's part'), an unfortunately taste-less image that other writers also lambasted (p. 103).[31] Nashe also claims that the mysterious gentlewoman, whom Harvey claims has supported him against Nashe, is actually Harvey's own invention.[32]

Even a relatively casual reading of *Pierces Supererogation* reveals it to be full of undigested learning, demonstrating that Harvey is more a thief than an author, someone who does not have the ability to transform what he reads and create something new, but instead relies on authorities to hide his own shortcomings. Nashe rebuts the charge of atheism that Harvey has levelled against him, and an accusation that he is impoverished because of his poor writing. Nashe concludes that '*Hydras*' heads I should go about to cut off . . . if I should undertake to run throughout all the foolish frivolous reprehensions & cavils he hath in his Book' (p. 128). *Have with You* ends with Nashe defending him-self from the criticism that he fell out with other writers, such as Christopher Marlowe, Henry Chettle and Robert Greene. He includes a letter from Chettle exonerating him of doing him any wrong (p. 131), and one from Thorius, who had defended Harvey, stating now that he would not have done so had he been in possession of all the facts. He also defends

Harvey's old enemies Andrew Perne and John Lyly, before concluding that it is now late and the court has gone to dinner.

Have with You is stuffed full of inventive insults, such as the claim that Harvey's massive letters have caused the poor carter forced to transport them to complain that he has cracked three axles and that they would be better suited to making mud walls, mending highways or damming quagmires: 'Letters, do you term them? They may be Letters patents well enough for their tediousness: for no lecture at Surgeons Hall upon an Anatomy may compare with them in longitude. Why, they are longer than the Statutes of clothing, or the Charter of *London*' (p. 34). Nashe is also adept at imagining ridiculous names for Harvey, as he does in *Strange News*, playing on Harvey's connection to the Angel Gabriel and inventing epithets for him, many based on literary characters: Gabriel Jobbernoul, Gamaliel Hobgoblin, Braggadochio Glorioso, Gilgilis Hobberdehoy, Gabriell Hoeilglasse, Gregory Habberdine, Gabriel Hangtelow, Timothy Tiptoes, Infractissime Pistlepragmos, Dragobert Coppenhagen, Domine Dewse-ace, Gobin a grace ap Hannikin, Gregorie Huldricke and other imaginatively insulting soubriquets.[33]

Comic enjoyment aside – and there is a great deal of such pleasure to be had in *Have with You* – the strongest satirical passages are probably those directed at Harvey's absurd language. In the dedicatory epistle Nashe asserts that if anyone spends a quarter of the time they might have spent reading the romances of Barnabe Rich (one of the many second-rate authors that Nashe treats with casual disdain) 'in mumping upon *Gabrielism* . . . I'll be bound, body and goods, thou wilt not any longer sneakingly come forth with a rich spirit and an admirable capacity, but an *enthusiastical spirit* & a *nimble entelechy* [a spirit realized as a body]' (p. 17). Put another way, readers who waste too much time reading Harvey rather than profitably reading other authors will end up believing that his Ciceronianisms are, in fact, the natural way to speak English. 'Mumping' is an expressive Nashe coinage, capturing the hesitant, inarticulate nature of Harvey's language as the speaker struggles to articulate words clearly and meaningfully, hamstrung by their pointless and misleading grandeur.

In many ways, the sharpest passages are hardly written by Nashe at all, but are compilations of Harvey's own words followed by the comments of the interlocutors, struggling to control their laughter. Near the start of the oration the following passage appears, made up entirely of quotations from *Pierces Supererogation* and *A New Letter*:

ORATION

Omitting (sicco pede) *my encomiastical Orations and mercurial and martial discourses of the terribility of war, in the active & chivalrous vain, every way comparable with the Cavalcads of* Bellerophon, *or* Don Alphonso d'Avalos, *my Seraphical visions in Queen Poetry, queint theoricks, melancholy projects, and pragmatical discourses; whose beau-desert and rich economy the inspiredest Heliconists &* Arch-patrons *of our new Omniscians have not sticked to equipage with the ancient Quinquagenarians,* Centurions *and* Chiliarchs: *notwithstanding all which* Ideas *of monstrous excellency, some smirking Singularists, brag Reformists and glicking Remembrancers (not with the multiplying spirit of the Alchumist, but the villainist) seek to be masons of infinite contradiction; they (I say) with their frumping* Contras, *tickling*

interjections, together with their vehement incensives and allectives,
as if they would be the only A per se a's, or great A's of puissance,
like Alexander *(whom yet some of our modern Worthies' disdain*
to have sceptred the est Amen *of valure,) commense redoubtable*
Monomachies against me, and the dead honey-bee, my brother.

    Bentiv: A *per se, con per se, tittle est Amen!* Dost thou not
feel thy self spoiled? why, he comes upon thee (man)
with a whole Horn-book.

    Import: What a supernatural *Hibble* de *beane* it is, to
call his brother a dead honey-bee!

    Consil: I laughed at nothing so much as that word
Arch-patrons. Go thy ways, thought I; thou art a Civilian,
and maist well fetch metaphors from the Arches, but
thou shalt never fish any money from thence whilest
thou liv'st. (pp. 45–6)[34]

The interlocutors all find different elements of Harvey's words
especially ridiculous: his pedantic insistence on grammar that
actually reminds them of the most basic means of learning
to write, the hornbook; the lack of rhetorical skill that dooms
such speeches to failure should they ever be used in the civilian
law courts; the ludicrous neologisms to dress up familiar
words and concepts; and, most pathetically, the comparison
of his dead brother, John, to a honey bee.[35] The last point
might seem rather mean-spirited, even cruel, but it is surely
a response to Harvey's comments on the death of Robert
Greene in *Four Letters.* Nashe knows that he can satirize Gabriel
Harvey rather well, but that he does not need to because his
opponent does such a good job himself. He simply has to
allow Harvey to speak and guide the reader's reactions. There

is more substance to Harvey than Nashe allows — as he surely knew — and their quarrel may well be enshrined as a composite character, Ingenioso, in the Parnassus plays.[36] Even so, it is a sign of his success and Harvey's failings as a writer that, even if few people have read *Have with You* since the 1590s, based on their understanding of his other works, principally *The Unfortunate Traveller* and *Lenten Stuff*, they assume that the man who wrote English as well as he did in those works must have triumphed in their quarrel.

FIVE

Fiction

ashe is still best known for his longish work of prose fiction, *The Unfortunate Traveller* (1594). It is his only work of fiction, a stark contrast to the prodigious quantity of prose produced by his slightly older friend Robert Greene, who died at a similar age but who produced more than 35 works of romance and cony-catching literature (representing the harsh and cynical reality of life on London's streets) in just under a decade (1583–92). This dubious achievement enabled him to become the first professional writer in English.[1] Nashe may have had a complicated and not entirely straightforward relationship with Greene, possibly because he thought the older man wrote too much.[2] That would not, however, explain why Nashe – whose literary talents would seem to have been ideal for prose fiction – wrote only one such work.

A series of possible explanations present themselves. In *Lenten Stuff* Nashe represents himself as a writer, but for drama.[3] He may well have transferred his energies to drama and have been writing works that either are not extant or have not yet been identified as his.[4] It may be significant that after the flurry of works that appeared in the early 1590s Nashe published only two new works after *The Unfortunate*

Traveller, Have with You to Saffron Walden and *Lenten Stuff*, a marked slowing down of his literary output. Perhaps, as Charles Nicholl has argued, he suffered a breakdown, a 'crack up'.[5] If so, this may have been caused by the criticism of *Christ's Tears over Jerusalem*, referred to in the letter to William Cotton; the strain of the feud with Gabriel Harvey (although there is no sign in Nashe's writings that the quarrel affected him); or perhaps something more mundane – that, like his older contemporary Edmund Spenser, Nashe had a source of income that made him less reliant on his writing for a living.[6]

The explanation for the uniqueness of *The Unfortunate Traveller* may be literary. Perhaps Nashe felt there was a problem with writing in the way he had been; he may have felt dissatisfied with his work and believed that he had to try something new and more adventurous. Certainly, in his relatively short writing career Nashe tries a wide variety of genres, a further pointed contrast to Greene, who energetically produced more works in a narrow range of genres. Nashe frequently reminds readers that he is a serious writer whose work really matters to him and who wants to push the boundaries of what it is possible to write. Very little prose fiction of substance and originality by any author appeared between 1594 and Nashe's death six years later. The great works that characterize Elizabethan prose – including those by Greene – had already appeared: imitations of Heliodorus; John Lyly's *Euphues: The Anatomy of Wit* (1578); Sir Philip Sidney's *Arcadia* (1593); the collections of tales by William Painter and George Pettie (1566, 1576); and Thomas Lodge's *Rosalind* (1590). *The Unfortunate Traveller*, a work that cleverly combines cony-catching trickster literature and the picaresque with romance and travel

writing, could be seen as literature that is simultaneously
cynical and nostalgic and so marked the end of a tradition,
rather than a newly revitalized genre.[7]

The Unfortunate Traveller narrates the adventures of the
roguish Jack Wilton, a soldier in Henry VIII's invading army
in France (1513). Jack returns from the campaign, but after an
outbreak of plague – a perennial theme in Nashe's works – he
flees to Europe, where he witnesses the Battle of Marignano
(1515), at which the French forces under François I decisively
defeated the Swiss confederation. He then heads on to
Münster, where he observes the terrible effects of the civil
wars in Germany after the Anabaptists under John of Leiden
seize the city and are besieged by the Holy Roman Emperor,
Charles V (1500–1558), and the Duke of Saxe-Lauenburg,
Magnus I (1470–1543) (this took place in 1535, demonstrating
that Nashe showed little interest in historical chronology).

Urs Graf, *Battlefield of Marignano*, 1521, pen in black.

Attempting to return to England, Jack joins his former master Henry Howard, the Earl of Surrey (1516/17–1547), at 'Middleborough' (Middelburg, Holland), and decides instead to accept 'the lottery of travel'.[8] They journey through Europe to Italy, where they stop at Venice and Florence. Here Jack leaves Surrey and heads down to Rome. After a series of violent and troubling encounters, and witnessing too many executions, he marries his courtesan, Diamante, flees Italy and rejoins Henry VIII's army as he meets the French king, François I, at the Field of the Cloth of Gold (7–24 June 1520).[9]

Nashe intermingles fact and fiction in his narrative, so that the absurd, impossible chronology and imaginary journey of Surrey to defend the honour of the 'fair Geraldine' (Elizabeth Fitzgerald, Countess of Lincoln, daughter of the Earl of Kildare (1527–1590), the Fitzgeralds being known as the Geraldines) are set against the background of real places and events.[10] And, of course, Nashe knew that Surrey never travelled to Italy in his short life, although he spent a year in France (1532–3). Surrey did write a sonnet for Elizabeth, in which he commented, 'Bright is her hue, and Geraldine she hight', which led to the nickname 'the fair Geraldine'. She was ten at the time and Surrey, a relative, was trying to help her family choose a suitable match for her.[11]

The Unfortunate Traveller directly confronts the questions any traveller had to ask: was travel worthwhile? What did one learn from travelling?[12] Even by the standards of Elizabethan fiction, *The Unfortunate Traveller* is a work dominated by paranoia, secrets and the fear of coming to harm in a relentlessly hostile world. Jack Wilton is a non-voluntary or involuntary

Master of the Countess of Warwick (attrib.), *The Fair Geraldine*,
c. 1575, oil on panel.

traveller, someone who – in common with most English people who travelled abroad in the sixteenth century – does so because he is connected to the army or a great lord's entourage.[13] He is also a picaresque rogue, able to flourish in a series of unpromising environments because he can exploit conditions to his advantage, understanding that being distanced from home enables him to ignore established social norms and act unscrupulously to protect himself and, when possible, profit. The piety of a humanist education counts for little in a brutal world structured by military conflict and street crime, a point that Nashe made repeatedly in his attacks on the Harvey brothers.

Jack is also extremely lucky in ways that a reader understands are implausible for an unfortunate traveller, one of the many ironies that structure the story. In his opening paragraph, Jack signals his conscious inversion of established patterns of learning: 'What stratagemical acts and monuments do you think an ingenious infant of my years might enact? You will say, it were sufficient if he slur a die, pawn his master to the utmost penny, and minister the oath of the pantofle artificially'.[14] In other words, a sensible man in his shoes learns how to cheat, expropriate and, most significantly, lie. The 'acts and monuments' that someone needs when trying to keep their head above water in the army are not those found in John Foxe's history of the martyrs of the Protestant church, *The Acts and Monuments of the Christian Church* (1563), but rather wit, verbal dexterity and the ability to think on one's feet under pressure whatever the morality of the situation.[15]

Jack's first two 'jests' indicate how he plans to use his experiences of travel. First, he dupes an alehouse-keeper who sells cider and cheese to the soldiers, described grandiosely as a 'Lord of misrule' (p. 210), one of the many who followed the army to exploit the opportunities it created. Jack tells him that 'It is buzzed in the King's head that you are a secret friend to the Enemy, and under pretence of getting a License to furnish the Camp with cider and such like provant, you have furnished the Enemy, & in empty barrels sent letters of discovery and corn innumerable' (p. 214). In a world dominated by spying and lying, the claim is only too plausible. It probably also alludes to the secret communications between Mary, Queen of Scots and her supporters who wished to assassinate Elizabeth and place Mary on the throne; those messages were hidden in a beer barrel, the discovery of which led to Mary's execution on 8 February 1587.[16] The cider-seller's error is that he is wise enough to believe that treachery is omnipresent but foolish enough to trust Jack, a lesson that also unsettles the reader, who does not know how far to credit Nashe's narrative. In one sense, this dilemma is surely that posed by fiction itself: can we believe what we read?

In this case, early on in the narrative, questions are posed and little harm is done. Jack persuades the cider-seller that the best way to offset the king's judgement that he is 'a miser and a snudge [sponger]' (p. 215) is to give his cider free to the whole army. The cider-seller does so and, drunk himself, seeks out the king and professes his loyalty. The startled monarch extracts the story of the hoax, as a consequence Jack is whipped for his 'holiday lie', and the army 'made themselves merry with it many a Winter's evening after' (p. 216).

The second jest is more disturbing, and indeed episodes in *The Unfortunate Traveller* increase in seriousness as Jack moves south through Europe towards Rome. He persuades an 'ugly mechanical Captain' (p. 217) that he has been chosen to assassinate the king of France. He is instructed to pretend to be an English traitor and so bluff his way into the French camp and gain the enemy's trust. Needless to say, his story is easily exposed, and he escapes torture on the wheel only because he is too ridiculous to be a credible threat. The captain is whipped by the French and sent back to the English camp, Jack having now inflicted the suffering he experienced on someone else. The French send a boast back to their English enemies: 'they were shrewd fools that should drive the Frenchman out of his Kingdom and make him glad, with Corinthian *Dionisius*, to play the Schoolmaster' (pp. 224–5). The story of Dionysius, the tyrant who was transformed into a proper king after he became a humble schoolmaster for a while, was a standard example in English humanist treatises, demonstrating the power of education to curb the excesses of over-mighty government.[17] Here the moral force of the story is negated because it is cast as a military boast; only a more powerful enemy – if the English should defeat them – can make them trade their weapons for schoolbooks.

Jack stands as a figure of the untrustworthy and malign counsellor whose advice is designed to cause disaster to those foolish enough to listen to it. He sees himself as 'God's scourge from above' (p. 226), the term surely borrowed from Marlowe's *Tamburlaine*, in which the violent conquering protagonist defines himself as the 'scourge of god'.[18] At this point Jack seems master of his destiny. When persuading the captain that he has been chosen for a special mission, he lies: 'I see in your face, that you were born, with the swallow, to feed flying, to get much treasure and honour by travel' (p. 221), words that will return to haunt him on his own travels in Europe. As Jack witnesses more terrifying sights and spectacles, the reader has to work ever harder to understand whether what he encounters is truth or fiction and what moral and educational significance his experiences have (if any).

Near the end of the work, Jack witnesses two graphically described executions of the unrepentant criminals Zadoch (in Rome) and Cutwolfe (Bologna). These are surely based on first-hand experience, given the frequency with which early modern executions were staged, but both soon become fantastic accounts, flights of fancy that are a testament to the author's ability to produce the disturbing effects of the truly grotesque. Zadoch's death in particular can be read as an unsettling set piece:

> To the execution place was he brought, where first and foremost he was stripped, then on a sharp iron stake fastened in the ground, had he his fundament pitched, which stake ran up along into his body like a spit, under his arm-holes two of like sort, a great bonfire they made round about him, wherewith his flesh roasted not burned: and ever as with the heat his skin blistered, the fire was drawn aside, and they basted him with a mixture of Aqua fortis, alum water, and Mercury sublimatum, which smarted to the very soul of him, and searched him to the marrow. Then did they scourge his back parts so blistered and basted, with burning whips of red hot wire: his head they noynted over with pitch and tar, and so enflamed it. To his privy members they tied

streaming fireworks, the skin from the crest of his shoulder, as also from his elbows, his huckle bones, his knees,
his ankles they plucked and gnawed off with sparkling
pincers: his breast and his belly with seal skins they
grated over, which as fast as they grated & rawed, one
stood over and lav'd with smity's cindry water and *aqua
vito*: his nails they half raised up, and then underpropped
them with Sharp pricks like a taylor's shop window half
open on a holiday: every one of his fingers they rent
up to the wrist: his toes they brake off by the roots, and
let them still hang by a little skin. In conclusion, they had
a small oil fire, such as men blow light bubbles of glass
with, and beginning at his feet, they let him lingeringly
burn up limb by limb, till his heart was consumed, and
then he died. Triumph women, this was the end of the
whipping Jew, contrived by a woman, in revenge of two
women, her self and her maid. (pp. 316–17)

Early modern executions throughout Europe were, hardly
surprisingly, brutal and terrifying events, designed to cow
potentially hostile populations into submitting to authority.[19]
Protestant and Catholic martyrologies, which circulated widely
in the 1590s, show terrible images of heretics burning at the
stake and mutilated bodies to remind readers of the horror
the faithful endured to maintain true religion.[20] Tearing the
flesh off the criminal's body with red-hot pincers was common
in France, as contemporary English pamphlets noted.[21] Severed
heads and body parts frequently adorned most city walls to
remind citizens of the fate of traitors.[22] However, there surely
is a point at which Nashe's description changes from what

most contemporary readers would have recognized as familiar,
even normal, practice – or the sort of judicial killing that they
imagined took place in other European states – to a horrifying
fantastic spectacle.[23]

The first sentence describing a stake entering Zadoch's
anus is undoubtedly taken from the descriptions of Turkish
executions recounted by travellers such as Fynes Moryson.[24]
The burning surely resembles the strategy of burning heretics during Mary's reign, abandoned by Elizabeth, who classi-
fied opposition as treason and chose hanging, drawing and
quartering as the primary method of execution.[25] The next
sentence describing the basting with 'a mixture of Aqua fortis,
alum water, and Mercury sublimatum' (nitric acid, alum and
mercury sulphate), all chemicals used by alchemists, should
arouse suspicions in the reader that this is not an account of
an execution that anyone has ever witnessed. But it is the
description of anointing the victim's head with tar that is then
set alight and the attachment of fireworks to his penis that
confirms any lingering suspicions that we are now reading a
grotesque fantasy. From this sentence onwards the description becomes ever more far-fetched, so that when Zadoch's
mutilated fingers look like the open shutters of a tailor's shop
we know that this cannot be a testimony of an actual event.
The bathos of the moral at the end brings the reader back to
the reality of the criminal's death, but also forces the question
of whether such punishment is appropriate, real or just. *The
Unfortunate Traveller* works as a satire not of society as such, but
of the ways in which society is represented. Nashe is especially
astute on the power that images, fictional and factual, have
over a reader who does not have the ability to challenge the

representations they encounter. This was a significant problem, especially at a time when very few people outside the aristocracy had the freedom to travel unless they were 'unfortunate travellers'. We process material and think we know things because we have digested received images that we are then able to refigure as knowledge. If we are relying on the evidence of what others have told and shown us, our understanding of the world is always mediated and we can never be sure whether we really know anything, whether the world deceives us or we deceive it.[26]

The problem is represented in spectacular terms when Jack is rescued from the gallows by an anonymous banished English earl who knows that he did not murder Heraclide, 'a noble & chaste matron', who commits suicide after she is raped by Bartol, 'a desperate Italian' working with Esdras of Granada, 'a notable Bandetto, authorized by the pope because he had assisted him in some murthers' (p. 287). The episode is a carefully constructed mixture of classical myth, the story of the rape of Lucrece (which led to the founding of the Roman Republic), and voguish popular tales of Italian villainy, gathered by William Painter, George Pettie and others in their sensationalist collections.[27] Rome, which no major English writer apart from Anthony Munday visited between Sir Thomas Wyatt's diplomatic missions (1526–7) and the young John Milton's grand tour (1638–9), was very much a city of the mind for English readers, as Nashe makes clear.[28] Jack is about to fall victim to a fate that many English men and women imagined would probably be theirs if they were to spend any time in the eternal city, the epicentre of the Catholic world. He is saved by yet another piece of absurdly good fortune,

when the earl tells the authorities that he has encountered
Bartol, 'grievously wounded and bloody' (p. 297), in a barber's
shop where he confessed to the crime, having ended his part-
nership with Esdras after a duel fought over Bartol's courtesan.
This testimony is enough to save Jack.[29] Of course, we know
that such strange coincidences and twists of fortune rarely
occur outside fiction.

The earl then provides Jack with a long speech on the perils
of overseas travel, advising him that as he can return home,
unlike the earl, he should do so as soon as possible. The earl
argues that nothing useful can be learned from travel that could
not have been acquired more easily and safely by other means:

> Alas, our Englishmen are the plainest dealing souls
> that ever God put life in: they are greedy of news, and
> love to be fed in their humours and hear themselves
> flattered the best that may be ... Rats and mice engen-
> der by licking one another, he must lick, he must crouch,
> he must cog [cheat], lie and prate, that either in the
> Court or a foreign Country will engender and come
> to preferment ... Some allege, they travel to learn wit,
> but I am of this opinion, that as it is not possible for
> any man to learn the Arte of Memory, whereof *Tully,*
> *Quintillian, Seneca, and Hermannus Buschius* have written so
> many books, except he have a natural memory before:
> so is it not possible for any man to attain any great wit
> by travel, except he have the grounds of it rooted in
> him before ... What is here but we may read in books
> and a great deal more too, without stirring our feet out
> of a warm study. (pp. 298–9)

The earl associates travel with the vices that result from lying. The excessive greed for news, here meaning novelty and newfangledness as much as the latest information, makes the English gullible and easily deceived by unscrupulous flatterers eager to swindle them. The desire for success in foreign courts leads to even more reprehensible behaviour: fawning, sycophancy and ingrained duplicity. Travel is associated not simply with unreliable narration but also, more significantly, with a corrosive influence on the personality of the traveller, who becomes more dishonest and mendacious as a result.

However, as this section of the speech continues, the nature and balance of the argument change and the alert reader may feel more at odds with the development of the earl's thinking. The earl argues that claims that travel will lead to new knowledge or the development of new understanding are entirely without foundation. People either are predisposed to something or will be unable to master its complexities, like the art of memory. This is surely excessively pessimistic and deluded. The art of memory could be learned, as so many manuals instructed readers, but perhaps the earl thinks Jack is too ignorant to know of them.[30] More significantly, he surely cannot really believe that, however pointless so much travel was – the grand tour often being a means of allowing young men to sow their wild oats by indulging in sex tourism under the guise of enculturation and preparation for adulthood – travellers learned nothing at all except vice.[31]

The last sentence cited here would appear to undercut the argument of the earl and force the reader to worry about the nature of the purported eyewitness accounts of travel literature. It would be true that one could learn everything through reading books and never be forced to venture into the wider world if one could trust those books to tell the truth. Of course, books have their limitations as testimony, as do eyewitness accounts and personal observation.[32] It would seem that the earl validates their use as a means of avoiding travel rather than because he particularly values them, especially if we remember that he claims that books on the art of memory are of little use because one cannot learn such skills. We should also remember that neither the earl nor Jack is an entirely willing traveller. While Jack is a non-voluntary traveller as a soldier and as part of the Earl of Surrey's entourage, the earl is an involuntary traveller, banished from his homeland for unstated reasons but surely as a result of bad behaviour. According to the courtier Sir Thomas Palmer, involuntary travellers were banished for two reasons: 'for breach of Laws in Court' or 'of such as the Prince upon just indignation banisheth the Land for a time certain or not; whereby such are forced to travel'.[33] Most probably, we are to assume that the anonymous earl is a Catholic exile, since there were many such exiled communities in major European cities.[34] His refusal to learn and his belief that he knows all the answers already would seem to suggest a stubbornness and wilful ignorance that would make him an unreliable witness who should be treated with suspicion by Jack and the reader.

As the earl's speech develops, the logic of his argument disintegrates, issuing a challenge to the reader, who has to decide whether to accept what he says. Just as our perception of what is happening in the description of the execution of Zadoch changes as we read, so does our understanding of the earl's words, a characteristic feature of Nashe's writing. The earl argues that travel teaches the traveller nothing because the different countries and peoples of Europe exhibit particular characteristics that are already in the public domain and are easy to know and understand. Why would anyone need to travel to the countries in question, at great expense and with the possibility of the terrible consequences that Jack has experienced, in order to discover nothing new? The earl poses a series of rhetorical questions: 'What is there in *France* to be learned more than in *England*, but falsehood in fellowship, perfect slovenry, to love no man but for my pleasure, to swear *Ah par la mort Dieu*, when a man's hams are scabbed?' (p. 300). Spain is no better, and the earl complains that travellers simply bring back the latest fashions and a series of absurd, ill-informed opinions of no consequence denigrating England in comparison: 'if you urge him [the traveller] more particularly wherein it exceeds, he can give no instance but in *Spain* they have better bread than any we have' (pp. 300–301). Italy has even more pernicious effects on the English traveller. From there he brings back a ridiculous series of affected gestures, kissing his 'hand like an ape, cringe his neck like a starveling [someone who is starving], and play at hey passe repasse come aloft, when he salutes a man' (p. 301), apparently trivial problems that are signs of the much greater sins of pride and insincerity. He also learns 'the art of atheism, the art of epicurising, the art of whoring, the art of poisoning, the art of Sodomitry', all of which makes him 'an excellent Courtier, a curious carpet knight . . . a fine close lecher, a glorious hypocrite' (p. 301). The Danes and the Dutch need little attention, being nations of drunks who 'do nothing but fill bottomless tubs, & will be drunk & snort in the midst of dinner' (p. 301).

The earl has provided a series of standard descriptions that the reader will recognize, but given that very few readers of *The Unfortunate Traveller* would have had a chance to visit the countries described (Nashe included), there is no means of disputing the earl's descriptions other than by reading other travellers' accounts. The work itself, especially the lurid and sensational sections recounting Jack's adventures in Italy, simply confirms what the earl asserts.[35] The earl's claims are mainly what would have been available in contemporary travel accounts. The comments on Italy recall Roger Ascham's exhortation to his countrymen not to travel abroad and risk being infected by Italian vice, such as the fussiness of agonizing over 'whether a man lust to wear Shoe or pantofle'.[36] According to Ascham, 'three proper opinions' characterize all Italians: 'open contempt of God's word: in a secret security of sin: and in a bloody desire to have all taken away, by sword or burning, that be not of their faction' (K1r). The reader of *The Unfortunate Traveller* will not learn anything new from the earl's words, nor from the descriptions he provides of the French, Dutch or Danes.[37] The description of Spain may be more challenging, given the necessarily limited contact with Spain in the later sixteenth century. The revelation that the main problem with travelling to Spain was the import of ridiculous fashions is certainly at odds with rather more serious accounts of the experience of mercenaries fighting in the Spanish armies in their European wars, or the fate of prisoners at the hands of the Inquisition.[38] The earl's rapid tour through the nationalities of Europe is comic in its reliance on stereotypes that supply obvious humorous effects, in part at the earl's expense. However, it is also comic in an Aristotelian sense, conspicuously representing people as worse than they really are.[39]

The earl's account forces the reader to consider the value of testimony and whether it can provide useful knowledge. *The Unfortunate Traveller* is, as its title indicates, written in the wake of the experience of the wider world for Europeans in the sixteenth century, as the Renaissance went global and individuals had to assimilate diverse forms of knowledge, information and testimony that challenged their understanding, but which probably contained as much falsehood and untruth as it did reliable information.[40] The same applies to Jack's own observations of Europe, in particular his representation of Rome. Rome loomed large in the English literary and cultural imagination, but it existed as an imagined urban space, a cityscape that everyone and no one knew, that provided a powerful image of how a city that was both ancient and modern might look. Of course, as modern and contemporary thinkers and theorists of the city after Lewis Mumford constantly remind us, our understanding of the great cities of the world – New York, Beijing, Istanbul, Mexico City, London – is inevitably fictional even if we do happen to live in these cities.[41] What really matter are the 'urban imaginaries', images of cities that determine how we think of them as they are and in relation to other major populated areas. There can be no safe distinction between the factual and the fictional in anyone's imaginative engagement with the city. As Andreas Huyssen, following Italo Calvino, has stated, 'no real city can ever be grasped in its present or past totality by any single person.'[42] The travelogue is just that, never a substitute for knowledge.

Jack waxes lyrical about the wonderful gardens he encounters in Rome (possibly referring to the Farnese Gardens, designed in 1550, but more likely based on Nashe's reading and imagination):

I saw a summer banqueting house belonging to a merchant, that was the marvel of the world, & could not be matched except God should make another paradise. It was built round of green marble like a Theater with-out: within there was a heaven and earth comprehended both under one roof; the heaven was a clear overhanging vault of crystal, wherein the Sun and Moon, and each visible Star had his true similitude, shine, situation, and motion, and, by what enwrapped art I cannot conceive, these spheres in their proper orbs observed their circular wheelings and turnings, making a certain kind of soft angelical murmuring music in their often windings & going about; which music the philosophers say in the true heaven by reason of the grossness of our senses, we are not capable of. For the earth, it was counterfeited in that likeness that Adam lorded it out before his fall. (pp. 282–3)[43]

Rome is replete with astonishing beauty that appears to undo the Fall. But, of course, as is ever the way with Nashe, things are not quite what they seem. The passage is probably a parody of Sir Philip Sidney's famous comments in his *Defence of Poesy* about poetry overcoming nature and enabling us to return to heaven through its creation of a golden world.[44] Sidney's tract was not printed until 1595. However, Nashe had written the preface to a pirated edition of Sidney's sonnet sequence *Astrophil and Stella* in 1591, so would have had more opportunity than most to access Sidney's treatise, which was circulating widely in manuscript.

Nevertheless, it is not long before Jack's time in Rome turns much uglier with an outbreak of the plague. Nashe is referring to a real epidemic, one in 1522, which had a terrible impact (again, Nashe's chronology does not work, since *The Unfortunate Traveller* opened with Jack taking part in Henry VIII's campaign in France, which took place in 1513). We move rapidly from the beauties of the summerhouse to the horror of summer plague:

> So it fell out, that it being a vehement hot summer when I was a sojourner there, there entered such a hotspurd plague as hath not been heard of: why it was but a word and a blow, Lord have mercy upon us, and he was gone. Within three quarters of a year in that one city there died of it a hundred thousand: Look in *Lanquets* Chronicle and you shall find it. To smell of a nosegay, that was poisoned, and turn your nose to a house that had the plague, it was all one. The clouds like a number of cormorants that keep their corn till it stink and is musty, kept in their stinking exhalations, till they had almost stifled all *Rome's* inhabitants. Physicians' greediness of gold made them greedy of their destiny. (p. 286)

Nature, imitated and tamed in the garden, returns with a vengeance to decimate Rome. The precious metals that were used to enable man to supersede the beauties of the natural world are now handed over to unscrupulous – and unsuccessful – doctors. Jack provides us with the sort of horrifying details that authenticate accounts of such catastrophic epidemics:

> one grave was the sepulchre of seven score, one bed was the altar whereon whole families were offered . . .
> Some died sitting at their meat, others as they were asking counsel of the physician for their friends. I saw at the house where I was hosted a maid bring her master warm broth for to comfort him, and she sink down dead her self ere he had half eat it up. (pp. 286–7)

Of course, as in all travellers' tales, such details can just as easily be made up as based on the observations of an eyewitness. But what Jack sees here probably had been witnessed by Nashe. London was subject to frequent outbreaks of the plague, notably that in the summer of 1592, which seems to have cast a shadow over Nashe's writing career. Nashe had undoubtedly seen many examples of houses boarded up to keep the victims from spreading the disease, with the words 'Lord Have Mercy Upon Us' written as a desperate warning.[45] Nashe connects London and Rome through the fear of the plague. He quibbles on the River Tiber and Tyburn, the site of the London gallows from 1196 to 1783, inviting his readers to think about these imagined cityscapes together, as he describes Jack's feelings on escaping from Rome: 'Oars nor wind could not stir nor blow faster, than we toiled out of *Tiber*; a number of good fellows would give size ace and the dice, that with as little toil they could leave Tyburn behind them'

(p. 318). The term 'size ace and the dice' is obscure, but clearly means 'all they possess' (p. 292), as well as reminding us that Jack starts the novel when first in the army in France, boasting of his ability to cheat at dice (p. 217). Jack is a trickster who gambles with his life, a real possibility for the reckless poor anywhere, as his narrator had already pointed out in *Christ's Tears over Jerusalem*. Complaining of the disastrous effects of usury, Nashe asks,

> What is left for a man to do, being consumed to the bare bones by these greedy Horseleeches, and not having so much reserved as would buy him Bread, but either to hang at Tyburn, or pillage and reprisal where he may? Huge numbers in their stinking Prisons they have starved, & made Dice of their bones for the devil to throw at dice for their own souls.[46]

In contrast to what the banished earl alleges, through his travels Jack manages to escape from the grisly fate that awaits his kind in London. However, the reader is surely aware that this is a literary fantasy, and has no basis in a common reality. What is real is the fate of those without property who have to make a living by their wits, and the constant threat of the plague in cities such as London and Rome.

What, then, is the moral of *The Unfortunate Traveller*, a work that employs the language of morality and religion throughout? What can a reader take away from the text that is true and real? Renaissance readers were used to the commonplace that fiction provided them with a world that was more instructive than the real one, and that literature could and should help one to live better.[47] Nashe explores these assumptions and pushes them to their limits. *The Unfortunate Traveller* can be read as a work that warns readers of the dangers of travel, or one that alerts them to the fact that without seeing anything for themselves they are dependent on the observations of others, which may be dubious and misleading. Its moral may be that crime does not pay, as the fates of Zadoch and Cutwolfe demonstrate; or, that in such an immoral and cruel world, crime is the only option left to many. Perhaps all countries and all cities are really the same, more or less. In the end, the reader has to decide how to read the work and sift what may be fact from what is probably fiction, a task that is designed to produce better, more astute and properly sceptical readers who do not believe everything they hear or see.

One of the intriguing – and terrifying – elements of the work is that it seems to point no particular moral other than the need for Jack to look after number one. At the conclusion, we have no idea whether Jack has learned anything from his travels: 'All the conclusive epilogue I will make is this; that if herein I have pleased any, it shall animate me to more pains in this kind' (p. 328). Are these the words of a man who has understood that the world is a dangerous and delusive place that provides delights that are unstable at best and damning at worst? Or those of a trickster who realizes that eventually one's luck runs out, at which point it is time to make discretion the better part of valour? Are we supposed to condemn Jack as an unreliable narrator and wayward soul who has got away with something a little less serious than murder? Or is Nashe pointing a more class-based moral, suggesting that Jack's chutzpah is what it takes to get on if one starts out with next to nothing? Nashe leaves the question of repentance and redemption open, forcing the reader to wonder whether Jack's self-serving behaviour is the best way to survive in a world that will never do him any favours, or whether he survives as long as he does simply because he is lucky and anyone who emulates him is more likely to suffer a grisly fate. Is Jack an unfortunate traveller simply because he has to go out into the world, something that all of us who do not live in enclosed communities have to do? Or are his experiences strange and atypical, making him both unlucky, in that he suffers terrible traumas, and lucky, because he survives them? Of course, *The Unfortunate Traveller* is fiction, and it consciously mixes up time schemes, blends real and fictitious events, and represents outrageously implausible experiences. For Steve Mentz, '*The Unfortunate Traveller* is a dishonest romance,' dishonest because it is about dishonesty, but also, more significantly, because it does not conform to the dictates of most contemporary fiction and so forces us to 'recognize the dishonesty of other fictions'.[48] In the end, it is the readers who are forced to decide what they take away from the text.

SIX

Late Writing, Mature Style

t is hard to claim that a man who had only just reached the age of thirty had developed a 'late style'.[1] *Lenten Stuff* is not the work of a writer thinking about his imminent demise, and in any case all of Nashe's work had been written under the threat of death from plague. In fact, he announces that he plans to write a satirical work, *The Barbers Warming Pan*, in response to Richard Lichfield's *The Trimming of Thomas Nashe*, which may or may not be a serious threat, but was a clear sign that the Nashe–Harvey quarrel was not yet over (as the authorities recognized).[2] *Lenten Stuff* does, however, mark a departure in his work, a movement towards a more confident, polyphonic structuring of narratives and an easy transition from one narrative strand to another, as well as an understanding that he could write long, complicated sentences that performed the same action in miniature.[3] Looking back to *Have with You to Saffron Walden*, we might describe *Lenten Stuff* as Nashe's mature style pointing to what he might have achieved in English prose had he lived longer and been permitted to continue writing. Retrospectively, what we have is later style cut off in its prime.

In *Lenten Stuff* Nashe explains that he has fled to Great Yarmouth to escape the unwelcome attention of the authorities after the scandal of *The Isle of Dogs*. Hoping that he might be forgiven, he writes in praise of the town that has taken him in and afforded him refuge. The first section of *Lenten Stuff* gives a history of Great Yarmouth from its origins as a fishing village to a medieval powerhouse able to govern itself because of its contribution to the navy. Nashe details the city's wealth and its impressive architecture. He then turns to the lucrative herring trade that underpins the town's fortune, a commodity more valuable than anything else that England produces – even wool, grain, iron, dairy products and so on. Nashe explains how herring must be cured by smoking, which turns the fish gold, a sign of its extraordinary value.[4] He explains its origin as the king of fish via a retelling of Marlowe's poem *Hero and Leander*, in which Hero is the herring and Leander a ling, Hero making an annual pilgrimage to Great Yarmouth to remember her beloved. The herring protects other fish in their war against the birds. The narrator then explains the story of the first smoked herring, the process of curing being discovered when a poor fisherman in a small shed lit a fire in winter that turned his catch red. Licensed by the king to show off his discovery, the fisherman travels to Rome, where the pope, eager to consume the king of fish, has his cook prepare a rather old and smelly herring, which he is convinced is an evil spirit that he has to exorcise. The narrator notes that many will be sceptical of his tale (quibbling on the significance of the red herring as a story designed to throw people off the scent), but that it has persuaded him of the truth of alchemy. He then lists some herring proverbs and explains their part in the history of English rebellions, with Jack Cade and Jack Straw both having ways of processing herrings named after them.[5] *Lenten*

Stuff concludes with the narrator berating other writers for not giving the herring enough attention, and so warning hostile critics that his is a serious subject and not simply a flight of fancy as they might assume.[6]

On the first page of *Lenten Stuff*, Nashe recounts the events leading up to his writing the book in a series of neat twists and reversals, after he fled London: 'the strange turning of the Isle of Dogs from a comedy to a tragedy two summers past with the troublesome stir which happened about it . . . is a general rumour that hath filled all England, and such a heavy cross laid upon me, as had well near confounded me' (pp. 152–3). In his profound misery, Nashe went 'beyond my greatest friends' reach to recover me', and was forced into 'exile', where 'the silliest miller's thumb or contemptible stickele-bank of my enemies is as busy nibbling about my fame as if I were a dead man thrown amongst them to feed upon' (p. 153). This is a densely allusive and subtly nuanced opening passage, which shows how things can be turned and transformed by will and by fate. The tenor of the passage seems downbeat, perhaps even humble in its acknowledgement of the reversals of fortune, as comedy becomes tragedy. But, of course, this

Great Yarmouth, *c.* 1570.

was no accident, as the lost play must have upset many people. Nashe's fate looks bad if we read what he has written superficially, but his words suggest that his misfortune and the persecution he suffers are really signs of his importance and achievement, which go beyond what even he had imagined beforehand. In his apparent abjection, Nashe judges himself to be the figure whose actions create rumours that fill all of England, leading to an exceedingly cheeky comparison of himself to Christ carrying the Cross. Opponents such as Gabriel Harvey might think Nashe is a trivial writer who debases knowledge, but the rest of the nation disagrees and casts its eyes towards him. Nashe, pretending to be humiliated, is actually showing that what he does eclipses and obliterates apparently important works that others praise. In fact, it is his enemies – again, the principal target is Harvey – who are trivial in their complaints against him, unable to realize the significance of what he has achieved. What people think is important is actually trivial, and what they imagine to be trivial is really important. They might imagine – or hope – that he is dead, but, in writing *Lenten Stuff*, he will show them how profound he can be if only read properly.

One of the subtexts of *Lenten Stuff* is the enthusiastic praise Harvey had heaped on Richard Hakluyt's vast collection of English voyages and discoveries, *The Principal Navigations, Voyages and Traffiques of the English Nation*, the first edition of which was published in 1589, and an expanded edition of which appeared around the time that *Lenten Stuff* was published. This was a work that Nashe knew well and cited frequently. Hakluyt's volume collected as many sources of English overseas travel as the editor could find to exhort his fellow countrymen to support the nascent colonial ventures to the Americas in the 1580s and so protect the Protestant Reformation against the Catholic Empire of Spain in the southern half of the continent.[7] In *Pierces Supererogation* Harvey launched a carefully prepared attack on Nashe, first praising the most worthy contemporary writers: 'England, since it was England, never bred more honourable minds, more adventurous hearts, more valorous hands, or more excellent wits, than of late.'[8] He contrasts the serious work of George Gascoigne, Thomas Drant, George Turbervile, and Roger Ascham to the 'phantasticall bibble-bables' of Nashe, which 'might have bene tolerated in a green, and wild youth' (undoubtedly a reference to Robert Greene's death and his friendship with Nashe).[9] The list culminates in Harvey's praise of Hakluyt, as he urges his reader to

> read the report of the worthy Western discourses, by the said Sir Humphrey Gilbert: the report of the brave West-Indian voyage by the conduction of Sir Francis Drake: the report of the horrible Septentional discoveries by the travail of Sir Martin Frobisher: the report of the politique discovery of Virginia, by the Colony of Sir Walter Raleigh: the report of sundry other famous discoveries, & adventures, published by M. Richard Hacklut in one volume, a work of importance: the report of the hot welcome of the terrible Spanish Armada to the coast of England, that came in glory, and went in dishonour: the report of the re-doubted voyage into Spain, and Portugal, whence the brave Earl of Essex, and the two valorous Generals, Sir John Norris, and

Sir Francis Drake[,] returned with honour: the report
of the resolute encounter about the Isles Azores, betwixt
the Revenge of England, and an Armada of Spain; in
which encounter brave Sir Richard Grenville most
vigorously & impetuously attempted the extreamest
possibilities of valour and fury.[10]

Harvey is reading Hakluyt exactly as Hakluyt intended, citing
his great compilation as a means of demonstrating the heroic
history of the English, seeking out far-flung places to colonize
and so civilize, thus protecting their shores against hostile
invaders.

Harvey continues, citing examples of English trade
spreading abroad, concluding by weighing up 'the course of
Industry' and 'consequents of Travail', which 'found profit to
be our pleasure, provision our security, labour our honour,
warfare our welfare', against what Nashe and his ilk produce,
'corrupt pamphlets . . . paultring fidle-faddles'.[11] The long
passage concludes with a reference to 'the ruins of Troy' discovered by Alexander, which inspires the great conqueror to
demand the 'Harp of Achilles' to lead him to further military
glory. Harvey is arguing that his fellow Englishmen should
adopt similar attitudes in contrast to the debilitating fare
offered them in the pamphlets of Nashe and Greene. The
central reference is to the *Iliad*, the great epic that is now transferred through the familiar process of *translatio imperii* from
ancient Greece to contemporary England. Harvey is further
contrasting the folio volume to the pamphlet, the serious to
the trivial, the inspirational work to the debilitating, the
national to the local, and what he is doing to what Nashe is

doing.[12] His aim is to create a genuine public sphere of writers all contributing to the advancement of England and English culture in their various ways, which does not preclude Nashe's methods, but does involve attacking his scurrilous and wasteful aims.

To counter Harvey's grand imperial rhetoric *Lenten Stuff* takes as its subject an everyday object, the red herring, traditionally ordinary fare eaten by the poor (and by the better off as a form of penance in Lent), and shows how it is actually the worthy focus of heroic legend, one of the most noble foodstuffs, a glory that sustains the nation.[13] Again, especially given the title of his previous work, there is a pointed contrast between Nashe and Harvey, the latter coming from a more upmarket place, one that obtained its name from the crocuses grown there. Saffron was a valued commodity that produced yellow dye, a colour of high status, one of the key jokes against the social-climbing Malvolio in *Twelfth Night*.[14] In imitation of Harvey, Nashe assembles ponderous lists of different categories of important and valuable examples of intellectual property, weaving together different textual elements, styles and registers to make his points. He describes his journey to Yarmouth in terms familiar to any reader of romance, as 'variable Knight arrant adventures and outroads and inroads, at great Yarmouth in Norfolk I arrived in the latter end of Autumn'. Adopting one of his earlier pseudonyms, Nashe then proclaims that 'this is a predestinate fit place for Piers Penniless to set up his staff in' (p. 154).

Nashe's range of allusions carefully echoes Harvey's chain of connections in *Pierces Supererogation*. In a provocatively disgusting image, Nashe compares the effects of the hospitality

he receives in Great Yarmouth to a well-known story about
Homer:

> Took I up my repose, and there met with such kind
> entertainment and benign hospitality when I was *Una*
> *litera plusquam medicus*, as Plautus saith, and not able to live
> to my self with my own juice, as some of the crumbs of
> it, like the crumbs in a bushy beard after a great banquet,
> will remain in my papers to be seen when I am dead and
> under ground; from the bare perusing of which, infinite
> posterities of hungry Poets shall receive good refreshing,
> even as Homer by Galataeon was pictured vomiting in
> a basin (in the temple that Ptolomy Philopater erected
> to him) and the rest of the succeeding Poets after him
> greedily lapping up what he dis-gorged. (pp. 154–5)

Nashe does not say that he consumes so much that he is sick;
the actual comparison is between the crumbs that he leaves
behind in his papers and Homer vomiting, the leavings of
each poet being greedily consumed by subsequent writers.
But the nature of the comparison invites the reader to make
this connection and to conclude that even Nashe behaving at
his lowest is more valuable than other writers' most highbrow
efforts. Furthermore, there is surely a reference to the death
of Robert Greene, expiring after a 'surfeit of pickle herring
and Rhenish wine'. Harvey made the allegation (which Nashe
denied by arguing that the meal had taken place too long before
Greene's death for it to have been a factor), and later enshrined
it in his joke in *Pierces Supererogation* about Nashe's green and
wild youth.[15]

Nashe is picking up Harvey's citations of Homer and Homeric themes at key points throughout *Pierces Supererogation*, designed to emphasize his own seriousness and the frivolity of Nashe's work.[16] This point is secured by the next reference to Homer as 'That good old blind bibber of Helicon', a direct quotation from Harvey.[17] Nashe deliberately plays on the more lowbrow stories of Homer's life, bringing Harvey's exalted register back to the demotic, but also demonstrating that there is an erudition that can undermine the pretensions of the literary social climber while signalling the user's rootedness in the stuff of everyday life, rather than the pointless mobility of imperial expansion. While Harvey wants to think about the *Iliad*, Nashe would like to remind readers that there was another side to Homer.

What links both references — a suppressed but vital connection — is Homer's other epic of travel, the *Odyssey*. Nashe deliberately skirts around this in developing the comparison between himself and Homer, by making two negative comparisons. First, he states: 'I allege this tale to show how much better my luck was than Homer's, (though all the King of Spain's Indies will not create me such a niggling Hexameter-founder as he was)' (pp. 155–6). Then, a few sentences later, he claims: 'I am no Tiresias or Calchas to prophecy, but yet I cannot tell, there may be more resounding bell-metal [strong alloy] in my pen then I am aware, and if there be, the first peal of it is in Yarmouths' (p. 156). Nashe is showing that he knows everything about Homer, both his epics and the slightly sordid tales of his personal life, producing the last before revealing his literary sophistication. His epic tale of Yarmouth is to be set against the epics of ancient Greece, as well as the epics and romances of the modern world, which have inspired the Spanish to conquer the New World.[18]

Nashe was in Yarmouth until at least January or February 1598, and was then probably somewhere outside London writing *Lenten Stuff*, which, as we have seen, was entered into the Stationers' Register on 11 January 1599.[19] As his more familiar readers would have known, Nashe was from Lowestoft, an origin he announces while discussing the Suffolk coastline towards the end of the work.[20] He describes the course of the River Waveny, which marks the border between Norfolk and Suffolk and, with the River Yare, creates an island as it meanders towards the North Sea: 'The head Town in that Island is *Leystofe*, in which be it known to all men I was born' (p. 205). Throughout *Lenten Stuff*, he refers to the long-running conflict between the two coastal towns.

In his substantial history of Great Yarmouth Nashe describes a historic dispute between the towns, which forced the king to intervene: 'Richard the second upon a discord twixt Leystofe and Yarmouth, after diverse law-days and arbitrary mandates to the counties of Suffolk and Norfolk directed about it, in proper person 1385 came to Yarmouth, and, in his parliament the year ensuing, confirmed unto it the liberties of Kirtley [Kirkley] road (the only motive of all their contention)' (p. 165). Nashe further outlines the significance and extent of the liberties of the borough, explaining how central they are to the town's identity, wealth and power:

> The liberties of it on the fresh water one way, as namely from Yarmouth to *S. Toolies* in Beckles water, are ten mile, and from Yarmouth to Hardlie cross another way,

> ten mile, and, conclusively, from Yarmouth to Waybridge
> in the narrow North water ten mile; in all which fords
> or *Meandors* none can attach, arrest, distress, but their
> officers; and if any drown themselves in them, their
> Crowners sit upon them. (pp. 166–7)

The granting of liberties defined the power of the town, as
Phil Withington has pointed out: 'An urban "liberty" was, first
and foremost, a territorial jurisdiction in which peculiar rights,
customs, properties, and privileges granted to or claimed by
burgesses were legitimate.'[21] What Nashe does not say, but
which would have informed an alert reader's understanding
of these passages, is that the bitter and protracted dispute
between Lowestoft and Great Yarmouth was based on this
particular question of liberties. Yarmouth asserted its ancient
liberties and Lowestoft resisted these, claiming that they were
an infringement of its own, the specific bone of contention
being the control of the Kirkley Road, and the right to collect
tolls on it, which the corporation of Lowestoft claimed was
unfairly impeding its ability to trade in herring.[22]

Nashe does not take sides in the dispute, but it may temper
and contextualize our understanding of his enthusiastic
endorsement of Great Yarmouth as his protection from the
powerful punitive apparatus of the capital. *Lenten Stuff* sees the
herring – especially when preserved through smoking as red
herring – as the staple food that has made England powerful,
preserved its liberties and sustained its people. Fishing was
vitally important not just in producing food in a period of
continual scarcity, but also in determining the demography of
Europe.[23] This was especially relevant in England, a country

with a long coastline and access to substantial fish stocks. There were serious arguments put forward to increase fish consumption in order to protect the industry.[24] In 1580 the soldier-writer Robert Hitchcock (*fl.* 1573–1591) had argued that developing herring fishing in particular would solve a host of England's economic and social problems, supplementing diet, boosting exports and providing useful work for sturdy beggars and criminals.[25] In the early seventeenth century John Keymer, a client of Sir Walter Raleigh who also worked for Sir Robert Cecil, made his celebrated claim 'that his Majesty's Seas are far richer then the King of *Spain's Indies*, and there is more made of Fish, taken by the *French, Biskers, Portugal, Spaniards, Hollanders, Hamburgers, Beemers, Embdeners, Scottish, Irish*, and *English* in one year, then the King of *Spain* hath in four years out of the *Indies*'.[26] Commentators have duly noted that 'No European government took as much interest in fishing as the English except the state of Holland,' which helps us to understand why a Dutch pamphlet on herring might be translated into English.[27] Herring, long a staple of the English and Scottish diet, especially on the east coast where there was ready access to the vast North Sea stocks of this prolific fish, were particularly important in the late 1590s and were much discussed.

According to Nashe, the herring fisheries are far more important to the long-term success of England than the much-trumpeted claims for the significance of transoceanic voyages, overseas trade and colonies; indeed, it is the red herring that makes these possible.[28] In a well-informed description of the staple commodities of England and northern Europe, Nashe gives the red herring its central place:

That English merchandise is most precious which no country can be without: if you ask *Suffolk, Essex, Kent, Sussex, or Lemster, or Cotswold*, what merchandise that should be, they will answer you it is the very same which *Polidore Virgil* calls *Verè aureum vellus*, the true golden fleece of our wool and English cloth, and nought else; other engrating upland cormorants will grunt out it is *Grana paradise* ['grains of paradise'] our grain or corn, that is most sought after. The Westerners and Northerners [will say] that it is lead, tin and iron. Butter and cheese, butter and cheese, saith the farmer: but from every one of these I dissent and will stoutly bide by it, that, to trowel in the cash throughout all nations of christendom, there is no fellow to the red herring. The French, Spanish and Italian have wool enough of their own whereof they make cloth to serve their turn, though it be somewhat coarser than ours. For corn, none of the East parts surpasseth us; of lead and tin is the most scarcity in foreign dominions, and plenty with us, though they are not utterly barren of them. As for iron, about *Isenborough* and other places of *Germany* they have quadruple the store that we have. As touching butter and cheese, the *Hollanders* cry by your leave we must go before you, and the *Transalpiners* with their lordly *Parmasin* (so named of the city of *Parma* in Italy where it is first clout-crushed and made) shoulder in for the upper hand as hotly; when as, of our appropriate glory of the red herring, no region twixt the poles artick and antartic may, can, or will rebate from us one scruple. (pp. 178–9)

This is an erudite passage designed to convince the reader that England has enough to survive if it looks inwards and values its own commodities, deliberately focusing on ordinary stuff that sustains everyday life.[29] Polydore Vergil (*c.* 1470–1555) was a native of the Italian city of Urbino who came to England in 1502 and was the foremost humanist historian of English history; *Grana Paradise* were the 'capsules of *Amomum Melegueta*, a kind of pungent spice brought from Africa', referred to in Hakluyt's *Principal Navigations*.[30] Nashe refers to both in order to show not only that learned scholars will come to England and value its 'stuff', but that English corn is worth far more than the exotic spices valued so highly by the proponents of imperial expansion. The passage is learned in its faux pedantry, ranging from the proverbial (the Dutch love butter and cheese), to the self-evident (Parmesan cheese comes from Parma), to the well informed (there are substantial wool trades in France, Italy and Spain, and the Germans have a great deal of iron).[31] In the end, Nashe argues, all such commodities, important as they are, exist in the shadow of the herring as a force for sustaining life and enabling a nation to thrive.

The red herring of *Lenten Stuff* is that what it claims to be is largely true: the work looks like an allegory that disguises and/or displaces its real focus, but its ostensible subject is sincere. It really is as much about herring as it is about Nashe's own life, his social class, his quarrel with Harvey and his literary wit. Or, rather, it is about all these things, but they cannot be separated from the history of English herring-fishing. In basic personal terms, Nashe is acutely aware that Lowestoft developed as a town because of the significance of the herring as a staple part of the English diet; Great Yarmouth, which took him in when he was hounded out of London, has a similar history.[32] Herring was an especially valuable and desirable fish because of its abundance and proximity to the shore during the breeding season, which meant that it was nowhere near as dangerous or expensive to fish as its main rival, cod, and did not require substantial investment in a large and technologically advanced ship that could travel a long way from shore.[33] Great Yarmouth, accordingly, has an exceptionally large fishing fleet of small boats so that 'six hundred reasonable barks and vessels of good burden (with a vantage) it hath given shelter to at once in her harbour' (p. 157).

Lenten Stuff, however, was written when the East Anglian fishing industry was in a position of precarious success, dependent on the ability of merchants to transport preserved fish to overseas markets such as Leghorn (Livorno), where red herring was regarded as a 'particular delicacy', as well as to the English interior.[34] Not only were there internal disputes between her ports, but there were significant threats from a powerful rival that would, in a few years, eclipse Yarmouth's success.[35] English writers often argued that the Dutch had a major advantage because they had a more technologically advanced fleet than the English (which enabled them to argue for more investment in shipbuilding), but the real problem for the English was probably salt, which was vital for making herring transportable, however preserved.[36] Herring were emptied on to the quay at Lowestoft and Yarmouth and preserved and salted there, a further advantage they had over cod, which had to be salted at sea, significantly increasing the investment required by the owner of the boat.[37] There were a series of problems with the supply of salt in England, in marked contrast to the situation in the Netherlands, which had an abundant supply.[38]

Nashe would seem to have had some awareness of this threat in connecting the Dutch to a particular taste for salted herring, even while he praises the great success of the English: 'On no coast like ours is it [herring] caught in such abundance, no where dressed in his right cue but under our Horizon; hosted, roasted, and toasted here alone it is, and as well powdered and salted as any Dutchman would desire' (p. 179). Two pages later the production of salt is placed at the heart of the industries' flourishing because of the success of the herring trade:

> Carpenters, Shipwrights, makers of lines, ropes, and cables, dressers of Hemp, spinners of thread, and net weavers it gives their handfuls to, sets up so many salt-houses to make salt, and salt upon salt; keeps in earnings the Cooper, the Brewer, the Baker, and numbers of people, to gill, wash, and pack it, and carry it and recarry it. (p. 180)

Lenten Stuff shows the careful structural balance of the English economy fuelled by one commodity, a successful but vulnerable society that must be reminded of exactly where its priorities should lie. The work is a literary red herring precisely because it concerns the stuff of the real world and urges its readers to pay close attention to things they invariably dismiss as being beneath their notice.

Lenten Stuff contains a long and humorous homage to Christopher Marlowe, with an imaginative and bizarre retelling of the story of Hero and Leander a year after Marlowe's unfinished poem was published, and six years after his death. In the story, adapted from the work of the sixth-century poet Musaeus Grammaticus, the lovers Hero and Leander live on opposite sides of the Hellespont. In the summer, Leander swims nightly across the dangerous straits, and Hero lights a lamp to guide her lover. They agree not to meet in winter, but Leander, seeing a light from Hero's tower, nevertheless attempts to swim across, gets lost and drowns. Seeing his dead body on the shore, Hero throws herself down so that she can die and be with her love.

In Nashe's version Hero becomes the red herring and Leander a ling, the deeper-water fish found in the North Sea and the Atlantic between Scotland, Scandinavia and Iceland.[39] Both were popular fish, and were often interchangeable in recipes, served with mustard, as Nashe points out at the end of his tale. It was easy to find common recipes for both to be eaten on the important fish days that William Cecil promoted to protect and encourage the industry, as in Thomas Dawson's *The Good Housewife's Jewel* (1587).[40]

Nashe introduces the story of Hero and Leander as one that can replace the real history of the red herring, a tale which he asserts would require a volume as long as Holinshed's *Chronicles*, framing the story in terms of his readers in Great Yarmouth, who may not have heard of Musaeus or Marlowe. This enables him to shuttle backwards and forwards between the local and the global, but Nashe reminds his readers that what is offered to them exists primarily in print: 'Two faithful lovers they were, as every apprentice in Paul's churchyard will tell you for your love, and sell you for your money' (p. 195), the balance of the last two clauses expressing familiar cynicism. Nashe lets knowing readers understand that he has Marlowe's poem to hand, mentioning that Leander lives in Adibos and Hero in Sestos, and that she was a 'Venus priest', all of which is taken from the opening three pages of Marlowe's poem, reading 'Venus priest' as 'Venus nun'.[41] Nashe adds his own local narrative imagining their parents at loggerheads 'and their towns that like Yarmouth and Leystoffe were still at wrig wrag, & sucked from their mothers teats serpentine hatred one against each other' (p. 195), referring to the fishing wars between the two towns, and making his own experience central, having been born in Lowestoft but taking refuge in Great Yarmouth.[42] Marlowe is celebrated, but it is Marlowe conspicuously moulded into a form that Nashe controls. He picks up the lurid and knowing erotic tone of Marlowe's original, with the description of Leander's white skin, which would tempt barbarous Thracian soldiers and the most chaste hunters.[43] However, he removes Marlowe's humorous references to same-sex desire, concentrating instead on the sublimated sexual desire of the young woman (which is also in Marlowe's poem, but by no means as prominent):

> Or Leander you may write upon, and it is written upon, she liked well, and for all he was a naked man, and clean despoiled to the skin, when he sprawled through the brackish suds to scale her tower, all the strength of it could not hold him out. O ware a naked man, Cithereas [Venus's] Nuns have no power to resist him: and some such quality is ascribed to the lion. Were he never so naked when he came to her, because he should not scare

her, she found a means to cover him in her bed, & for he might not take cold after his swimming, she lay close by him, to keep him warm. (p. 196)

The sly voyeurism in Marlowe's poem has become conspicuously heterosexual in Nashe's version. Male readers can enjoy the sexual awakening of young women, a common theme of pornography in this period, which, of course, Nashe also produced in 'The Choice of Valentines'.[44]

However, there is a tenderer side to Nashe's fantasy, with the lovers actually wanting to change into sea creatures and being rewarded by becoming fish, something that is not obviously present in Marlowe's poem. When Leander swims off, Hero is troubled that he may drown, but when she does catch a little slumber towards cockcrow, 'she dreamed that Leander and she were playing checkstones [a children's game] with pearls in the bottom of the sea' (p. 197). In Marlowe's poem, Leander is nearly dragged to the seabed by Neptune in a homoerotic marine encounter that mingles sex and death.[45] In Nashe's retelling, the fear of a watery grave is replaced with playful pleasure, the magnetic attraction of the land where the fish live, because, as he puts it in his perverse reflection on the significance of dreams, 'Hero hoped, and therefore she dreamed . . . her hope was where her heart was' (p. 197). Hero drowns herself as she rushes into the sea when she sees Leander's corpse washed up on the shore and is dragged under. In a parodic Ovidian-Marlovian moment, Hero and Leander are transformed into a red herring and a ling, so that on Fridays and Saturdays they can meet at the table. Hero's nurse expires with grief and her reward is to be transformed into mustard seed, a fitting reward because 'she was a shrewish snappish bawd, that would bite off a man's nose with an answer and had rumatic sore eyes that ran always.' After death she can accompany the lovers, as she did in life, linking them as a common condiment, so 'that *Hero & Leander*, the Red Herring and Ling, never come to the board without mustard, their waiting maid' (p. 200). In recipe books such as A. W.'s *A Book of Cookery Very Necessary for All Such as Delight Therein* (published in 1587 and reprinted in 1591) we see herring and ling together, next to mustard, which is surely what Nashe had in mind as a fitting conclusion to his retelling of Marlowe's story.

Nashe demonstrates that he was eager to take on the mantle of Marlowe, showing how he could honour the dead writer as well as promote his own – very different – literary identity. Marlowe's transgressive retelling of Musaeus, which emphasizes the pleasures of liberty and licence that could be discovered in the classics, is in turn retold as an absurd fable, a central feature in a work that, like so much in Nashe, is unsettling because it is hard to gauge its register and understand how it should be read. Of course, the very act of producing such powerful, disturbing writing was designed to remind readers what literature could do, what Marlowe had done, and what Nashe was doing through his rereading of Marlowe.

For all its comic bluster and many layers of irony, *Lenten Stuff* is a deeply serious work that thinks about the nation and the movement that is required to understand as well as sustain it. Many writers were eager to establish and represent exactly what England was and how it should be conceived, as it became possible to survey, quantify and chart the nation, draw up its boundaries and compare it to its neighbours, rivals and

A
Book of Cookrye:

very neceſſary for all ſuch
as delight therein.

(∴)

Gathered by A. W.

And now newlye enlarged
with the ſeruing in of
the Table.

With the proper Sauces
to each of them con-
uenient.

✱

IMPRINTED
At London by Edward
Allde. 1587.

Tart.

Ginger bread.

Fritters.

Seruice for fish dayes.

Butter.

A Sallet with hard Egges.

Potage of sand Eeles and Lamprons.

Red Hering græn broyled sugar strewed

White Hering.　　　　　　　　(vpon.

Ling.　　　　　　　Sauce Mustard.

Haburdine.

Salt Salmon minced, sance Mustard and

　　Uinagre and a little Sugar.

Powdred Cunger.

Shad.　　　　　　　Sauce Uinagre,

Mackrel.

Whiting, sance with Liuer and Mustard.

Plaice, sauce Sorel. or Wine and Salt,

　　or Uinagre.

Thorne back, sance liuer and mustard,

　　pepper, & salt strewed vpon it after it

　　is brused.

Fresh Cod, Sauce Gréensauce.

Bace.

Mullet.

Eeles vpon Sops.

Roches vpon Sops.

Perch.　　　　　　　　　　　　Pike

Pages from A. W., *A Book of Cookrye: very necessary for all such as delight therin* (1587).

distant outposts. The urgency became more apparent in the
1590s as the Tudor dynasty neared its end and the English
wanted to know who they were and where they lived.[46] *Lenten
Stuff* is a humorous reminder of what people needed to know
and what was often left out of what he clearly saw as grandi-
ose and dangerously deluded visions of imperial expansion.
Towards the end of the work, Nashe conjures a fantastic vision
of the red herring becoming a dried flying fish travelling as
far as the limits of the Old World:

> the red herring flies best when his wings are dry: through-
> out Belgia, high Germany, France, Spain, and Italy he
> flies, and up into Greece and Africa, South and South-
> west, Estrich-like, walks his stations, and the Sepulcher
> Palmers or Pilgrims, because he is so portable, fill their
> Scrips [bag or pouch] with them, yea, no dispraise to
> the blood of the Ottomans, the Nabuchedonesor of
> Constantinople and Giantly Antaeus, that never yawneth
> nor sneezeth. If so, should be square] but he afrighteth
> the whole earth, gormandizing, muncheth him up for
> his imperial dainties. (p. 192)

The style of the sentence becomes ever more inflated as the
herring proceeds on his epic journey, a parody of the movements of the bravest English explorers. A key point is that
travel requires sustenance, and so cannot be undertaken without preserved food, almost invariably dried. Here, however,
the herring's progress is represented as if it were an end in
itself. Nashe is reminding readers that they must not lose sight
of what they have at home or of its importance, and that what

seems more important is invariably nourished by something that is easy to overlook. Too much food makes those who over-indulge sick, even if their leavings are as valuable as those of Homer or Nashe. Nevertheless, everyone needs to be sustained in leaner times by Lenten stuff, which is why the Yarmouth fleets are so much more valuable than their more celebrated counterparts.

Epilogue

ashe's reputation crystallized soon after his death, and has remained more or less the same ever since. The character Ingenioso, one of the dominant figures in the three Parnassus plays first performed at the University of Cambridge and London in 1598–1602, is largely based on Nashe.[1] He first appears in the final act of the satirical university drama *The Pilgrimage to Parnassus*, to warn the two would-be writers, Philomusus and Studioso, that the path they have chosen to follow will be a hard one if his experience is at all typical:

> What, I travel to Parnassus? Why, I have burnt my books, splitted my pen, rent [torn] my papers, and cursed the cozening arts, that brought me up to no better fortune. I, after many years study, having almost brought my brain into a consumption, looking still, when I should meet with some good Maecenas, that liberally would reward my deserts, I fed so long upon hope, till I had almost starved. Why, our empty handed satin suits do make more account of some foggy Faulkner, then of a witty scholar, had rather reward a man for setting of a hair, than a man of wit for making of a poem. Each long

eared ass rides on his trappings and thinks it sufficient
to give a scholar a majestic nod with his rude noddle.
Go to Parnassus? Alas, Apollo is banckrout [bankrupt],
there is nothing but silver words & golden phrases for a
man; his followers want the gold, while tapsters, ostlers,
carters, and cobblers have a foaming paunch, a belching
bag . . . Turn home again, unless you mean to . . . curse
your witless heads in your old age for taking themselves
to no better trades in their youth.[2]

In this semi-accurate pastiche of his style Nashe is truthful,
honest and acerbic, not caring who hears what he says because
his dedication is to the truth, not popular opinion. He might
want reward but he will not compromise in order to get it;
therefore, he eventually runs out of options and has to give
up writing.

There is something fitting in Nashe being celebrated for
his writing in this Cambridge drama, since he may well have
begun his writing career with one himself, *Terminus et non terminus*, and he was always loyal to and fascinated by his alma
mater. However, it is, at best, a partial and distorted assessment
of Nashe, one that ignores his complicated relationship with
what Alexandra Halasz has termed the 'marketplace of print',
and it takes his representation of himself from *Piers Penniless*
onwards – as an impoverished scholar railing against the ills
of the world – at face value, an easily reproduced thumbnail
sketch.[3] John Taylor the 'water poet' (1578–1653), a prolific
autodidact who saw himself as Nashe's heir, summoned the
ghost of Tom or Thomas Nashe to help him counter the
claims of the Puritans soon after the start of the Civil War.[4]

Looking back to the Marprelate Quarrel, Nashe's Ghost states: 'I spurred at *Flattery*, I lov'd *Truth*, I despised Riches, yet I liv'd and died Rich enough to be a poet. And So much shall suffice to tell thee what I was.'[5] Taylor may have simplified Nashe's complicated position in the 1590s, but he understood enough about his writing to characterize him as a defender of the established church against attacks by schismatic factions of Puritans; he also understood that he was one of a number of writers who had established an English tradition of writing ('Old *Chaucer*, *Sidney*, *Spenser*, *Daniel*, *Nash*,/ I dip'd my finger where they us'd to wash'), and that his chief attribute was his satirical wit ('I'll whip him ['a depraving Emblamist'] with a yerking Satyr's lash,/ Fang'd like th'invective muse of famous *Nash*').[6]

That picture of Nashe was long accepted and was enshrined in R. B. McKerrow's pioneering edition, one that established bibliographical principles for twentieth-century scholars.[7] McKerrow represented Nashe as a writer of great wit and ability but not truly profound, a guide to the age in which he lived rather than someone – like Shakespeare (although he is not mentioned) – who stood for all time:

> In invective he stands perhaps without a rival: as a satirist of manners he had talent rather than genius, wit rather than wisdom; in eloquence and in profundity of thought he was surpassed by many a man long forgotten; he was indeed often faulty in language and crude in ideas, often careless, often ignorant, but what he saw he could describe, and what he thought he said in most effective words.[8]

With tongues firmly planted in cheeks in imitation of Nashe's fractious and skewed attitude to authority, a team of American editors boldly reversed his outsider status in dubbing the 1590s 'the Age of Nashe'.[9] As they acknowledge, they were building on the ground-breaking revisionist scholarship of the 1980s: Neil Rhodes's *Elizabethan Grotesque*, Charles Nicholl's *Cup of News*, Jonathan Crewe's *Unredeemed Rhetoric* and Lorna Hutson's *Thomas Nashe in Context*. A new Nashe was established, one whose 'restless and relentless invention' was much more in tune with contemporary literary values.[10] But, of course, as I hope this short book has demonstrated, there was – and is – still more to say about a writer who played such a crucial role in establishing the nature of English commercial theatre, the identity of the Church of England and English prose style, as well as satire, fiction and polemic.

CHRONOLOGY

1567	Nashe born in Lowestoft
1569–70	Northern Rebellion
1570	Papal Bull excommunicates Elizabeth as illegitimate and declares that loyal Catholics should try to depose her, dividing the English Catholic community
23–24 August 1572	Massacre of St Bartholomew's Day in Paris
1573/4	Nashe family moves to West Harling, Norfolk
1577	Holinshed's *Chronicles*
1578	John Lyly, *Euphues: The Anatomy of Wit*
1579	Edmund Spenser, *The Shepheardes Calender*
1580	First edition of Michel de Montaigne's *Essays*. Jesuit mission sent to England; Francis Drake completes circumnavigation of the world
1582	Nashe matriculates at St John's College, Cambridge
1583	Richard Harvey, *An Astrological Discourse upon the Great and Notable Conjunction of the Two Superior Planets, Saturn and Jupiter*
1585	Elizabeth sends troops to help the Dutch forces fight the Spanish
1586	Nashe graduates from Cambridge. Death of Sir Philip Sidney after he is wounded at the Battle of Zutphen (17 October)
1586–8	With Robert Mills, *Terminus et non terminus* (lost)
1587	Marlowe, *Tamburlaine* Execution of Mary, Queen of Scots (8 February)

1588	Nashe leaves Cambridge
	Defeat of the Spanish Armada
1588–90	Marprelate Controversy
1589	*The Anatomy of Absurdity*; Preface to *Menaphon*;
	An Almond for a Parrot; *Countercuffe Given to Martin*
	Junior (?); *The Return of Pasquill* (?); Richard Hakluyt,
	The Principal Navigations of the English Nation
1590	*Pasquills Apologie* (?). Richard Harvey, *The Lamb of God*;
	Edmund Spenser, *The Faerie Queene, I–III*
1590–99	Nashe–Harvey quarrel
1591	Preface to Sidney's *Astrophil and Stella*; collaboration
	on *Henry VI, Part One*; Adam Foulweather,
	A Wonderful Astrological . . . Prognostication (?)
1591–3	'The Choice of Valentines'
1592	*Piers Penniless, His Supplication to the Devil*; *Strange*
	News. *Summer's Last Will and Testament* performed at
	Croydon Palace. Gabriel Harvey, *Four Letters and*
	Certain Sonnets; Robert Greene/Henry Chettle,
	A Groatsworth of Wit
1592–3	Outbreak of plague in London
1593	Nashe imprisoned; released by Sir George Carey
	and stays in Carisbrooke Castle, Isle of Wight
	(1593–4). *Christ's Tears over Jerusalem*. Gabriel Harvey,
	Pierces Supererogation; Sir Philip Sidney, *The Countess of*
	Pembroke's Arcadia
1594	*The Terrors of the Night*; *The Unfortunate Traveller*; *Dido,*
	Queen of Carthage
1594–1603	Nine Years War in Ireland
1595	Visit to Lincolnshire, probably to see Robert Mills
1596	*Have with You to Saffron Walden*; letter to William
	Cotton. Sir John Harington, *A New Discourse about*
	a Stale Subject: The Metamorphosis of Ajax
1597	With Ben Jonson, *Isle of Dogs*; possibly with
	Ben Jonson, *The Case Is Altered* (?). Nashe
	flees to Great Yarmouth. Richard Lichfield,
	The Trimming of Thomas Nashe; Shakespeare,
	Henry IV, Part One (?)

1599	*Nashe's Lenten Stuff*. Bishops' Ban (1 June); construction of the Globe Theatre
1600	Tommaso Garzoni's *The Hospital of Incurable Fooles* (?); *Summer's Last Will* published
1600/1601	Nashe dies
c. 1601	*The Return from Parnassus*, which provides an epitaph for Nashe

LIST OF ABBREVIATIONS

AHR	*Agricultural History Review*
BJJ	*Ben Jonson Journal*
BSRS	*Bulletin of the Society for Renaissance Studies*
CD	*Comparative Drama*
DC	*Dutch Crossing*
DSH	*Digital Scholarship in the Humanities*
ELH	*English Literary History*
ELR	*English Literary Renaissance*
EMLS	*Early Modern Literary Studies*
ES	*English Studies*
ET	*Early Theatre*
FMLS	*Forum for Modern Language Studies*
HER	*English Historical Review*
JEGP	*Journal of English and Germanic Philology*
JEH	*Journal of Ecclesiastical History*
MLN	*Modern Language Notes*
MLQ	*Modern Language Quarterly*
MP	*Modern Philology*
MRDS	*Medieval and Renaissance Drama in England*
N&Q	*Notes and Queries*
Nashe, *Works*	Thomas Nashe, *The Works of Thomas Nashe*, ed. R. B. McKerrow, revd F. P. Wilson, 5 vols (Oxford, 1966)
NJES	*Nordic Journal of English Studies*
ODNB	*The Oxford Dictionary of National Biography*, online edition
P&P	*Past and Present*

PBSA	*Papers of the Bibliographical Society of America*
PMLA	*Publications of the Modern Language Society of America*
PQ	*Philological Quarterly*
R&R	*Renaissance and Reformation/Renaissance et Reforme*
RES	*Review of English Studies*
SCJ	*Sidney Circle Journal*
SEL	*Studies in English Literature, 1500–1900*
SLI	*Studies in the Literary Imagination*
SP	*Studies in Philology*
SQ	*Shakespeare Quarterly*
Stationers' Register	Edward Arber, ed., *A Transcript of the Registers of the Company of Stationers of London, 1554–1640*, 5 vols (London, 1875–94)
STC	A. W. Pollard, G. R. Redgrave and Katharine F. Pantzer, *A Short-Title Catalogue of Books Printed in England, Scotland and Ireland, and of English Books Printed Abroad 1475–1640*, 3 vols (London, 1976–91)
TLS	*Times Literary Supplement*
Wiggins, *Drama*	Martin Wiggins, in association with Catherine Richardson, *British Drama, 1533–1642: A Catalogue*, 10 vols (Oxford, 2011–)
YES	*Yearbook of English Studies*

Some of the quotations in the text have been amended in line with modern spelling conventions to help readers who are unfamiliar with early modern English.

REFERENCES

Introduction: Nashe's Life, Interests and Circle

1 'The Oxford Authorship Site', www.oxford-shakespeare.com/ nashe.html (accessed 19 July 2021), argues that the Earl of Oxford, who was really Shakespeare, was also Nashe.

2 *All Is True* (dir. Kenneth Branagh, 2018).

3 In Roland Emmerich's film *Anonymous* (2011), Nashe is described as a 'heavy-set, a hard-drinking satirist'.

4 C. S. Lewis, *English Literature in the Sixteenth Century* (London, 1954), p. 416.

5 Edward Chaney, *The Evolution of the Grand Tour: Anglo-Italian Cultural Relations Since the Renaissance* (London, 1998).

6 Richard MacKenney, *Sixteenth-Century Europe: Expansion and Conflict* (Basingstoke, 1993).

7 On Richard and John Harvey, and Robert Greene, see the respective ODNB entries. John Harvey died relatively young and appears not to have offended Nashe in any particular way other than through his siblings; Richard, a clergyman, was known for his puritanical views and rather unfortunate prophecies, and is attacked by Nashe for these failings, as well as for sexual hypocrisy.

8 Nashe died almost immediately afterwards; Harvey lived on until 1631, but retreated to his home town, Saffron Walden, and published nothing more. For details of Harvey's life, see Virginia Stern, *Gabriel Harvey: His Life, Marginalia and Library* (Oxford, 1979).

9 See Alexandra Walsham, *Church Papists: Catholicism, Conformity and Confessional Polemic in Early Modern England* (Aldershot, 1999).

10 On Nashe's life, see Charles Nicholl, *A Cup of News: The Life of
    Thomas Nashe* (London, 1984), and the ODNB entry by the same
    author.

11 Richard Lichfield, *The Trimming of Thomas Nashe* (London, 1597),
    sig. G3r; Nicholl, *Cup of News*, pp. 36–7.

12 Andrew Hadfield, 'Marlowe and Nashe', ELR, LI/2 (2021), pp. 1–27.

13 For more details, see Chapter Four.

14 On Lyly, see Andy Kesson, *John Lyly and Early Modern Authorship*
    (Manchester, 2014); G. K. Hunter, *John Lyly: The Humanist as
    Courtier* (Cambridge, MA, 1962). On Munday, see Tracey Hill,
    Anthony Munday and Civic Culture (Manchester, 2004), and Donna
    B. Hamilton, *Anthony Munday and the Catholics, 1560–1633* (Aldershot,
    2005), which read evidence of Munday's work and character in
    strikingly different ways.

15 On the discovery of the press, see Chapter One.

16 Nashe early style is 'Euphuistic', heavily indebted to John Lyly's
    prose fiction *Euphues: The Anatomy of Wit* (1578) and *Euphues and His
    England* (1579), characterized by studied parallel clauses, antitheses
    and copious alliteration.

17 On the tennis court quarrel, see Alan Stewart, *Sir Philip Sidney:
    A Double Life* (London, 2011), pp. 215–16.

18 Gary Taylor, 'Shakespeare and Others: The Authorship of *Henry VI,
    Part One*', MRDS, 7 (1995), pp. 145–205. See Chapter Three.

19 Nashe, *Works*, I, p. 212. See Chapter Three.

20 Nashe, *Works*, III, p. 220. See Chapter Three.

21 For a reading of Shakespeare's interest in Nashe, see Neil Rhodes,
    Elizabethan Grotesque (London, 1980), ch. 6.

22 Gabriel Harvey, *Pierces Supererogation; or, A New Prayse of the Old Ass*
    (London, 1593), p. 45.

23 See Chapter Six. For discussion, see Andrew Hadfield, *Lying in Early
    Modern Literature and Culture* (Oxford, 2017), pp. 243–5.

24 See Chapter Two.

25 Wiggins, *Drama*, III, pp. 444–7. Children's companies – also
    called boys' companies – were popular in Elizabethan London,
    often working in more enclosed indoor stages than many adult
    companies. See Reaveley Gair, *The Children of Paul's: The Story of a
    Theatre Company, 1553–1608* (Cambridge, 1982).

26 See Kate De Rycker, 'Commodifying the Author: The Mediation of Aretino's Fame in the Harvey–Nashe Pamphlet War', *ELR*, 49 (2019), pp. 145–71.

27 Samuel Fallon, *Paper Monsters: Persona and Literary Culture in Elizabethan England* (Philadelphia, PA, 2019), ch. 4.

28 Zachary Lesser, 'Walter Burre's *The Knight of the Burning Pestle*', *ELR*, XXIX/1 (1999), pp. 21–43.

29 Beatrice Groves, 'Laughter in the Time of Plague: A Context for the Unstable Style of Nashe's "Christ's Tears over Jerusalem"', *SP*, CVIII/2 (2011), pp. 238–60.

30 On Wolfe, see the *ODNB* entry; Harry R. Hoppe, 'John Wolfe, Printer and Publisher, 1579–1601', *The Library*, 14 (1933), pp. 241–87.

31 Brian Cummings, ed., *The Book of Common Prayer: The Texts of 1549, 1559 and 1662* (Oxford, 2011), p. 132; William P. Haugaard, *Elizabeth and the English Reformation: The Struggle for a Stable Settlement of Religion* (Cambridge, 1968), ch. 4.

32 Richard McCabe, *'Ungainefull Arte': Poetry, Patronage and Print in the Early Modern Era* (Oxford, 2016), pp. 82–5.

33 Ibid., part 1. See also Eleanor Rosenberg, *Leicester: Patron of Letters* (New York, 1955), ch. 1.

34 Nashe, *Works*, I, p. 310.

35 Katherine Duncan-Jones, 'Christs Teares, Nashe's "Forsaken Extremities"', *RES*, XLIX/194 (1998), pp. 167–80.

36 Nashe, *Works*, II, pp. 158–9. For details, see Nashe, *Works*, II, p. 4; Nicholl, *Cup of News*, pp. 170–73.

37 Nashe *Works*, II, pp. 158–9.

38 Nashe, *Works*, III, p. 7; Matthew Steggle, *Digital Humanities and the Lost Drama of Early Modern England: Ten Case Studies* (Abingdon, 2015), ch. 1.

39 See Chapter Three.

40. I owe this insight to Eric Vivier.

41 *ODNB* entry on 'Nashe'.

42 Neil Rhodes, 'On Speech, Print, and New Media: Thomas Nashe and Marshall McLuhan', *Oral Tradition*, XXIV/2 (October 2009), n.p.; Jennifer Richards, *Voices and Books in the English Renaissance: A New History of Reading* (Oxford, 2019), ch. 5.

43 See Chapter Six.

44 C. G. Harlow, 'Nashe's Visit to the Isle of Wight and His
    Publications of 1592–4', RES, XIV/55 (1963), pp. 225–42.

45 Nicholl, *Cup of News*, pp. 224–6, *passim*; Richards, *Voices and Books*,
    ch. 5; Kate De Rycker, 'Thomas Nashe and the Print Shop:
    Looking for Clues in the Archive', *The Collation*, 20 December
    2016, https://collation.folger.edu.

46 Henry Chettle/Robert Greene, *Greene's Groatsworth of Wit: Bought with
    a Million of Repentance*, ed. D. Allen Carroll (Binghamton, NY, 1994);
    ODNB entries on Chettle, Williams and Campion by Emma Smith,
    Francis J. Bremer and David Lindley; Nashe, *Works*, III, p. 195.

47 'The City of Cambridge: Inns', in *A History of the County of Cambridge
    and the Isle of Ely*, vol. III: *The City and University of Cambridge*, ed. J.P.C.
    Roach (London, 1959), pp. 115–16, available at British History
    Online, www.british-history.ac.uk, accessed 29 January 2021.

48 Nashe, *Works*, III, p. 95.

49 Ibid., p. 6.

50 Andrew Hadfield, 'Shakespeare, Nashe, and the Famous Victories
    of Henry V', N&Q LXV/1 (2018), pp. 67–9.

51 Nashe, *Works*, V, pp. 192–6. For comment, see E. D. Macerness,
    'Thomas Nashe and William Cotton', RES, XXV (1949), pp. 342–6;
    Katherine Duncan-Jones, 'Thomas Nashe and William Cotton:
    Parallel Letters, Parallel Lives', EMLS, XIX/1 (2016), https://extra.
    shu.ac.uk/emls.

52 Nashe, *Works*, V, p. 194.

53 I.M.W. Harvey, *Jack Cade's Rebellion of 1450* (Oxford, 1991).

54 William Shakespeare, *The First Part of the Contention (Henry VI, Part
    Two)*, IV.ii, in *The Norton Shakespeare*, ed. Stephen Greenblatt, Walter
    Cohen, Jean E. Howard and Katharine Eisaman Maus (New York,
    2008). All subsequent references are to this edition.

55 Jason Scott-Warren, 'The Privy Politics of Sir John Harington's
    New Discourse of a Stale Subject, Called the Metamorphosis of Ajax', SP,
    XCIII/4 (1996), pp. 412–42.

56 See the ODNB entry by Jason Scott-Warren; Jason Scott-Warren,
    Sir John Harington and the Book as Gift (Oxford, 2001), p. 59.

57 Nashe, *Works*, III, p. 177. See Chapter Four.

58 Andrew Hadfield, 'Nashe and *The Isle of Dogs*', N&Q 68 (2021),
    pp. 89–90.

59 Ian Donaldson, 'The Isle of Dogs (Lost Play)', in *The Cambridge Edition of the Works of Ben Jonson*, ed. David Bevington, Martin Butler and Ian Donaldson, 7 vols (Cambridge, 2012), vol. I, pp. 101–9; William Ingram, *A London Life in the Brazen Age: Francis Langley, 1548–1602* (Cambridge, MA, 1978), pp. 167–96; Misha Teramura, 'Richard Topcliffe's Informant: New Light on *The Isle of Dogs*', RES, LXVIII/283 (2017), pp. 44–59.

60 ODNB entry on 'Nashe'; Ian Donaldson, *Ben Jonson: A Life* (Oxford, 2011), ch. 7.

61 Andy Wood, 'Tales from the "Yarmouth Hutch": Civic Identities and Hidden Histories in an Urban Archive', P&P, CCXXX, Supplement 11 (2016), pp. 213–30.

62 James Travis Jenkins, *The Herring and the Herring Fisheries* (London, 1927), chs 4–5; Robert Tittler, 'The English Fishing Industry in the Sixteenth Century: The Case of Great Yarmouth', *Albion*, IX/I (1977), pp. 40–60.

63 But see Kristen Abbott Bennett, 'Red Herrings and the "Stench of Fish": Subverting "Praise" in Thomas Nashe's *Lenten Stuffe*', R&R, XXXVII/I (2014), pp. 87–110.

64 ODNB entry on 'Nashe'.

65 Nashe, *Works*, III, pp. 175–6.

66 On Burby and Danter, see STC, III, pp. 32, 49. See also Judith K. Rogers, 'John Danter', in *The British Literary Book Trade, 1475–1700*, ed. James K. Bracken and Joel Silver (Washington, DC, 1999), pp. 71–7.

67 On King, see the ODNB entry.

68 Nashe, *Works*, III, p. 151.

69 See *Stationers' Register*, III, pp. 677–8; Richard McCabe, 'Elizabethan Censorship and the Bishops' Ban of 1599', YES, XI (1981), pp. 188–93.

70 See the ODNB entry by Jason Scott-Warren.

71 On Nashe and Rabelais, see Rhodes, *Elizabethan Grotesque*, pp. 42–4, *passim*; Alan D. McKillop, 'Some Early Traces of Rabelais in English Literature', MLN, XXXVI/8 (1921), pp. 469–74.

72 J. B. Leishman, ed., *The Three Parnassus Plays, 1598–1601* (London, 1949), p. 245.

73 ODNB entry on 'Nashe'.

74 Katherine Duncan-Jones, "'They say a made a good end": Ben Jonson's Epitaph on Thomas Nashe', *BJJ*, III/1 (1996), pp. 1–19.

75 Nashe, *Works*, III, p. 222.

76 Kathy Eden, *Friends Hold All Things in Common: Tradition, Intellectual Property and the Adages of Erasmus* (New Haven, CT, 2001).

77 Nashe, *Works*, III, p. 213.

78 Nicholl, *Cup of News*, pp. 9–10.

79 Nashe, *Works*, III, p. 20.

80 *ODNB* entry on 'Nashe'.

1 Religion

1 The literature on the Reformation is vast. Two splendid recent accounts are Peter Marshall, *Heretics and Believers: A History of the English Reformation* (New Haven, CT, 2017), on England, and Diarmaid MacCulloch, *Reformation: Europe's House Divided, 1490–1700* (London, 2003).

2 Joseph L. Black, ed., *The Martin Marprelate Tracts: A Modernized and Annotated Edition* (Cambridge, 2008), introduction, p. lix. Subsequent references to this edition are in parentheses in the text.

3 There was also a theatrical response; see Jill Ingram, "'Hick Scorners Jestes": Thomas Nashe, Martin's Month's Mind and the Tudor Dramatic Tradition', *ELR* (forthcoming). I am grateful to Professor Ingram for sharing this essay in advance of publication.

4 Charles Nicholl, *A Cup of News: The Life of Thomas Nashe* (London, 1984), pp. 15, 20; Isaac Herbert Jeayes, ed., *Letters of Philip Gawdy of West Harling, Norfolk, and of London to Various Members of His Family, 1579–1616* (London, 1906), p. 65.

5 For discussion, see Black, ed., *Marprelate Tracts*, introduction, pp. lxii–lxiv.

6 Nashe, *Works*, I, p. 62.

7 Ibid., III, p. 342.

8 Ibid., III, pp. 342–3.

9 On the anxieties and fears of invasion in the post-Armada period, see Carol. Z. Weiner, 'The Beleaguered Isle: A Study of Elizabethan and Early Jacobean Anti-Catholicism', *P&P*, LI/1 (1971), pp. 27–62.

10 Black, ed., *Marprelate Tracts*, introduction, pp. liv–lv.

11 Black, ed., *Marprelate Tracts*, introduction, pp. xxxiv–xlvi.

12 Nashe, *Works*, III, p. 171.

13 Eiléan Ní Chuilleanáin, 'The Debate Between Thomas More and William Tyndale, 1528–33: Ideas on Literature and Religion', *JEH*, XXXIX/3 (1988), pp. 382–411.

14 Nicholas Tyacke, *Anti-Calvinists: The Rise of English Arminianism, c. 1590–1640* (Oxford, 1987); Nigel Smith, *Literature and Revolution, 1640–1660* (New Haven, CT, 1994).

15 See Introduction.

16 Andrew Hadfield, 'Shakespeare: Biography and Belief', in *The Cambridge Companion to Shakespeare and Religion*, ed. Hannibal Hamlin (Cambridge, 2019), pp. 18–33.

17 For accounts of the revolt, see Norman Cohn, *The Pursuit of the Millennium: Revolutionary Millenarians and Mystical Anarchists of the Middle Ages*, revd edn (London, 1970), ch. 12; Anthony Arthur, *The Tailor-King: The Rise and Fall of the Anabaptist Kingdom of Munster* (New York, 1999).

18 Nashe, *Works*, II, pp. 234–6.

19 C. A. Patrides and Joseph Wittreich, eds, *The Apocalypse in English Renaissance Thought and Literature: Patterns, Antecedents and Repercussions* (Manchester, 1984).

20 See Introduction; and, for one example, Andrew Hadfield, 'Spenser and Religion – Yet Again', *SEL*, LI/1 (2011), pp. 21–46.

21 Nashe, *Works*, III, pp. 320–21.

22 Sir Philip Sidney, *An Apology for Poetry (or The Defence of Poesie)*, ed. Geoffrey Shepherd, revd Robert Malsen (Manchester, 2002).

23 William Garrett Crane, *Wit and Rhetoric in the Renaissance: The Formal Basis of Elizabethan Prose Style* (New York, 1960).

24 Marcia B. Hall and Tracey E. Cooper, eds, *The Sensuous in the Counter-Reformation Church* (Cambridge, 2013).

25 Nashe, *Works*, III, p. 318.

26 Beatrice Groves, 'Laughter in the Time of Plague: A Context for the Unstable Style of Nashe's *Christ's Tears over Jerusalem*', *SP*, CVIII/2 (2011), pp. 238–60.

27 Nashe, *Works*, II, p. 123.

28 Patrick Collinson, *The Elizabethan Puritan Movement* (London, 1967), p. 27.

29 The adjective is not a Nashe coinage, but was used in
    theological disputes. It may have been first used by the Catholic
    controversialist Thomas Stapleton (1535–1598): *A Counterblast to
    M. Hornes Vayne Blast against M. Fekenham* (London, 1567), **4v.

30 See Chapter Five.

31 Peter McCulloch, Hugh Adlington and Emma Rhatigan, eds,
    The Oxford Handbook of the Early Modern Sermon (Oxford, 2011).

32 Jennifer Richards, *Voices and Books in the English Renaissance: A New
    History of Reading* (Oxford, 2019), ch. 3; Arnold Hunt, *The Art of
    Hearing: English Preachers and Their Audiences, 1590–1640* (Cambridge,
    2010).

33 Botcher, n. 1, *OED*, 1, 2.a.

34 See Christopher A. Hill, 'Thomas Nashe's Imitation of Christ',
    Prose Studies, 28 (2006), pp. 211–21.

35. For further discussion, see Brian Cummings, *The Literary Culture of
    the Reformation: Grammar and Grace* (Oxford, 2002).

36 The belief in balance between extremes appears in numerous
    aspects of early modern thought. On medicine, see Margaret
    Healy, *Fictions of Disease in Early Modern England: Bodies, Plagues, Politics*
    (Basingstoke, 2002); on architecture, see Rudolf Wittkower,
    Architectural Principles in the Age of Humanism (London, 1971).

37 See Introduction.

38 For details of her life, see the *ODNB* entry by Elaine V. Beilin.
    See also E. A. Strathmann, 'Lady Carey and Spenser', *ELH*, 11
    (1935), pp. 33–57.

39 Nashe, *Works*, 1, p. 342.

40 See Jonathan Crewe, 'This Sorrow's Heavenly: *Christ's Tears* and the
    Jews', in *The Age of Thomas Nashe: Text, Bodies and Trespasses of Authorship
    in Early Modern England*, ed. Stephen Guy-Bray, Joan Pong Linton
    and Steve Mentz (Farnham, 2013), pp. 27–43.

41 Beatrice Groves, *The Destruction of Jerusalem in Early Modern English
    Literature* (Cambridge, 2017), ch. 6.

42 A useful comparison might be made with Ben Jonson's *The Devil Is
    an Ass* (1616), in which the junior devil Pug begs to be allowed back
    to hell he cannot cope with the extent of sin in London.
    The literary relationship between Nashe and Jonson was especially
    important for Jonson, and Nashe's influence continued long after

his death; see, for example, Katherine Duncan-Jones, 'City Limits: Nashe's "Choice of Valentines" and Jonson's "Famous Voyage"', *RES*, 56 (2005), pp. 247–62.

43 Jeremiah 9:17–18, 21.

44 Shakespeare, *Hamlet*, v.i.171–2.

45 Christopher Marlowe, *Tamburlaine*, v.i–ii, in *Tamburlaine the Great, Parts One and Two*, ed. Anthony B. Dawson (London, 2003).

46 Nashe, *Works*, I, pp. 34, 39. Nashe's exact source here is not known. I am grateful to François Quiviger for his advice here.

47 On combining disparate sources in Renaissance images and writing, see Stephen Campbell, *The Cabinet of Eros: Renaissance Mythological Painting and the Studiolo of Isabella D'Este* (New Haven, CT, 2004), p. 2; Elliott M. Simon, *The Myth of Sisyphus: Renaissance Theories of Human Perfectibility* (Madison, WI, 2007), ch. 6.

2 Early Style

1 Charles Nicholl, *A Cup of News: The Life of Thomas Nashe* (London, 1984), p. 37.

2 See Kirk Melnikoff, 'Thomas Hacket and the Ventures of an Elizabethan Publisher', *The Library*, 10 (2009), pp. 257–71.

3 Nicholl, *Cup of News*, p. 43. On Golding and Kyd, see the ODNB entries; on the reference to Kyd in *Menaphon*, see Andrew Hadfield, 'The Ur-Hamlet and the Fable of the Kid', *N&Q* LIII/1 (2006), pp. 46–7; for the *Strange News* reference, see Nashe, *Works*, I, p. 271.

4 On Blount, see the ODNB entry. On the relationship between the pirated edition of *Astrophil and Stella*, Nashe, Blount and the Sidney circle, see Henry Woudhuysen, *Sir Philip Sidney and the Circulation of Manuscripts, 1558–1640* (Oxford, 1996), pp. 371–84.

5 Nashe, *Works*, I, p. 5.

6 The reference is actually to Juvenal, *Satires*, II.24–7 (as McKerrow points out: Nashe, *Works*, IV, p. 4).

7 Nashe, *Works*, IV, p. 4.

8 Rosalie Colie, *Paradoxia Epidemica: The Renaissance Tradition of Paradox* (Princeton, NJ, 1966).

9 Compare the use of the word to describe *Lenten Stuff* (see Chapter Three).

10 See, for example, Alcuin Blamires, ed., *Women Defamed and Women Defended: An Anthology of Medieval Texts* (Oxford, 1992).

11 Peter Mack, *Elizabethan Rhetoric: Theory and Practice* (Cambridge, 2002), p. 35.

12 William Hansen, *Handbook of Classical Mythology* (Santa Barbara, CA, 2004), p. 37.

13 Peter Mack, *Renaissance Argument: Valla and Agricola in the Traditions of Rhetoric and Dialectic* (Leiden, 1993), pp. 3–5, *passim*.

14 Paul J. du Plessis, *Borkowski's Textbook on Roman Law*, 6th edn (Oxford, 2020), p. 127.

15 Nashe, *Works*, IV, p. 19; Lee Patterson, *Chaucer and the Subject of History* (Madison, WI, 1991), p. 291.

16 George Puttenham, *The Art of English Poesie*, ed. Frank Whigham and Wayne C. Rebhorn (Ithaca, NY, 2007), p. 271.

17 On Nashe's satire of Spenser, see Andrew Zurcher, 'Getting It Back to Front in 1590: Spenser's Dedications, Nashe's Insinuations, and Raleigh's Equivocations', *SLI*, XXXVIII/2 (2005), pp. 173–98.

18 See Introduction and Chapter Four; Nicholl, *Cup of News*, p. 99.

19 See Chapter One.

20 Nashe may not have a particular biblical story in mind here; the closest – the well-known episode of Susannah and the Elders – has the lecherous, corrupt elders falsely accusing Susannah of adultery before their deception is uncovered.

21 On knights of the post, see Burton A. Milligan, 'A Note on Knights of the Post', *MLN*, LXI (1946), pp. 247–51; Sandra Clark, *The Elizabethan Pamphleteers: Popular Moralistic Pamphlets, 1580–1640* (London, 1983), pp. 56–7. 'Eritus' is Eric Ragnnarsson (*c.* 820–*c.* 850). Nashe's source is Saxo Grammaticus' *Danica Historia* (Frankfurt, 1576), pp. 82–3 (Nashe, *Works*, IV, p. 145; see also n. 23 below).

22 Geoffrey Bullough, *Narrative and Dramatic Sources of Shakespeare*, 8 vols (London, 1966–75), vol. VII, pp. 60–79.

23 Saxo Grammaticus, *The History of the Danes, Books I–IX*, ed. and trans. Hilda Ellis Davidson and Peter Fisher, 2 vols (Cambridge, 1979, 1980), vol. I, p. 151.

24 Starch was expensive, and so having a sizable ruff was a sign of ostentatious wealth; to spade a beard was to cut it into a fashionable point.

25 Aristotle, *Physics*, IV, 6–9.

26 Jennifer Clement, 'The Art of Feeling in Seventeenth-Century English Sermons', *ES*, XCVIII/7 (2017), pp. 675–88.

27 For more discussion, see Andrew Hadfield, *John Donne: In the Shadow of Religion* (London, 2021).

28 On Elderton, see the *ODNB* entry.

29 For more discussion, see Neil Rhodes's pioneering *Elizabethan Grotesque* (London, 1980).

30 The connection between intelligence and night terrors indicates that Nashe's most likely source was Marsilio Ficino's *De Vita Libri Tres* (1480–89); see Carol V. Kaske and John R. Clark, ed. and trans., *Three Books on Life* (Tempe, AZ, 2002), pp. 125–7. I owe this point to François Quiviger.

31 Stephen D. Bowd, *Renaissance Mass Murder: Soldiers and Civilians During the Italian Wars* (Oxford, 2018); Roger B. Manning, *An Apprenticeship in Arms: The Origins of the British Army, 1585–1702* (Oxford, 2006), pp. 57, 60, 198, *passim*; Thomas Arnold, *The Renaissance at War* (London, 2001), pp. 60–67, *passim*.

32 Raymond Fagel, 'Gascoigne's *The Spoyle of Antwerp* (1576) as an Anglo-Dutch Text', *DC*, 41 (2017), pp. 101–10. Fagel shows how Gascoigne relied on Dutch texts as well as his own observations.

33 The imagined battle was a standard subject in Renaissance art; see Peter Paret, *Battles* (Chapel Hill, NC, 1997), p. 1. I owe this point to François Quiviger.

34 Murray W. Bundy, '"Invention" and "Imagination" in the Renaissance', *JEGP*, XXIX/4 (1930), pp. 535–45.

35 On *Summer's Last Will*, see Chapter Three.

36 On McKerrow's reaction, see Andrew Hadfield, 'R. B. McKerrow, Horace Hart and Nashe's "The Choice of Valentines"', *N&Q*, 64 (2017), pp. 154–5; Linda Grant, *Latin Erotic Elegy and the Shaping of Sixteenth-Century English Love Poetry* (Cambridge, 2019), p. 124. Grant finds more of interest in the poem than do many Nashe critics, and Stephen Guy-Bray and Jan Pong Linton point out that it is taught more frequently now than it once was: 'Postscript: Nashe

Untrimmed: The Way We Teach Him Today', in *The Age of Thomas Nashe: Text, Bodies and Trespasses of Authorship in Early Modern England*, ed. Stephen Guy-Bray, Joan Pong Linton and Steve Mentz (Farnham, 2013), pp. 169–82.

37 For the manuscript circulation, see Nashe, *Works*, III, pp. 397–402; for its significance as pornography, see Grant, *Latin Erotic Elegy*, ch. 4; Sandra Friesen, 'The Rise and Fall of Seigneur Dildoe: The Figure of the Dildo in Restoration Literature and Culture', PhD thesis, University of Victoria, 2017, pp. 80–95.

38 Grant, *Latin Erotic Elegy*, p. 123.

39 William Keach, *Elizabethan Erotic Narratives: Irony and Pathos in the Ovidian Poetry of Shakespeare, Marlowe, and Their Contemporaries* (New Brunswick, NJ, 1976). On Marlowe's influence on Nashe, see Andrew Hadfield, 'Marlowe and Nashe', *ELR*, LI/2 (2021), pp. 22–7.

40 Ian Moulton, *Before Pornography: Erotic Writing in Early Modern England* (Oxford, 2000), p. 17.

41 Christopher Marlowe, *Doctor Faustus*, ed. Roma Gill (Oxford, 1990), 13.61–73.

42 See Chapter Three.

43 Ovid, *Amores*, 3.7.1–16.

3 The Theatre

1 On Drayton, see the ODNB entry.

2 Michael Drayton, "To my most dearely-loved friend Henry Reynolds Esquire, of *Poets & Poesie*", ll. 111–18, in *The Battaile of Agincourt* (1617), 2Dv.

3 See the *Lost Plays Database*, https://lostplays.folger.edu (accessed 13 July 2021).

4 See Introduction.

5 On university dramatic culture in the period, see Frederick Boas, *University Drama in the Tudor Age* (Oxford, 1914). On Watson, see the ODNB entry.

6 On Legg, see the ODNB entry. Nashe had undoubtedly seen Legg's play *Richardus Tertius*, to which he refers in *Have with You*: Nashe, *Works*, III, p. 13.

7 Nashe, *Works*, III, p. 80. Edward Forsett, *Pedantius*, ed. E.F.J. Tucker (Hildesheim, 1989). Forsett (1553–1630) later became a politician and author of political tracts, and was one of the prosecutors of the Gunpowder Plotters in 1605; see the ODNB entry.

8 See Andrew Hadfield, *Edmund Spenser: A Life* (Oxford, 2012), pp. 76–9.

9 Wiggins, *Drama*, II, pp. 321–2; Virginia Stern, *Gabriel Harvey: His Life, Marginalia and Library* (Oxford, 1979), pp. 40–46.

10 Wiggins, *Drama*, II, pp. 264–5.

11 Forsett, *Pedantius*, ed. Tucker, introduction, p. xxii.

12 See Chapter Five.

13 Paul H. Kocher, 'Some Nashe Marginalia Concerning Marlowe', *MLN*, LVII/1 (1942), pp. 45–9; Paul H. Kocher, 'Nashe's Authorship of the Prose Scenes in *Faustus*', *MLQ*, III/1 (1942), pp. 17–40; Kate De Rycker, 'Thomas Nashe and the Print Shop: Looking for Clues in the Archive', *The Collation*, 20 December 2016, https://collation.folger.edu, accessed 21 July 2021.

14 Wiggins, *Drama*, II, p. 426.

15 Christopher Marlowe, *Doctor Faustus*, ed. Roma Gill (Oxford, 1990), 1.47–8.

16 Kocher, 'Some Nashe Marginalia', pp. 46, 48.

17 Marlowe, *Doctor Faustus*, ed. Gill, 1.90–91.

18 See Kocher, 'Nashe's Authorship'; Wiggins, *Drama*, II, p. 419; *Christopher Marlowe and his Collaborator and Revisers, Doctor Faustus: A and B Texts (1604 and 1616)*, ed. David Bevington and Eric Rasmussen (Manchester, 1993), p. 72. See also Jacqueline Stanhope Hoefer, 'A Refutation of Paul H. Kocher's Claim that Thomas Nashe Wrote the Prose Scenes in Christopher Marlowe's *Dr Faustus*', MA thesis, Washington University, 1955.

19 Katherine Duncan-Jones has argued that Robert Greene was Nashe's co-author; see *Shakespeare: Upstart Crow to Sweet Swan, 1592–1623* (London, 2011), pp. 38–48. For evidence of the performance, see Charles Nicholl, *A Cup of News: The Life of Thomas Nashe* (London, 1984), pp. 135–9; Patricia Posluszny, ed., *Thomas Nashe's 'Summer's Last Will and Testament': A Critical Modern-Spelling Edition* (Frankfurt, 1989), introduction, pp. 9–10.

20 Duncan-Jones, *Upstart Crow*, p. 46.

21 Nashe, *Works*, III, p. 291 (ll. 1841–9).

22 See Jennifer Richards, *Voices and Books in the English Renaissance: A New History of Reading* (Oxford, 2019), ch. 5.

23 See Introduction; Andrew Hadfield, 'Commentary: How Lamentable, Thomas Nashe's Dog Days', *TLS*, 5817 (25 September 2014), pp. 14–15.

24 Nicholl, *Cup of News*, p. 137; Posluszny, *Summer's Last Will*, introduction, p. 10.

25 Glynne Wickham, Herbert Berry and William Ingram, eds, *English Professional Theatre, 1530–1660* (Cambridge, 2000), p. 312.

26 On Will Somers, see the ODNB entry; John Southworth, *Fools and Jesters at the English Court* (London, 1998), pp. 91–103.

27 See Introduction.

28 H. E. Malden, ed., *A History of the County of Surrey*, vol. II (London, 1905), p. 334; Mavis E. Mate, *Trade and Economic Developments, 1450–1550: The Experience of Kent, Surrey and Sussex* (Woodbridge, 2006), pp. 48, 70.

29 F. P. Wilson, *The Plague in Shakespeare's London* (Oxford, 1927), pp. 77–9; Vanessa Harding, 'Burial of the Plague Dead in Early Modern London', in *Epidemic Disease in London*, ed. J.A.I. Champion (London, 1993), pp. 53–64.

30 W. G. Hoskins, 'Harvest Fluctuations and the English Economy, 1480–1619', *AHR*, 12 (1964), p. 32.

31 On 6 September 1592 the Thames dried out and could be crossed on foot in many places; see John Stow, *Annals* (London, 1615), p. 764 (cited in Nashe, *Works*, IV, pp. 426–7).

32 Ronald Hutton, *Stations of the Sun: A History of the Ritual Year in Britain* (Oxford, 2001), ch. 33.

33 Wilson, *Plague*, pp. 61, 63–4.

34 Andrew Hadfield, 'How to Read Nashe's "Brightness Falls from the Air"', *FMLS*, LI/3 (2015), pp. 239–47.

35 Philippe Aries, *The Hour of Our Death*, trans. Harriet Weaver (New York, 1981), pp. 105–10, *passim*.

36 John A. Wagner, *Historical Dictionary of the Elizabethan World* (Abingdon, 2011), p. 64.

37 Peter Gibbard, 'Breaking Up the Line: The Sententious Style in Elizabethan Blank Verse', *MP*, CXII/2 (2014), pp. 312–35. For an

argument that Nashe owes much to Marlowe in *Summer's Last Will*, see Per Sivefors, 'Underplayed Rivalry: Patronage and the Subtext of *Summer's Last Will and Testament*', *NJES*, IV/2 (2005), pp. 65–87.

38 For the evidence, see Brian Vickers, 'Incomplete Shakespeare: or, Denying Co-Authorship in *1 Henry VI*', *SQ*, LVIII/3 (2007), pp. 311–52; Gary Taylor and Rory Loughnane, 'The Canon and Chronology of Shakespeare's Works', in *The New Oxford Shakespeare: Authorship Companion*, ed. Gary Taylor and Gabriel Egan (Oxford, 2017), pp. 513–14.

39 Vickers, 'Incomplete Shakespeare', pp. 336–7.

40 Stephen Greenblatt, Walter Cohen, Jean E. Howard and Katharine Eisaman Maus, eds, *The Norton Shakespeare* (New York, 2008), pp. 230, 319, 465.

41 More generally, see Bart van Es, *Shakespeare in Company* (Oxford, 2013).

42 Taylor and Loughnane, 'Canon and Chronology', pp. 513–17. Much of the evidence is still disputed, although not Nashe's role in the first version of the play.

43 Peter Saccio, *Shakespeare's English Kings: History, Chronicle, Drama*, 2nd edn (Oxford, 2000), pp. 106–13.

44 Maurice Charney, 'The Voice of Marlowe's Tamburlaine in Early Shakespeare', *CD*, XXXI/2 (1997), pp. 213–23.

45 The reference is Suetonius, *Lives of the Caesars*, 6.

46 H. J. Oliver notes that 'there are more than a dozen words that are found elsewhere in Nashe but not in Marlowe, and at least three classical allusions to which Nashe's other works offer closer parallels than do Marlowe's': Christopher Marlowe, *'Dido, Queen of Carthage' and 'The Massacre at Paris'*, ed. H. J. Oliver (London, 1968), introduction, pp. xxii–xxiii. On computational tests for attribution, see, for example, Darren Freebury-Jones and Marcus Dahl, 'Searching for Thomas Nashe in *Dido, Queen of Carthage*', *DSH*, XXXV/2 (2020), pp. 296–306; Ruth Lunney and Hugh Craig, 'Who Wrote *Dido, Queen of Carthage*?', *MS*, I (2020), https://journals.shu.ac.uk.

47 Park Honan, *Christopher Marlowe: Poet and Spy* (Oxford, 2005), p. 99.

48 John Ford, *The Collected Works of John Ford*, vol. II, ed. Brian Vickers (Oxford, 2016), introduction, p. 10.

49 Martin Wiggins, 'When Did Marlowe Write *Dido, Queen of Carthage?*', *RES*, LIX/241 (2008), pp. 521–41; Wiggins, *Drama*, II, p. 244; Glynn Wickham, Herbert Berry and William Ingram, eds, *English Professional Theatre, 1530–1660* (Cambridge, 2000), p. 260.
50 Marlowe, '*Dido*' and '*Massacre*', ed. Oliver, p. 6.
51 See Introduction.
52 See Chapter Six.
53 See Introduction.
54 Robert Miola, in *The Works of Ben Jonson*, ed. David Bevington, Martin Butler and Ian Donaldson, 7 vols (Cambridge, 2012), vol. I, p. 3.
55 Ian Donaldson, *Ben Jonson: A Life* (Oxford, 2011), pp. 109–11.
56 Miola, in *Jonson*, vol. I, pp. 5–6.

4 Gabriel Harvey

 1 Nashe, *Works*, III, p. 320.
 2 This account is indebted to R. B. McKerrow, 'The Harvey–Nashe Quarrel' (Nashe, *Works*, V, pp. 65–110); Donald J. McGinn, *Thomas Nashe* (Boston, MA, 1981), chs 8–10; Charles Nicholl, *A Cup of News: The Life of Thomas Nashe* (London, 1984), *passim*; Jennifer Richards, *Rhetoric and Courtliness in Early Modern Literature* (Cambridge, 2003), ch. 5.
 3 Nashe, *Works*, I, p. 303; III, p. 80. See also Chapter Two.
 4 Cited in Nashe, *Works*, V, p. 180.
 5 It is possible that Nashe's address to Richard Lichfield, the barber of Trinity College, prefacing *Have with You to Saffron Walden* looks back to this slight.
 6 John Lyly, *Pap with an Hatchet*, ed. Leah Scragg (Manchester, 2015), p. 59.
 7 Nashe, *Works*, V, p. 77.
 8 Ibid., I, p. 196.
 9 See Introduction; Bernard Capp, 'Harvey, Richard', *ODNB*.
10 Gabriel Harvey, *Four Letters and Certaine Sonnets* [1592], ed. G. B. Harrison (1922; repr. Edinburgh, 1966), pp. 81–2.
11 Nashe, *Works*, II, p. 12.
12 Gabriel Harvey, *A New Letter of Notable Contents* (London, 1592), sigs B3r, C2v.

13 Harvey, *Pierces Supererogation*, sig. Z3v. See also Nashe, *Works*, V,
    pp. 93–4.

14 Harvey, *Pierces Supererogation*, sig. Z4r. See also Nashe, *Works*, V, p. 94.

15 Nashe, *Works*, I, pp. 290–91.

16 Jennifer Richards, *Rhetoric* (London, 2007), p. 109. On the history
    of Ciceronianism and the debates it generated, see Peter Mack,
    A History of Renaissance Rhetoric, 1380–1620 (Oxford, 2011), pp. 166–9.

17 'Are we turned Turks, and to ourselves do that/ Which heaven
    hath forbid the Ottomites?' (*Othello*, II.iii.153–4).

18 See Introduction.

19 See Chapter Six.

20 See Chapter Six.

21 See Introduction.

22 Nashe, *Works*, III, pp. 92–3.

23 See Introduction.

24 Richard Lichfield, *The Trimming of Thomas Nashe* (London, 1597),
    sigs F1v, F3v.

25 William Desmond, *Cynics* (London, 2006), p. 3.

26 For more on *Trimming*, see Rebecca Hasler, '"Tossing and turning
    your booke upside downe": *The Trimming of Thomas Nashe*, Cambridge,
    and Scholarly Reading', *RS*, XXXIII/3 (2019), pp. 375–96.

27 The best outline and guide is McGinn, *Nashe*, pp. 132–51.

28 Nashe, *Works*, III, p. 5.

29 See Introduction.

30 On Harvey's pride in his Italianate appearance, see Virginia Stern,
    Gabriel Harvey: His Life, Marginalia and Library (Oxford, 1979), p. 42.

31 Barnabe Barnes, *Parthenophil and Parthenophe* (London, 1593), sonnet
    63 (sig. F4r). See also the criticism of John Marston, *The Scourge of
    Villainy* (London, 1598), sig. G4v.

32 For discussion, see Matthew Steggle, 'Gabriel Harvey, the Sidney
    Circle, and the Excellent Gentlewoman', *SCJ*, XXII (2004),
    pp. 115–30.

33 See the list in Nicholl, *Cup of News*, p. 143.

34 For analysis see Nashe, *Works*, IV, pp. 323–4.

35 Hornbooks were primers for study that could be held by children
    in one hand as they learned how to form letters. English law is
    predominantly based on common law, but there were civil law

courts in early modern England; see Martin Vranken, *Western Legal Traditions: A Comparison of Civil Law and Common Law* (Alexandria, NSW, 2015). Harvey had trained as a civilian lawyer but never practised (Stern, *Harvey*, pp. 68–9). The Arches was the site of the ecclesiastical law courts.

36 P. B. Roberts, 'Underemployed Elizabethans: Gabriel Harvey and Thomas Nashe in the Parnassus Plays', *ET*, XXI/2 (2018), pp. 49–70; Travis L. Summersgill, 'Harvey, Nashe and the Three Parnassus Plays', *PQ*, XXI (1952), pp. 94–5. On the plays, see also the Epilogue.

5 Fiction

1 Kirk Melnikoff and Edward Gieskes, eds, *Writing Robert Greene: Essays on England's Notorious First Professional Writer* (Aldershot, 2008); Lori Humphrey Newcomb, *Reading Popular Romance in Early Modern England* (New York, 2001).

2 Edwin Haviland Miller, 'The Relationship of Robert Greene and Thomas Nashe', *PQ*, 33 (1954), pp. 353–67; Lorna Hutson, *Thomas Nashe in Context* (Oxford, 1989), pp. 64–7, 120–21.

3 See Chapter Six.

4 See Chapter Three.

5 Charles Nicholl, *A Cup of News: The Life of Thomas Nashe* (London, 1984), ch. 12.

6 Andrew Hadfield, *Edmund Spenser: A Life* (Oxford, 2012), ch. 9.

7 Steve Mentz, *Romance for Sale in Early Modern England: The Rise of Prose Fiction* (Aldershot, 2006), chs 6 and 7. On the vogue for Heliodorus, see Victor Skretkowicz, *European Erotic Romance: Philhellene Protestantism, Renaissance Translation and English Literary Politics* (Manchester, 2010); on the picaresque, see Harry Sieber, *The Picaresque* (London, 1977); on cony-catching literature, see Gamini Salgādo, *The Elizabethan Underworld* (London, 1977), and Salgādo, ed., *Cony-Catchers and Bawdy Baskets: An Anthology of Elizabethan Low Life* (Harmondsworth, 1972).

8 Nashe, *Works*, II, p. 243.

9 Donald J. McGinn, *Thomas Nashe* (Boston, MA, 1981), pp. 87–103; Geoffrey Elton, *Reformation Europe, 1517–1559* (London, 1963), pp. 38, 100–101; J. J. Scarisbrick, *Henry VIII* (London, 1988), pp. 74–80.

10 Andrew Hiscock, 'Blabbing Leaves of Betraying Paper: Configuring the Past in George Gascoigne's *The Adventures of Master F. J.*, Thomas Nashe's *The Unfortunate Traveller*, and Thomas Deloney's *Jack of Newberry*', *English*, LII/202 (2003), pp. 1–20.

11 For the legend of the 'fair Geraldine' and Nashe's part in the dissemination of the story, see William A. Sessions, *Henry Howard, The Poet Earl of Surrey: A Life* (Oxford, 2003), pp. 187–99.

12 See Andrew Hadfield, ed., *Amazons, Savages and Machiavels: Travel and Colonial Writing in English, 1550–1630* (Oxford, 2001), part 1.

13 On voluntary, involuntary and non-voluntary travel, see Thomas Palmer, *An Essay of the Meanes How to Make Our Travailes, into Forraine Countries, the More Profitable and Honourable* (London, 1606); Emily Thomas, *The Meaning of Travel: Philosophers Abroad* (Oxford, 2020), pp. 40–41.

14 Nashe, *Works*, II, p. 209. The oath of the pantofle (a slipper or old shoe) was taken to initiate freshmen at university and probably new courtiers at court.

15 A copy of Foxe's work was placed in every cathedral church in England and Wales, so the allusion would have been recognized by all Nashe's readers.

16 For details of the Babington Plot, see John Guy, *My Heart Is My Own: The Life of Mary Queen of Scots* (London, 2004), ch. 29.

17 Rebecca Bushnell, *A Culture of Teaching: Early Modern Humanism in Theory and Practice* (Ithaca, NY, 1996), pp. 35–7.

18 Roy Battenhouse, 'Tamburlaine, the Scourge of God', *PMLA*, LVI/2 (1941), pp. 337–48.

19 Michel Foucault, *Discipline and Punish: The Birth of the Prison*, trans. Alan Sheridan (Harmondsworth, 1977), ch. 2.

20 Anne Dillon, *The Construction of Martyrdom in the English Catholic Community, 1535–1603* (Farnham, 2002).

21 Anon., *A Spectacle for Usurers and Succers of Poor Folkes Bloud, Whereby they may see, Gods just dislike and revenge, upon their uncharitable and Unciuill oppression, with a horrible murther committed by a young man, that hanged his owne Mother in August last* (London, 1606).

22 J. A. Sharpe, *Crime and the Law in English Satirical Prints, 1600–1832* (Cambridge, 1986), pp. 56–7.

23 Neil Rhodes, *Elizabethan Grotesque* (London, 1980), p. 43.

24 Charles Hughes, ed., *Shakespeare's Europe: Unpublished Chapter of Fynes Moryson's Itinerary* (London, 1903), p. 67.

25 Eamon Duffy, *Fires of Faith: Catholic England Under Mary Tudor* (New Haven, CT, 2009), pp. 76–8.

26 Antonio Barrera-Osorio, *Experiencing Nature: The Spanish American Empire and the Early Scientific Revolution* (Austin, TX, 2006), p. 120.

27 Andrew Hadfield, 'Prose Fiction', in *A New Companion to English Renaissance Literature and Culture*, ed. Michael Hattaway, 2 vols (Oxford, 2010), vol. II, pp. 423–36.

28 Andrew Hadfield, 'Renaissance England's Views of Rome', *BSRS*, XXXII/2 (October 2015), pp. 9–12.

29 McGinn, *Nashe*, p. 95.

30 On the art of memory, see Frances A. Yates, *The Art of Memory* (Harmondsworth, 1966).

31 Ian Littlewood, *Sultry Climates, Travel and Sex Since the Grand Tour* (London, 2001).

32 Frances E. Dolan, *True Relations: Reading, Literature, and Evidence in Seventeenth-Century England* (Philadelphia, PA, 2013), pp. 9–10.

33 Palmer, *Travel*, p. 8.

34 Katy Gibbons, *English Catholic Exiles in Late Sixteenth-Century Paris* (Woodbridge, 2011).

35 Michael J. Redmond, *Shakespeare, Politics and Italy: Intertextuality on the Jacobean Stage* (Farnham, 2009), pp. 40–43.

36 Roger Ascham, *The Scholemaster* (London, 1570), sig. KIr.

37 For the relevant descriptions, see Ton Hoenselaars, *Images of Englishmen and Foreigners in the Drama of Shakespeare and His Contemporaries* (Cranbury, NJ, 1992); Jean-Christophe Mayer, 'Representing France and the French in Early Modern English Drama', in *Representing France and the French in Early Modern English Drama*, ed. Jean-Christophe Mayer (Newark, NJ, 2008), pp. 21–46.

38 Geoffrey Parker, *The Army of Flanders and the Spanish Road, 1567–1659* (Cambridge, 1972), ch. 7.

39 D. A. Russell and Michael Winterbottom, eds, *Classical Literary Criticism* (Oxford, 1989), p. 53.

40 Jerry Brotton, *The Renaissance Bazaar: From the Silk Road to Michelangelo* (Oxford, 2002); Jyotsna G. Singh, ed., *A Companion to the Global*

Renaissance: English Literature and Culture in the Era of Expansion (Oxford, 2009).

41 Lewis Mumford, *The City in History: Its Origins, Its Transformations, and Its Prospects* (New York, 1968).

42 Andreas Huyssen, ed., *Other Cities, Other Worlds: Urban Imaginaries in a Globalizing Age* (Durham, NC, 2008), p. 3.

43 John Dixon Hunt writes that the Farnese Gardens 'finely epitomized the English experience of modern Italian gardens created in and out of classical predecessors'; see *Garden and Grove: The Italian Renaissance Garden in the English Imagination, 1600–1750* (Philadelphia, PA, 1996), p. 27.

44 Sir Philip Sidney, *A Defence of Poetry*, ed. J. A. van Dorsten (Oxford, 1966), p. 24.

45 F. P. Wilson, *The Plague in Shakespeare's London* (Oxford, 1927), p. 61.

46 Nashe, *Works*, II, p. 93.

47 Lorna Hutson, 'Fortunate Travelers: Reading for the Plot in Sixteenth-Century England', *Representations*, 41 (Winter 1993), pp. 83–103.

48 Steve Mentz, *Dishonest Romance: Greene and Nashe* (2006), p. 184.

6 Late Writing, Mature Style

1 See Edward Said, *On Late Style: Music and Literature Against the Grain* (London, 2006), and, for the early modern period, Gordon McMullan, *Shakespeare and the Idea of Late Writing: Authorship in the Proximity of Death* (Cambridge, 2007).

2 Nashe, *Works*, III, p. 153.

3 For a related but different claim, see Ann Rosalind Jones, 'Inside the Outsider: Nashe's *Unfortunate Traveller* and Bakhtin's Polyphonic Novel', *ELH*, L/1 (1983), pp. 61–81.

4 Robert Appelbaum, *Aguecheek's Beef, Belch's Hiccup, and Other Gastronomic Interjections: Literature, Culture, and Food Among the Early Moderns* (Chicago, IL, 2006), pp. 211–18.

5 On Jack Cade, see Introduction; Jack Straw was a leader of the Peasants' Revolt in 1381, the most dangerous challenge to the authority of the late medieval English monarchy.

6   For a more detailed summary, see Donald J. McGinn, *Thomas Nashe*
    (Boston, MA, 1981), pp. 152–60.

7   For a recent analysis of the importance of Hakluyt's volume, see
    Daniel Carey and Claire Jowitt, eds, *Richard Hakluyt and Travel
    Writing in Early Modern Europe* (Farnham, 2012).

8   Harvey, *Pierces Supererogation*, p. 47.

9   Ibid., p. 48.

10 Ibid., pp. 48–9.

11 Ibid., pp. 49–50.

12 For a splendid analysis, see Matthew Day, 'Hakluyt, Harvey, Nashe:
    The Material Text and Early Modern Nationalism', *SP*, CIV/3
    (2007), pp. 281–305.

13 See Joan Thirsk, 'The Farming Regions of England', in *The
    Agrarian History of England and Wales*, vol. IV: *1500–1640*, ed. Joan Thirsk
    (Cambridge, 1967), p. 46.

14 On saffron and Saffron Walden, see Joan Thirsk, 'Farming
    Techniques', ibid., p. 175; on yellow, see Ann Rosalind Jones and
    Peter Stallybrass, *Renaissance Clothing and the Materials of Memory*
    (Cambridge, 2000), pp. 63–85.

15 Gabriel Harvey, *Four Letters and Certaine Sonnets* [1592], ed. G. B.
    Harrison (1922; repr. Edinburgh, 1966), p. 13.

16 Harvey, *Pierces Supererogation*, pp. 10, 14, 17, 24, 28, 53, *passim*.

17 Ibid., p. 152.

18 See, for example, David Quint, *Epic and Empire: Politics and Generic
    Form from Virgil to Milton* (Princeton, NJ, 1992); Joan Pong Linton,
    *The Romance of the New World: Gender and the Literary Formations of English
    Colonialism* (Cambridge, 1998).

19 *STC*, II, p. 173; *Stationers' Register*, III, p. 45.

20 David Butcher, *Lowestoft, 1550–1750: Development and Change in a Suffolk
    Coastal Town* (Woodbridge, 2008), pp. 242, 294.

21 Phil Withington, *The Politics of Commonwealth: Citizens and Freemen in
    Early Modern England* (Cambridge, 2005), p. 89.

22 David M. Dean, 'Parliament, Privy Council, and Local Politics
    in Elizabethan England: The Yarmouth–Lowestoft Fishing
    Dispute', *Albion*, 22 (1990), p. 42. See also Robert Tittler, 'The
    English Fishing Industry in the Sixteenth Century: The Case of
    Great Yarmouth', *Albion*, IX/1 (1977), pp. 40–60; R.C.L. Sgroi,

'Piscatorial Politics Revisited: The Language of Economic Debate and the Evolution of Fishing Policy in Elizabethan England', *Albion*, XXXV/1 (2003), pp. 1–24.

23 A. R. Mitchell, 'The European Fisheries in Early Modern Europe', in *The Cambridge Economic History of Europe*, vol. V: *The Economic Organization of Early Modern Europe*, ed. E. E. Rich and C. H. Wilson (Cambridge, 1977), p. 135; Mark Kurlansky, *Cod: A Biography of the Fish that Changed the World* (London, 1999).

24 'Arguments in Favour of Establishing Wednesday as an Additional Fish Day, February, 1563', in *Tudor Economic Documents*, ed. R. H. Tawney and Eileen Powers, 3 vols (London, 1924), vol. II, pp. 104–10.

25 Robert Hitchcock, *A Pollitique Platt for the Honour of the Prince, the greate profite of the publique state, relief of the poore, preseruation of the riche, reformation of roges and idle persones, and the wealthe of thousandes that knowes not howe to liue* (London, 1580). On Hitchcock, see the ODNB entry.

26 John Keymer, *John Keymors Observation Made upon the Dutch Fishing about the Year 1601 demonstrating that there is more wealth raised out of herrings and other fish in His Majesties seas by the neighbouring nations in one year, then the King of Spain hath from the Indies* (London, 1664). On Keymer, see the ODNB entry.

27 Mitchell, 'European Fisheries', p. 178.

28 Day, 'Hakluyt, Harvey, Nashe', pp. 281–305; Andrew Hadfield, '*Lenten Stuffe*: Thomas Nashe and the Fiction of Travel', YES, XL/4 (2011), pp. 68–83.

29 Jason Scott-Warren, 'Nashe's Stuff', in *The Oxford Handbook of English Prose, 1500–1640*, ed. Andrew Hadfield (Oxford, 2013), p. 217.

30 Nashe, *Works*, IV, p. 395; Richard Hakluyt, *The Principal Navigations of the English Nation* [1589], ed. D. B. Quinn and R. A. Skelton, 2 vols (Cambridge, 1965), vol. I, p. 97.

31 On the reputation of the Dutch, see G. K. Hunter, 'Elizabethans and Foreigners', in *Shakespeare and Race*, ed. Catherine M. S. Alexander and Stanley Wells (Cambridge, 2000), p. 48; on wool, see Kristof Glamann, 'The Changing Patterns of Trade', in Rich and Wilson, *Cambridge Economic History of Europe*, vol. V, pp. 207–8, 249–56; on iron, see Domenico Sella, 'European Industries 1500–1700', in *The Fontana Economic History of Europe: The Sixteenth*

and Seventeenth Centuries, ed. Carlo M. Cipolla (London, 1974),
pp. 391–2.

32 Butcher, *Lowestoft*, ch. 8; Peter Clark and Paul Slack, *English Towns
in Transition, 1500–1700* (Oxford, 1976), pp. 48, 50.

33 Mitchell, 'European Fisheries', p. 139; Sgroi, 'Piscatorial Politics',
p. 8.

34 Mitchell, 'European Fisheries', p. 178; Butcher, *Lowestoft*, p. 169.

35 Tittler, 'English Fishing Industry', p. 59.

36 James Travis Jenkins, *The Herring and the Herring Fisheries* (London,
1927), p. 67.

37 A. W. Ecclestone and J. L. Ecclestone, *The Rise of Great Yarmouth:
The Story of a Sandbank* (Great Yarmouth, 1959), pp. 103–4; Jenkins,
Herring, p. 64; Butcher, *Lowestoft*, p. 168. Fishermen protected their
profits by curing as well as catching fish; see Butcher, *Lowestoft*,
p. 166.

38 Sgroi, 'Piscatorial Politics', p. 8; Mitchell, 'European Fisheries',
p. 181; Edward Hughes, 'The English Monopoly of Salt in the
Years 1563–71', *EHR*, XL/159 (1925), pp. 334–50; Butcher, *Lowestoft*,
p. 189.

39 Maryanne Kowalski, 'The Seasonality of Fishing in Medieval
Britain', in *Ecologies and Economies in Medieval and Early Modern Europe:
Studies in Environmental History for Richard C. Hoffmann*, ed. Scott G.
Bruce (Leiden, 2010), p. 128.

40 'Arguments in Favour'; Thomas Dawson, *The Good Housewife's Jewel*
(London, 1587), sigs A2v–A3r.

41 Christopher Marlowe, *The Poems*, ed. Millar McLure (London, 1968),
sestiad 1, l. 45.

42 Dean, 'Parliament', pp. 39–64.

43 Marlowe, *Hero and Leander*, sestiad 1, ll. 63–5.

44 Katherine Duncan-Jones, 'City Limits: Nashe's "Choice of
Valentines" and Jonson's "Famous Voyage"', *RES*, 56 (2005),
pp. 253–8. Duncan-Jones suggests that Jonson claimed a literary
kinship with Nashe similar to the one I am arguing Nashe claimed
with Marlowe.

45 Marlowe, *Hero and Leander*, sestiad 2, ll. 155–226.

46 See, in particular, Richard Helgerson, *Forms of Nationhood: The
Elizabethan Writing of England* (Chicago, IL, 1992), and Claire

McEachern, *The Poetics of English Nationhood, 1590–1612* (Cambridge, 1996), ch. 1.

Epilogue

1 J. B. Leishman, ed., *The Three Parnassus Plays, 1598–1601* (London, 1949), introduction, pp. 71–9. On the authorship of the plays, see Marjorie L. Reyburn, 'New Facts and Theories about the Parnassus Plays', PMLA, LXXIV/4 (1959), pp. 325–35. See also above, Chapter Four.

2 Leishman, *Parnassus Plays*, pp. 125–6.

3 Alexandra Halasz, *The Marketplace of Print: Pamphlets and the Public Sphere in Early Modern England* (Cambridge, 1997), ch. 3.

4 On Taylor's relationship to Nashe, see Bernard Capp, *The World of John Taylor the Water Poet, 1578–1653* (Oxford, 1994), pp. 83–6.

5 John Taylor, *Tom Nash, His Ghost* (London, 1643), p. 2.

6 John Taylor, *All the Works of John Taylor, the Water Poet* (London, 1630), sigs 2E6r, 2J2v.

7 G. Thomas Tanselle, *Bibliographical Analysis: An Historical Introduction* (Cambridge, 2009), ch. 1.

8 Nashe, *Works*, V, p. 1.

9 Stephen Guy-Bray, Joan Pong Linton and Steve Mentz, eds, *The Age of Thomas Nashe: Text, Bodies and Trespasses of Authorship in Early Modern England* (Farnham, 2013).

10 Steve Mentz, 'Introduction: The Age of Thomas Nashe', ibid., p. 7.

BIBLIOGRAPHICAL ESSAY

The standard edition of Nashe's works at present is the pioneering five-volume work edited by R. B. McKerrow, supplemented by F. P. Wilson, *The Works of Thomas Nashe* (Oxford, 1957). McKerrow's original four-volume edition, published 1904–10, was instrumental in establishing the nature and standard of bibliographical scholarship in the twentieth century. It is now being supplemented and updated by the Thomas Nashe Project based at Newcastle University, and a six-volume edition with Oxford University Press will appear in the near future, under the general editorship of Joseph Black, Andrew Hadfield, Jennifer Richards and Cathy Shrank. J. B. Steane's useful Penguin edition (1971), *The Unfortunate Traveller and Other Works*, contains six complete texts and extracts from five others, and is based almost entirely on McKerrow's editorial work, as is Stanley Wells's *Thomas Nashe: Selected Works* (London, 1964). *Thomas Nashe's 'Summer's Last Will and Testament': A Critical Modern-Spelling Edition* (Frankfurt, 1989), edited by Patricia Posluszny, is a readable text and has a helpful introduction and some useful notes. G. R. Hibbard's *Three Elizabethan Pamphlets* (London, 1951) has a useful introduction on pamphlets, and contains *Piers Penniless*.

The standard biography is Charles Nicholl's *A Cup of News: The Life of Thomas Nashe* (London, 1984), being revised at the time of writing for Oxford University Press; it is a lucid, thoughtful work written by an expert stylist with a hard nose for historical detective work. It also informs the same author's updated digest in the ODNB. Important recent discoveries have been made by Katherine Duncan-Jones: '"They say a made a good end": Ben Jonson's Epitaph on Thomas Nashe', *BJJ*, III/I (1996), pp. 1–19; and 'Thomas Nashe and William Cotton: Parallel Letters, Parallel Lives', *EMLS*, XIX/I (2016). Virginia Stern's *Gabriel Harvey: His Life, Marginalia and*

Library (Oxford, 1979) is an invaluable resource on Nashe's great rival, and Kirk Melnikoff and Edward Gieskes's collection *Writing Robert Greene: Essays on England's First Notorious Professional Writer* (Aldershot, 2008) contains valuable information and perspectives on another figure close to Nashe. Joseph Black's *The Martin Marprelate Tracts: A Modernized and Annotated Edition* (Cambridge, 2008) is a scholarly and readable resource that helps to explain the origins of Nashe's polemical style.

The Thomas Nashe Project at Newcastle University has a great deal of information about Nashe, his life, work, handwriting, bibliography, events and other relevant matters (https://research.ncl.ac.uk/thethomas-nasheproject). Louis Ule's *A Concordance to the Works of Thomas Nashe*, 2 vols (Hildesheim, 1997), despite its rather eccentric account of Nashe's life, is an incredibly useful tool for readers of Nashe. Georgia Brown's anthology of criticism *Thomas Nashe: The University Wits* (Aldershot, 2011) contains a generous selection of published essays and has sections on the Nashe–Harvey quarrel and *The Unfortunate Traveller*.

There are overviews of Nashe's life and literary achievement in G. R. Hibbard, *Thomas Nashe: A Critical Introduction* (London, 1962), Donald J. McGinn, *Thomas Nashe* (Boston, MA, 1981) and Stephen S. Hilliard, *The Singularity of Thomas Nashe* (Lincoln, NE, 1986). Jason Scott-Warren's 'Nashe's Stuff', in *The Oxford Handbook of English Prose, 1500–1640*, ed. Andrew Hadfield (Oxford, 2013), pp. 204–18, is a good introduction that explores the ways in which Nashe represents the world. Stephen Guy-Bray, Joan Pong Linton and Steve Mentz, eds, *The Age of Thomas Nashe: Text, Bodies and Trespasses of Authorship in Early Modern England* (Farnham, 2013), is a recent and diverse collection with some valuable essays. The most influential and important book dedicated to Nashe in recent years is Lorna Hutson's *Thomas Nashe in Context* (Oxford, 1989), which explores the connections between Nashe's literary production and the socio-economic nature of life in Elizabethan England, and, in particular, his relationship to popular culture and literary theory. It is especially strong on credit, patronage and the porous boundaries between work and holiday. Equally valuable and learned is Neil Rhodes's *Elizabethan Grotesque* (London, 1980), which is excellent on the comical and satirical milieu out of which Nashe's prose developed. Jennifer Richards's splendid, thought-provoking *Voices and Books in the English Renaissance: A New History of Reading* (Oxford, 2019) has a chapter on Nashe that explores the complicated balance between the written and the oral in his work. Richards's work builds on and rethinks many aspects of Marshall McLuhan's now published doctoral thesis, *The Classical Trivium: The Place of Thomas Nashe in the Learning of His Time* (Corte Madera, CA, 2006), originally completed in 1942, which uses Nashe to explore the nature and history of communication; Neil Rhodes's essay 'Orality, Print and Popular Culture: Thomas Nashe and Marshall McLuhan', in *Literature and Popular Culture in Early Modern England*, ed. Matthew Dimmock and Andrew Hadfield (Aldershot, 2009), pp. 29–44, is another important work on Nashe and written/oral culture. Alexandra Halasz's *The Marketplace of Print: Pamphlets and the Public Sphere in Early Modern England* (Cambridge, 1997) is good at situating Nashe within early modern print culture and the economics of publishing as well as among his contemporary pamphleteers: Thomas Dekker, Thomas Deloney, Gabriel Harvey and John Taylor. Reid Barbour's *Deciphering Elizabethan Fiction* (Newark, NJ, 1993) is a careful and lucid study of Nashe, Dekker and Robert Greene and the way such writers defined the boundaries of Elizabethan prose. Steve Mentz's *Romance for Sale in Early Modern England: The Rise of Prose Fiction* (Aldershot, 2006) has an interesting chapter on Greene and Nashe as authors eager to expose the ridiculous nature of romance, while David Margolies, *Novel and Society in Elizabethan England* (New York, 1985), has an interesting analysis of *The Unfortunate Traveller* (ch. 6). Jennifer Richards's *Rhetoric and Courtliness in Early Modern Literature* (Cambridge, 2003) is very good on the Nashe–Harvey quarrel and adds analysis to the outline first mapped out in McKerrow's edition. Joshua Phillips, *English Fictions of Communal Identity, 1485–1603* (Farnham, 2010), explores Nashe's relationship to and representation of his readers (ch. 6), as does Tamsin Badcoe in '"As Many Ciphers Without an I": Self-Reflexive Violence in the Work of Thomas Nashe', *MP*, CXI/3 (2014), pp. 384–407, which pays particular attention to Nashe's understanding of how his enemies saw – or might have seen – him. Lorna Hutson's 'Fictive Acts: Thomas Nashe and the Mid-Tudor Legacy', in *The Oxford Handbook of Tudor Literature, 1485–1603*, ed. Mike Pincombe and Cathy Shrank (Oxford, 2009), pp. 718–32, is a characteristically incisive analysis of Nashe's place in literary history.

Other works on Nashe have particular angles or approaches. Jonathan Crewe's *Unredeemed Rhetoric: Thomas Nashe and the Scandal of Authorship* (Baltimore, MD, 1982) is a complicated and fascinating exploration of the relationship between rhetoric and writing in the work of Nashe. James

Nielson's *Unread Herrings: Thomas Nashe and the Prosaics of the Real* (Frankfurt-am-Main, 1993) has some interesting insights into *The Unfortunate Traveller* and *Lenten Stuff*, but is an idiosyncratic post-structuralist reading of the works that is not always for the faint-hearted. Jürgen Schafer's *Documentation in the* OED: *Shakespeare and Nashe as Test Cases* (Oxford, 1980) has a useful (if now rather dated) analysis of Nashe words recorded in the OED, which demonstrates how inventive Nashe's use of language was and how an understanding of his ability to coin neologisms has shaped an understanding of the development of the English language.

Important work on the production of Nashe's texts is contained in Andrew Zurcher, 'Getting It Back to Front in 1590: Spenser's Dedications, Nashe's Insinuations, and Raleigh's Equivocations', SLI, XXXVIII/2 (2005), pp. 173–98; Chiaki Hanabusa, 'Notes on the Second Edition of Thomas Nashe's *The Unfortunate Traveller*', N&Q, 56 (2009), pp. 556–9; and 'The Printing of the Second Edition of Thomas Nashe's *The Unfortunate Traveller* (1594)', PBSA, CIV/3 (2010), pp. 277–97.

Criticism of Nashe's works, outside the larger surveys and monographs on particular subjects, largely concentrates on *The Unfortunate Traveller* and *Lenten Stuff*. Many works are not analysed in a particular critical essay. On the lost play *Terminus et non terminus*, see Matthew Steggle, *Digital Humanities and the Lost Drama of Early Modern England: Ten Case Studies* (Abingdon, 2015), ch. 1. On *An Almond for a Parrot*, see Jennifer Andersen, 'Thomas Nashe and Popular Conformity in Late Elizabethan England', R&R, XXV/4 (2001), pp. 25–43. Rachel Stenner's chapter 'St Paul's Churchyard and the Meanings of Print' in her *The Typographic Imaginary in Early Modern English Literature* (Abingdon, 2019) explores the relationship between *Piers Penniless* and the culture of print; Sam Fallon's 'Pierce Pennilesse and the Art of Distinction' in his *Paper Monsters: Persona and Literary Culture in Elizabethan England* (Philadelphia, PA, 2019), ch. 4, is a sophisticated and nuanced reading of Nashe's literary persona. The best account of the lost play *The Isle of Dogs* is in William Ingram, *A London Life in the Brazen Age: Francis Langley, 1548–1602* (Cambridge, MA, 1978), pp. 168–90. Karen Kettnich's 'Nashe's Extemporal Vein and His Tartonizing Wit', in Guy-Bray, Linton and Mentz, *The Age of Thomas Nashe*, pp. 99–114, is good on Nashe and clowning in relation to *Summer's Last Will* in particular. On *Summer's Last Will*, see also Sherri Geller, 'Commentary as Cover-Up: Criticizing Illiberal Patronage in Thomas Nashe's *Summer's Last Will and Testament*', ELR, XXV/2

(1995), pp. 148–78; and Marie Axton, '*Summer's Last Will and Testament*: Revels' End', in *The Reign of Elizabeth I: Court and Culture in the Last Decade*, ed. John Guy (Cambridge, 1995), pp. 258–73. For a recent reading of the 'Litany in Time of Plague', see Andrew Hadfield, 'How to Read Nashe's "Brightness Falls from the Air"', *FMLS*, LI/3 (2015), pp. 239–47. There is a recording of the performance of *Summer's Last Will and Testament* by Edward's Boys, directed by Perry Mills, at Archbishop Whitgift School, Croydon, on 30 September 2017 on the Thomas Nashe Project website. On 'The Choice of Valentines', see Ian Frederick Moulton, 'Transmuted into a Woman or Worse: Masculine Gender Identity and Thomas Nashe's "Choice of Valentines"', *ELR*, XXVII/1 (1997), pp. 57–88; Karen Newman, *Cultural Capitals: Early Modern London and Paris* (Princeton, NJ, 2007), ch. 8; Duncan Salkeld, *Shakespeare among the Courtesans: Prostitution, Literature, and Drama, 1500–1650* (Farnham, 2012), pp. 81–7; and Linda Grant, *Latin Erotic Elegy and the Shaping of Sixteenth-Century English Love Poetry* (Cambridge, 2019), ch. 4 (which is especially good on Nashe's reading of Ovid). The best essays on *Christ's Tears over Jerusalem* are Beatrice Groves, 'Laughter in the Time of Plague: A Context for the Unstable Style of Nashe's *Christ's Tears over Jerusalem*', *SP*, CVIII/2 (2011), pp. 238–60, which explores the frequently analysed relationship between the apparently jaunty tone and style of the work and its grim subject matter; and Philip Schwyzer, 'Summer Fruit and Autumn Leaves: Thomas Nashe in 1593', *ELR*, XXIV/3 (1994), pp. 583–619. On *The Terrors of the Night*, see Per Siverfors, '"All this tractate is but a dream": The Ethics of Dream Narration in Thomas Nashe's *The Terrors of the Night*', in Brown, *Thomas Nashe*, pp. 361–74.

On *The Unfortunate Traveller* as a fiction/novel, see Margaret Ferguson, 'Nashe's *The Unfortunate Traveller*: The "Newes of the Maker" Game', *ELR*, XI/2 (March 1981), pp. 165–82; Ann Rosalind Jones, 'Inside the Outsider: Nashe's *Unfortunate Traveller* and Bakhtin's Polyphonic Novel', *ELH*, L/1 (1983), pp. 61–81; Mihoko Suzuki, '"Signiorie ouer the Pages": The Crisis of Authority in Nashe's *The Unfortunate Traveller*', *SP*, LXXXI/3 (Summer 1984), pp. 348–71; and Alex Davis, *Renaissance Historical Fiction: Sidney, Deloney, Nashe* (Woodbridge, 2011), ch. 4. For a recent overview, see my 'Thomas Nashe, *The Unfortunate Traveller*', in *Handbook of English Renaissance Literature*, ed. Ingo Berensmeyer (The Hague, 2019), pp. 395–410. On *Lenten Stuff*, see, in particular, Jennifer Andersen, 'Blame-in-Praise Irony in *Lenten Stuff*', in Guy-Bray, Linton and Mentz, *The Age of Thomas Nashe*, pp. 45–62, and Kristen Abbott Bennett, 'Red Herrings and the "Stench of Fish": Subverting "Praise" in Thomas Nashe's *Lenten Stuff* ', *R&R*, XXXVII/I (2014), pp. 87–110, both of which attempt to get to grips with Nashe's slippery levels of irony; Matthew Day, 'Hakluyt, Harvey, Nashe: The Material Text and Early Modern Nationalism', *SP*, CIV/3 (2007), pp. 281–305, and Andrew Hadfield, '*Lenten Stuffe*: Thomas Nashe and the Fiction of Travel', *YES*, XLI/I (2011), pp. 68–83, explore the representation of travel in Nashe's work and his relationship to travel writing. Henry Turner's 'Nashe's Red Herring: Epistemologies of the Commodity in *Lenten Stuff* (1599)', *ELH*, LXVIII/3 (2001), pp. 529–61, explores how Nashe thinks about objects and things in the work. Aaron Kitch, *Political Economy and the States of Literature in Early Modern England* (Farnham, 2009), ch. 3, analyses Nashe's work in terms of recent interest in economic criticism.

The best essay on *The Trimming of Thomas Nashe* is Rebecca Hasler, '"Tossing and turning your booke upside downe": *The Trimming of Thomas Nashe*, Cambridge, and Scholarly Reading', *RS*, XXXIII/3 (2019), pp. 375–96.

ACKNOWLEDGEMENTS

My especial gratitude goes to the team on The Thomas Nashe Project, especially the general editors, Joe Black, Jennifer Richards and Cathy Shrank. Special thanks also to Kirsty Rolfe, my research associate who has been so brilliant, so nice to work with, and who reads Nashe so well, as well as Kate De Rycker, who has been another source of true knowledge. Also to Matthew Dimmock, Claire Loffman, Lucy Nicholas, Jason Scott-Warren, Emma Smith, Chris Stamatakis, Alan Stewart, Rachel White and Henry Woudhuysen. I have learned so much from all the above, as I have from Anna Brass, Colin Burrow, Martin Butler, Tom Cain, Suzanne Gossett, Lorna Hutson, David Kastan, Claire Loffman, Perry Mills, Charles Nicholl, Neil Rhodes and James Tucker. I am grateful to Michael Leaman and François Quiviger, who read an early draft of the manuscript and saved me from numerous errors. For answering specific queries, I am further grateful to Joe Black, Jason Scott-Warren, Alan Stewart and Henry Woudhuysen.

This book is dedicated to my friend Richard Shields (1961–2021), who, as I imagine Nashe to have been, was clever, witty, kind and a pleasure to have known.

PHOTO ACKNOWLEDGEMENTS

The author and publishers wish to express their thanks to the below sources of illustrative material and/or permission to reproduce it. Some locations of artworks are also given below, in the interest of brevity:

British Library, London: pp. 33 (Cotton MS Julius C III, fol. 280r), 60, 184 (Cotton MS Augustus I i 74); photo Nick Browning, courtesy Edward's Boys: p. 111; used by permission of the Folger Shakespeare Library, Washington, DC (CC BY-SA 4.0): pp. 41 (STC 12906, image 54126), 126 (STC 17441, image 9488), 151 (STC 18369 copy 2, image 68187); used by permission of the Folger Shakespeare Library, Washington, DC (STC 15447), photos Kate De Rycker: pp. 105, 106; The Frick Collection, New York: p. 21; from J. R. Green, *A Short History of the English People*, vol. II (New York and London, 1899), photo Harold B. Lee Library, Brigham Young University, Provo, UT: p. 134; from Francis Grose, *The Antiquities of England and Wales*, vol. III (London, 1775): p. 110; Kunstmuseum Basel: p. 160; Library of Congress, Prints and Photographs Division, Washington, DC: pp. 14, 28, 55; Musei Vaticani, Vatican City: p. 66; collection Museum aan de Stroom (MAS), Antwerp, photo Bart Huysmans & Michel Wuyts: p. 91; collection Museum Boijmans Van Beuningen, Rotterdam: pp. 78–9; National Galleries of Scotland, Edinburgh: p. 46; National Gallery of Ireland, Dublin: p. 162; Royal Collection Trust/© Her Majesty Queen Elizabeth II 2023: p. 73; from Sir Philip Sidney, *The Countesse of Pembroke's Arcadia* (London, 1590): p. 19; UK Churches/Alamy Stock Photo: p. 8; University of Leeds Library, photos © University of Leeds: pp. 202, 203.

INDEX

Page numbers in *italics* refer to illustrations

Aesop 142

Agrippa, Heinrich Cornelius 28, 120

All Is True (film, 2018) 9

America 186, 191

Anabaptism 53–6, 160

Anti-Martinist Tracts 12, 15–16, 44–53, 56, 71, 83, 122, 136

Antwerp, Siege of 91–2

Aretino, Pietro 20

Aristotle 76, 88

Aristotelian 174

Armada 51

Ascham, Sir Roger 174, 186

Audley End 150

Baker, Harry 109

Barnes, Barnabe 153

Bible 44, 48, 62, 68, 117

Bishops' Ban 12, 37–8, 52, 129

Black, Joseph 44

Blount, Charles 72–6, *73*

Book of Common Prayer 23

Burby, Cuthbert 37

Burre, Walter 22

Cade, Jack 32, 183

Calpurnia 80

Calvin, Jean 71

Calvino, Italo 175

Cambridge 71, 102–5, 152
    Dolphin Inn 30, 145
    see also University of Cambridge

Campion, Thomas 30

Carey, Elizabeth (1552–1618) 24–5, 64

Carey, Elizabeth (1576–1635) 27, 86

Carey, Sir George 25, 27, 34, 64, 86

Carey, Henry, Lord Hunsdon 34

Carfania 80

Carisbrooke Castle 27, *28*, 32

Catholicism 12, 23, 34, 43, 50, 51, 53, 58, 167, 169, 172, 186

Cecil, Sir Robert 193

Cecil, William, Lord Burghley 17

Charles v 160

Chettle, Henry 30, 153

Children of the Chapel 20, 127

Chrysostom, St John 87

Church of England 23, 43, 53, 209
Chute, Anthony 153
Cicero 141–2, 144
    Ciceronianism 148, 155
cod 196
colonies, colonialism 186, 193
Cookery, Book of 201, *202, 203*
Cooper, Thomas 44
Cotton, William 32–5, *33*, 159
Crewe, Jonathan 209
Croydon 112
    Croydon Palace 20–21,
        108, *110*

Danes 173
Danter, John 29–30, 37
Dekker, Thomas 38
de Vere, Edward, Earl of Oxford
    17, 133, 135, 150
Devereux, Penelope 72
Diodorus Sicilius 50
Diogenes the Cynic 147
Dionysius of Corinth 165
Donne, John 12, 88
Dowland, John 64
Drant, Thomas 186
Drayton, Michael 101
Dudley, Robert, Earl of Leicester
    34
Dutch, Holland, Netherlands
    53, 173, 193, 195, 197

East Anglia 36, 129, 143, 196
Egyptian mythology 70
Elderton, William 88
Elizabeth I 17, 21–2, 108, 113, 150,
    164, 168

Elton, Ben 9
empire 127, 185–8
Europe 165–8, 173–5, 193–4
Eurydice 79
execution 166–70

Farnese Gardens 176
Field of the Cloth of Gold 161
fishing 192–5, 196
Fitzgerald, Elizabeth, Countess
    of Lincoln ('fair Geraldine')
    161, *162*
Forsett, Edward 102–4
    Pedantius 102–4, 133
Foulweather, Adam 16
Foxe, John 28, 163
France, French 11, 32, 121–5,
    160, 161, 165, 167, 173, 174,
    177, 179, 195
    Wars of Religion 11
François I 160

Gaia Afrania 80
Ganymede 128
Garzoni, Tommaso, *Hospital
    of Incurable Fooles* 38
Gascoigne, George 92, 186
Gawdy family 48
Germany 11, 195
Globe Theatre 35
Golding, Arthur 71
Gosson, Stephen 58
grand tour 171
Grant, Linda 94
Great Yarmouth 36–7, 182–3, *184*,
    188–9, 190–92, 195, 199, 205
Greece 187, 190

Greene, Robert 12, 15, 18, 30,
    56, 71, 107, 122, 134, 153, 156,
    158, 159, 186, 187, 189–90

Hacket, Thomas 71
Hakluyt, Richard 27, 185–7, 195
Halasz, Alexandra 207
Hall, Joseph 37
Harington, Sir John 34–5, 149
Harvey, Gabriel 11–12, 15, 18,
    22–4, 27, 28, 30–31, 35,
    37–8, 82, 102–5, 132–57,
    151, 159, 185–90, 195
    Four Letters and Certain Sonnets
        18, 157
    Gratulationes Valdinenses 104
    New Letter of Notable Contents
        139, 155
    Pierces Supererogation 18, 20, 23,
        28, 82, 139–40, 142, 149,
        152, 155, 186, 189–90
    Three Proper, Witty and Familiar
        Letters 133
Harvey, John 12, 103, 150, 156
Harvey, Richard 11, 16–17, 88–9,
    103–4, 133–7, 146, 150
    Lamb of God 133–4
Heliodorus 159
Henry V 121, 124
Henry VI 32, 122
Henry VII 121
Henry VIII 21, 160, 161, 177
heresy 167
herring 36, 183–4, 188, 192–6,
    204
Hitchcock, Robert 193
Holinshed, Raphael 28, 34

Homer 76, 189–90, 205
Howard, Henry, Earl
    of Surrey 161, 172
Huntley, Dick 109
Hutson, Lorna 209
Huyssen, Andreas 175

Italy 161, 173–4, 195

Jeremiah 65–7, 66
Jerusalem 64–9
Jews 64
John of Leiden 53–6, 55, 160
Jonson, Ben 12, 18, 35, 38–40,
    114, 129–31
    The Case Is Altered 17, 131
Josephus 64–5
Jove (Jupiter) 78–80, 128
Julius Caesar 80
Juno 80, 128
Juvenal 28

Keymer, John 193
King, Humphrey 37
Kyd, Thomas 17, 71, 122

Lambeth Palace 20–21
Legge, Thomas 102
Leland, John 28, 105–7
Leovitius (Cyprian Leowitz)
    135
Lewis, C. S. 10, 29
Lichfield, Richard 12, 15, 30–32,
    37, 40, 145–8, 182
    The Trimming of Thomas Nashe
        15, 32, 145–7, 182
Ling 198, 200, 201

Livorno 196
Lodge, Thomas 159
London, Londoners 13, 20, 25–6,
    27, 64, 67, 83, 129, 152, 158,
    179, 206
Lord Chamberlain 34
    Lord Chamberlain's Men
    25, 34
Lord Pembroke's Men 131
Lord Strange's Men 17
Lowestoft 13, 36, 191–2, 195, 199
Luther, Martin 23
Lyly, John 15, 30, 44, 133, 135, 137,
    154, 159

McKerrow, R. B. 208
Magnus 1 160
Marignono, Battle of 160
Marlowe, Christopher 12, 15, 17,
    18, 27, 30, 67–8, 97–8, 107–8,
    119, 125–31, 153, 197–201
    Dr Faustus 97–8, 107–8
    Hero and Leander 183, 198–201
    Tamburlaine 67–8, 124, 165
Marprelate Tracts 16, 20, 43–53,
    60, 109, 117, 133, 208
Marston, John 37
Martial 39
Mary 1 168
Mary Stuart (Queen of Scots)
    164
Medusa 79
memory, art of 171
Mentz, Steve 181
Middelburg 161
Middleton, Thomas 37, 38
Millenarianism 56

Mills, Robert 15, 27, 30, 102
Milton, John 169
Minerva 79
More, Thomas 52
Mumford, Lewis 175
Munday, Anthony 15, 169
Münster Uprising 11, 53–6, 160
Musaeus 198, 201

Nashe, Margaret 13
Nashe, Mary 36
Nashe, Thomas
    anti-feminism 76–81
    appearance 40–41, 41
    Cambridge 13
    character 208
    Christianity 40, 70, 93
    drama 17–18, 21, 27, 34, 35,
        101–31, 144, 209
    friendship 18, 40
    handwriting 105–7, 105, 106
    pornography 18, 94–100
    printing 29–30, 109
    private life 41–2
    satire 20, 75, 127, 209
    sizar 13
    style 29, 63, 144–5
Nashe, Thomas, works
    Almond for a Parrot 16, 50–51
    Anatomy of Absurdity 13, 16, 52,
        70, 71–80, 86, 115, 129
    Astrophil and Stella, preface to 72
    'Choice of Valentines' 18,
        93–100, 149, 200
    Christ's Tears Over Jerusalem 12,
        22, 24, 25, 34, 52, 59–69,
        81, 139, 159, 179

Countercuff Given to Martin
  Junior (?) 48–50
Dido, Queen of Carthage 18–19,
  27, 72, 125–31, *126*
Have With You To Saffron Walden
  15, 16, 17, 24, 27, 29, 30–32,
  35, 40, 76, 102–5, 142–3,
  144–57, 159, 182
Henry VI, Part One 17, 120–25,
  126
Isle of Dogs 18, 27, 35, 37, 52,
  114, 128, 129, 131, 183
Menaphon, preface to 15, 56–7,
  107
Nashe's Lenten Stuff 13, 17, 35,
  36, 37, 39, 40, 52, 76, 128,
  129–30, 143, 157, 159,
  182–205
Piers Penniless 17, 20, 22, 81–6,
  124, 130, 135, 207
Strange News 18, 25, 71, 88,
  138–41, 144, 154
Summer's Last Will and Testament
  21, 27, 38, 93, 108–20,
  121, 122, 124, 125, 127, 129,
  146
Terminus et Non Terminus 15, 52,
  72, 102, 127, 207
Terrors of the Night 27, 86–93,
  129
The Unfortunate Traveller
  10–11, 22, 24, 37, 53–6,
  58, 61, 157, 158–81
Nashe, Tom 36
Nashe, William 13, 48
Nero 124
Newgate Prison 27, 83

Nicholl, Charles 41, 159, 209
North Sea 193, 198

Orpheus 79
Ovid 28, 71, 78, 94, 98–9,
  200

Painter, William 159, 169
Palmer, Sir Thomas 172
Parnassus plays 38, 39, 157,
  206–7
Peele, George 122
Penry, John 52
Perne, Andrew 103, 154
Pettie, George 159, 169
plague 22, 59, *60*, 67, 112–19, 152,
  160, 177–9
Plato 76
Plautus 131
Pope 47, 51
Privy Council 35, 37
Protestantism 12, 43, 47, 50, 53,
  58, 61, 163, 167, 186
Puritans 63, 117, 207
Puttenham, George 81

Quran 38, 68

Raleigh, Sir Walter 193
Reformation 12, 43, 51, 56,
  186
Rhodes 50
Rhodes, Neil 209
Rich, Barnabe 154
Richard III 102, 121
Robin Hood 134–5
Roman Republic 74

Rome 22, 61, 64, 127, 161,
     165, 175–9
Rose Theatre 17, 35
Russia 27

saffron 143, 188
Saffron Walden 38, 143, 152
salt 197
Sanford, James 28
satire 9, 16
Saxo Grammaticus 85
Saye, Lord 32
Shakespeare, William 12,
     17–18, 24, 25, 30, 121, 208
     Hamlet 85
     Henry IV, Part One 31, 32
     Twelfth Night 188
Sidney, Philip 17, 58, 72, 133,
     159, 176–7
     Arcadia 19
     Astrophil and Stella 72, 177
Sidney family 17
Skelton, John 20
Somers, Will 21, 109
Spain, Spanish 11, 51, 92, 173,
     174–5, 186, 191, 195
     Spanish Fury 92
Spencers of Althorp 64
Spenser, Edmund 20, 64,
     81–2, 103, 159
Stamford, Lincolnshire 15, 27
Stanley, Ferdinando, Lord
     Strange 17, 18, 24–5, 94, 95
Stationers' Company 71
     Stationers' Register 37,
          38, 56, 71, 191
Straw, Jack 183, 236n.5

Swiss 160
syphilis 40

Talbot, John, Earl of Shrewsbury
     121–5
Tantalus 69
Taylor, John 207–8
Terence 28
Thames (river) 35
Thorius, John 153–4
Throckmorton, Job 51
Tiber (river) 178–9
Tiresias 80, 190
Topcliffe, Richard 36
travellers, travelling 162–3,
     170–76, 178, 180–81
treason 167–8
Turbeville, George 186
Turkey, Turks 50, 168
Tyburn 83, 178–9
Tyndale, William 52

Udall, Nicholas 71
usury 179
University of Cambridge 11, 15,
     20, 29, 102, 206–7
     St John's College 13, 14, 32, 38
     Trinity College 12, 32, 102,
          104
     Trinity Hall 32

Vergil, Polydore 195
Virgil 28, 127
Vulcan 129

Warrington, Lancashire 51
Wars of the Roses 121

Watson, Thomas 18, 102
West Harling 13, 48
Whitgift, John, Archbishop of
     Canterbury 15, 20, 24, 37,
     45–8, *46*, 50, 108–9
Wight, Isle of 11, 27
Williams, Sir Roger 30
Withington, Phil 192
Wolfe, John 23, 30, 152
wool trade 195
Wriothesley, Henry, Earl of
     Southampton 24
Wyatt, Sir Thomas 169